Paul Verhoeven: Interviews

Conversations with Filmmakers Series
Gerald Peary, General Editor

Paul Verhoeven
INTERVIEWS

Edited by Margaret Barton-Fumo

University Press of Mississippi   Jackson

www.upress.state.ms.us

The University Press of Mississippi is a member of the Association of American University Presses.

All images © copyright Paul Verhoeven

Cover photo by Lex de Meester

Copyright © 2016 by University Press of Mississippi
All rights reserved

First printing 2016

∞

Library of Congress Cataloging-in-Publication Data

Names: Verhoeven, Paul, 1938– author. | Barton-Fumo, Margaret editor.
Title: Paul Verhoeven : interviews / edited by Margaret Barton-Fumo.
Description: Jackson : University Press of Mississippi, 2016. | Series: Conversations with filmmakers | Includes filmography and index.
Identifiers: LCCN 2016032570 | ISBN 9781496810151 (cloth : alk. paper)
Subjects: LCSH: Verhoeven, Paul—Interviews. | Motion picture producers and directors—Netherlands—Interviews.
Classification: LCC PN1998.3.V46 A5 2016 | DDC 791.4302/33092—dc23 LC record available at https://lccn.loc.gov/2016032570

British Library Cataloging-in-Publication Data available

Contents

Introduction   ix

Chronology   xxiv

Filmography   xxviii

How Could He?
    Ale Van Dijk / 1968   3

Blonde Greet Emigrates: *Business Is Business* Travels to Germany and the United States
    Ale Van Dijk / 1971   5

Turkish Delight and The Hague
    Nieuwsblad van het Noorden / 1973   9

I Distrust Anyone Who Pursues An Ideal
    Leeuwarder Courant / 1979   11

Paul Verhoeven on Sex and Violence in *The Fourth Man*
    Peter Slavenburg / 1983   16

Interview with Paul Verhoeven
    Mark Valen / 1984   22

Paul Verhoeven on the Violence in His Films
    Ariejan Korteweg and Bart Jungmann / 1985   29

Flesh and Blood
    Bertrand Borie / 1985   35

Man of Iron
    Brian Cronenworth / 1987   43

Paul Verhoeven Tackles Science Fiction
   Indra Bhose / 1988   47

Total Recall: Director Paul Verhoeven on His Mars Vacation with Arnold Schwarzenegger
   Bill Florence / 1990   55

The Vitality of Existence
   George Hickenlooper / 1991   57

Paul Verhoeven: An Interview
   Chris Shea and Wade Jennings / 1992   64

Beyond Flesh and Blood
   Jean-Marc Bouineau / 1994   80

Basic Cutting: Paul Verhoeven's *Basic Instinct*
   Laurent Bouzereau / 1994   85

Sex, Cinema, and *Showgirls*
   Paul Verhoeven / 1995   91

Showgirls: Shooting the Script
   Paul Verhoeven / 1995   102

The Showgirl Must Go On
   Dennis Hensley / 1995   104

Dreams of War
   Bill Warren / 1997   120

Interview with Paul Verhoeven
   Olivier Guéret / 1997   126

Dutchman's Breaches
   Brian D'Amato and David Rimanelli / 2000   130

The Master of Science Fiction Longs for a Break from Special Effects
   Douglas Eby / 2000   141

The Many Dreams of Paul Verhoeven
    Neil Young / 2002   144

Paul Verhoeven
    Bruce LaBruce / 2003   153

Paul Verhoeven: Back in Black
    Alex Simon / 2007   161

Devil's Advocate
    James Hughes / 2007   166

Jesus of Nazareth
    Rüdiger Sturm / 2009   173

49 Minutes with Paul Verhoeven
    Mark Jacobson / 2010   184

According to Verhoeven: *Vertigo*
    Rob van Scheers / 2011   186

My Filmviews Interviews . . . Paul Verhoeven
    Nostra / 2013   191

Verhoeven in Venice
    Margaret Barton-Fumo / 2014   195

Shooting *Elle*
    Margaret Barton-Fumo / 2015   202

Additional Resources   207

Index   209

Introduction

I first met Paul Verhoeven face-to-face in 2014 in Los Angeles at one of his favorite cafés—a bustling, characteristically sunny establishment in Venice Beach. In spite of having lived in the Netherlands for more than half of his life and maintaining a musical Dutch accent, Verhoeven could have passed for a native Angeleno, dressed in his trademark collared denim shirt with a cardigan sweater and stylish leather sneakers. Verhoeven appeared at home in this chic, distinctively West Coast American milieu, but as soon as we began the interview the complex facets of his identity were thrown into high relief. His intricate background and singular attitude radiate every one of his interviews going back as far as his early press clippings.

Most of Verhoeven's admirers consider his European identity a kind of pedigree, and the reason why all of his blockbusters seem to tout a certain *je ne sais quoi*. His personal history is remarkably diverse: Raised in German-occupied territory during WWII, Verhoeven holds a doctorandus in mathematics and physics with an emphasis on the theory of relativity. In recent years he has moonlighted as a published historian and the only non-theologian member of the Westar Institute's exclusive Jesus Seminar. He is known to movie buffs as the director of fast-paced, hyperbolic films that teem with cynicism while in person Verhoeven is as exuberant and straightforward as they come. He is an effortlessly garrulous interviewee, always willing to lay bare the ideas and influences that animate his work.

David Rimanelli, who considers the Dutchman to be his "favorite mass market auteur," observed in *Artforum* in 2000: "Part of the thrill of Verhoeven's American films derives from the narrative ambiguities and off-register tone common to all his work—a link, however unexpected, to the European art cinema of the '70s and to his youth." Verhoeven directed seven features before moving to California in 1986, where he would repeatedly top box-office records. Relatively little is known about Verhoeven's first seventeen (pre-*RoboCop*) years as a feature director, and so as a cursory introduction to his early career I've included six Dutch interviews dating from 1968-1985 that have been meticulously translated by Julia van den Hout. The form and content of these articles provide an interesting contrast to the later interviews in this collection because of their provenance, as newspaper clippings: the choice of questions directed at Verhoeven, the juicy titles of some of the interviews, and the occasionally stilted, "newsy" vernacular distinguish these entries from the latter material. They provide a brisk but fascinating portrait of the young director, as well as an illuminating peek at the logistics of the contemporary Dutch film industry.

"*Hoe kón hij?*" or, "How could he?" is the title of the first interview in the book, and notably establishes the thirty-year-old Verhoeven as a budding provocateur. Earlier that week, the VPRO (the Dutch public broadcasting station) abruptly cancelled the scheduled broadcast of *Portrait of Anton Adriaan Mussert*, Verhoeven's documentary about the 1930s leader of the NSB (the Dutch pro-fascist party) days before the program was scheduled to air. Verhoeven's supposedly unbiased presentation of interviews with Mussert's former NSB comrades and associates caused quite a controversy at the VPRO, which preemptively cancelled the broadcast at the behest of the celebrity historian Professor Lou de Jong, who had already profiled Mussert in his own television series a few years prior. It quickly becomes evident in the 1968 interview that the "he" of the title in fact refers to Mussert, as Verhoeven explains his interest in the man's ideological downfall: "The focus of my movie is not so much on Mussert's betrayal of his country but rather asks the question, 'How could such an intelligent man get to that point?'" Verhoeven's final word, however, is typically defiant: "Is it my fault that so much has changed at the VPRO [since I finished the documentary]? What good is all this commotion? Why all of the fuss about the release of this movie?" A young filmmaker who dared to present a Nazi sympathizer in a neutral light, embedded in a controversy over a film that hasn't even aired—clearly, the headline doubles as a shrill critique of Verhoeven himself: How *could* he? What nerve!

Published in the Saturday paper the weekend before the film's release in 1973, "*Turkish Delight* and The Hague" throws another jab at Verhoeven in anticipation of an expected controversy. Addressing an audience that was likely familiar with the best-selling source novel by Jan Wolkers, Verhoeven defended the numerous sex scenes in his upcoming film: "I thought it would be foolish not to show the audience everything that happens in the book. The book is by no means pornographic but thoroughly human. I wasn't afraid to show a great deal of realism." This comment marks an early instance of Verhoeven's association of sexual explicitness with "realism," and identification of his (Dutch) subject matter as a "human" topic. These are two key words that will recur throughout the book; in retrospective American interviews where he contrasts his intimate, "human" Dutch dramas with his big-budget American blockbusters, and in defense of other sex scenes in films like *Basic Instinct* and *Showgirls*, which he argues are shocking in their blunt, explicit "realism." They are concepts that Verhoeven will alter and develop over the course of his career, but always link to his Dutch identity—it is worth noting here the title of a 2007 interview with Verhoeven for the *Guardian*: "'Of course there are nude scenes . . . I'm Dutch!'"

The main takeaway from the *Turkish Delight* interview is Verhoeven's final say on his adaptation of the novel's heavy-handed symbolism: "I tried to prevent it from turning into an Antonioni-like movie, which I specifically wanted to stay away from. This movie was intentionally made for a mass audience. It is what I like to call a commercial film." Verhoeven's frequent dismissal of the predominately European art-house aesthetic is often delivered tongue-in-cheek, as he cites in subsequent interviews that his favorite filmmakers include Ingmar Bergman, Frederico Fellini, Sergei Eisenstein, and even Michael Haneke—all icons of what is now considered slow cinema. Tirelessly rational, Verhoeven was quick to categorize his successful 1973 film as an accessible, so-called commercial product although again, this is an assessment of *Turkish Delight* that does not hold water in the United States, where copious sex scenes and male full frontal nudity are anathema to box-office sales. Evidently, one culture's mainstream is another's soft-core underground.

Verhoeven reiterated his commercial bias with the following complaint about the surfeit of art-house cinema in the Netherlands to the *Leeuwarder Courant* in 1979: "The Dutch film industry is in danger of collapsing. Nine out of ten movies are art films. I have nothing against it, but they don't earn a penny. Eventually they won't be able to find investors anymore, and the Dutch film industry will go down the hole. I find this irresponsible. They shouldn't have to stop making art films, of course, but more commercial films must be made." One year later and Verhoeven's frustrations increased exponentially with the release of *Spetters*, his 1980 film about young motorcyclists. Though successful at the box-office per usual, the film managed to infuriate the press and hence the general public with its frank depiction of sex, a character who commits suicide after being confined to a wheelchair, and a homophobe who comes out as gay after being gang-raped by a group of men. A protest group formed under the title of the National Anti-Spetters Action Committee (NASA) and vilified Verhoeven in a public forum, claiming the film to be anti-gay, anti-women, and anti-invalid; he attempted to respond to their concerns on a popular Dutch talk show but was summarily overwhelmed as NASA activists jumped onstage and tried to kiss him, painting lipstick on his face while wheelchair-bound protesters hurled insults at him from the audience. Verhoeven speaks freely about the NASA protests in several of his interviews as a reference point for the backlash he experienced in the US against *Basic Instinct* and later *Showgirls*. Twenty years removed from *Spetters* in 2000, he divulged to Rimanelli and D'Amato in *Artforum* that it was by far the most upsetting experience of his career.

The public outrage in reaction to *Spetters* coincided with the buildup of acclaim for *Soldier of Orange* in the US, which had taken the Netherlands by storm the previous year. Based on Eric Hazelhoff Roelfzema's memoirs of his participance in the Dutch Resistance during WWII, *Soldier of Orange* collected the Los Angeles Film Critics' Award for Best Foreign Film and was nominated for a Golden Globe in 1980. According to Verhoeven's biographer Rob van Scheers, Steven Spielberg (who was initially wary of Verhoeven, having mistook *Turkish Delight* for pornography) was impressed by the action-packed *Soldier of Orange* and invited the Dutchman to come to Hollywood for a tour of the studios. After a series of false starts with a few executives and an awkward meeting with mega-fan Barbra Streisand, Verhoeven and his scriptwriter Gerard Soeteman returned to the Netherlands empty-handed. Van Scheers concludes his description of this Hollywood excursion with the astonishing disclosure that Spielberg originally intended to convince George Lucas to hire Verhoeven to direct *Return of the Jedi*, but changed his mind after he watched *Spetters* and was again repulsed by the film's sexual content.

The last film Verhoeven would direct in the Netherlands for a long time, and commonly recognized as the stylish precursor to *Basic Instinct*, *The Fourth Man* (1983) was his first concerted attempt at directing an "art film." Van Scheers described Verhoeven's quiet satisfaction once the film was released and the high-minded reviews began to roll in: "The director concluded that as long as the camera moved slowly, the light was filtered to a glossy pink, purple, and green, the main characters did not move too quickly and held each other enthralled with meaningful silences, the critics would write that film could also be art." *The Fourth Man* is indeed a gloomy, impressive film, loaded with religious and occult symbolism, complex staging and expressive cinematography. It is both visually striking and stark in its humor, and it represents a shrewd moment in Verhoeven's career. While *The Fourth Man* did not perform as well as his earlier "commercial" films, it turned a good profit and effectively revived the director's reputation in the Netherlands. Speaking a few years earlier to the *Leeuwarder Courant* about the overseas success of *Soldier of Orange*, Verhoeven gloated about the simple efficacy of well-designed *mise en scène*: "It's nonsense when people say that Dutch films are never picked up abroad. You just have to make sure that it is a commercial film and the set design looks good. That was the case with [his 1975 film] *Katie Tippel*. The script was weak and the dramaturgy wasn't very compelling . . . but the sets were beautiful and it portrayed the time period well. That's why the movie was successful abroad." This turned out to be true for *The Fourth Man*, which also caught the attention of the American studios and critics, convincing Mike Medavoy at Orion to invest in Verhoeven's talent.

Buoyed by his recent return to critical grace, Verhoeven admitted to his Dutch interviewer in 1983 after a few unproductive visits to Hollywood, "I prefer to work [in the Netherlands]. I'm bored in the US and I'm a little tired of the people there.

... But the movies I want to make will cost, I think, about fifteen million guilders. And in order to come up with that kind of money, it's necessary to get American investors." Medavoy came through with that amount and then some, securing over seven million dollars to finance *Flesh+Blood* (1985), which was at the time the equivalent of about twenty million guilders and nearly four times the budget of *Soldier of Orange*, the most expensive Dutch film ever made. In a concession to Orion's relative frugality, both parties agreed that the film would be shot in Spain with a Dutch/Spanish crew and a multi-national cast. Bertrand Borie's 1985 interview with Verhoeven for *Cinefantastique*, translated here by Alexandra Valentine Proulx, offers an in-depth discussion of this often overlooked, troubled film. The nearly four-month long shoot, which went a few weeks over schedule and about a million dollars over budget was an utter disaster, resulting in negligible ticket sales, and the end of Verhoeven's working relationship with his leading man, Rutger Hauer.

Plagued by miserable weather in a cold and snowy region of northern Spain, Verhoeven frequently lost his temper with an unfamiliar crew and a rowdy cast of American party animals. Still uncomfortable with the English language, Verhoeven struggled to communicate with the rebellious group and was dismayed when Rutger Hauer seemed to turn against him and side with the other actors in questioning his every command. As the star of the Dutch television series *Floris*, Hauer came into his own alongside his director Verhoeven, who went on to cast him in *Turkish Delight*, *Katie Tippel*, *Soldier of Orange*, and *Spetters*, in time eliciting the attention of the American industry, which led to Hauer's stumbling crossover to Hollywood. By the time production began on *Flesh+Blood*, Hauer had already appeared in *Blade Runner* and *Ladyhawke* and, believing himself to be a serious actor, reportedly conducted himself like a big shot on the set. In the long run this was a mistake for Hauer, who would struggle to break out as a leading man in Hollywood while Verhoeven quickly advanced to fame with his next film, *RoboCop* (1987).

Reading Verhoeven's comments about his professional breakup with Rutger Hauer is like witnessing the aftermath of a fractured romance. The two were close friends and colleagues for over fifteen years, and both actor and director have characterized their partnership as a love/hate relationship that came to a head during the production of *Flesh+Blood*. The two eventually patched up their differences but have yet to work together again. Verhoeven expressed an embittered fondness for Hauer to the *Leeuwarder Courant* in 1979 when the wounds were fresh: "Ever since *Floris* I've fallen for his charm. I recognize some of myself in him and I will always have a soft spot for him, although that is definitely affected now. Neither of us is eager to work together again." Verhoeven is resolutely candid when speaking about his often intense (but always strictly professional) relationships with his leading actors, examples of which can be found in the interviews conducted by Bill Florence (re: Arnold Schwarzenegger), Jean-Marc Bouineau (re: Sharon Stone), and Dennis Hensley (re: Elizabeth Berkley).

The title of the first American interview in the book, Brian Cronenworth's "Man of Iron," implicitly assigns Superman's alias to two figures: RoboCop, cyborg-star of "the summer's flashiest, smartest action movie" and Paul Verhoeven himself, "one of Hollywood's hottest directors . . . a mite overqualified for a robot-vigilante film." Cronenworth distinguishes Verhoeven from American directors like Spielberg, who follow an opposing trajectory and "start out making movies in popular genres, and then 'graduate' to serious period epics or to films based on distinguished novels." Verhoeven is especially canny in each of the interviews from this time period, revealing himself to be an accomplished, well-educated director, and a quick learner of special effects who worked with the young Rob Bottin to design an "elegant" suit for RoboCop inspired by Fritz Lang's *Metropolis*. His American interviewers are impressed with the "rather sweet undercurrent" of RoboCop's foregone humanity and the consensus that emerges from these interviews is that Verhoeven is a director who is capable of elevating comic book material into adult entertainment and able to ground Hollywood science fiction with his sophisticated wit.

RoboCop proved to be a massive sleeper hit, grossing over $53 million in ticket sales (and ultimately $120 million worldwide). Verhoeven began work soon after on *Total Recall* (1990) and while the film shoot in Mexico was hobbled by rampant stress and illness, the director struck a confident rapport with his new leading man, Austrian bodybuilder Arnold Schwarzenegger. Verhoeven's 1990 interview with Bill Florence for *Cinefantastique* is a tribute to the mega-star's talent and easygoing demeanor, in glaring contrast to Verhoeven's previous tug-of-war with Rutger Hauer on *Flesh+Blood*. *Total Recall* was the most expensive Hollywood production to date, and upon its release became the highest grossing film of all time with $120 million in domestic ticket sales (and $263 million worldwide).

Riding high on the success of his first two American-made films, Verhoeven spoke to George Hickenlooper in 1991 about his transition to the US and posited: "The world seems to be larger here. I don't want to say that the work [is] any better or more profound, but it's more diverse. In Holland they quickly grew intolerant of my work. Perhaps I was not politically correct enough." Verhoeven expounded further upon his frustrations with what he called the "pre-censorship situation" in the Netherlands during a 1991 talk at Ball State University that was published in *Post Script*. There he described how a government-appointed committee determined the funding of a film based on their approval of the script. Repeatedly compelled to defend his work, Verhoeven grew tired of arguing with the committee's chairman: the film critic Jan Blokker, who once complained of Verhoeven's "utterly repulsive mentality." In his capacity as chairman of the Productiefonds,

Blokker was a conservative proponent of nominally sophisticated, "artistic" films, and Verhoeven admitted to *Het vrije volk* in 1983 that he modeled the cynical, corpulent main character of *The Fourth Man* on his thoroughly "unpleasant" adversary, Blokker.

Without the dangling carrot of full government subsidy, there is no exact correlative to the Dutch "pre-censorship committee" in the American production system, although industry-imposed restrictions abound. The Motion Picture Association of America (MPAA) repeatedly instructed Verhoeven to make cuts to each of his American films, often several times over, in order to obtain an "R" rating. But Verhoeven's relationship with that committee was at times reluctantly cordial, as he explained to Laurent Bouzereau in 1994: "If you want to use the term censorship, which I'm hesitant to use, I think you would have to call it more of an economic censorship. They don't censor your movie. After showing the MPAA the first cut of *Basic Instinct*, they said this is great . . . please don't change it . . . They wanted to legitimize the NC-17." Verhoeven made that diplomatic statement to Bouzereau after he decided to disregard the committee's advice and cut *Basic Instinct* down to an R-rating. The film went on to gross $353 million worldwide, when it would have earned significantly less with the more restrictive NC-17. It is worth noting that Verhoeven toughened his assessment of the MPAA in later interviews, such as in 1995, when he admitted to Dennis Hensley that the act of toning down *Basic Instinct* in fact made him "very unhappy" and likened the experience to "cutting your own flesh a little bit."

Laurent Bouzereau's *The Cutting Room Floor* is an enlightening book that delves into the convoluted rites of the MPAA by painstakingly tracking the changes that were enforced on about twenty familiar films, from the scriptwriting stage to post-production. "Basic Cutting" is the final chapter of the book and the excerpt I've included focuses on Bouzereau's interview with Verhoeven after the triumphant release of *Basic Instinct*. There is a lot of insider information in "Basic Cutting" about the MPAA's elusive methods of working with production studios to allocate optional but effectively necessary letter-ratings. Verhoeven is well aware of the economic leverage wielded by the organization and indulges Bouzereau with a patient breakdown of the minute changes he made to the film in order to secure a more profitable R-rating. As it stood at the time, films with an NC-17 were financially knee-capped because the big theater chains would not screen them, television stations would not air their advertisements, and studios would hold back on promotional budgets and publicity. Most films with NC-17 ratings were (and still are) the result of an impasse in negotiations with the MPAA for an R, and usually wound up dead in the water following a meager theatrical release, or floundered in the no-man's land of the direct-to-video market. All the more reason why Verhoeven's strategic decision in 1994 to ensure complete creative control and film

Showgirls as an NC-17 film was a shockingly intrepid—and unprecedented—move. By agreeing to forfeit seventy percent of his fee, he became the first director in history to get pre-approval from a major studio to shoot an NC-17 film.

It appears as if this decision ultimately paid off, as *Showgirls* eventually grossed over $100 million after years of precipitating home video sales and a thriving cult reputation. It also survives as the highest-grossing NC-17 film of all time and to this day, it is head-and-shoulders above the second highest grossing film on the list, Philip Kaufman's *Henry & June* (1990), which grossed $11.6 million to *Showgirls*'s $20.4 million in ticket sales. Fans and the mainstream press recently heralded the film on the occasion of the twentieth anniversary of its theatrical release, but long before its eventual record-breaking gross *Showgirls* was Verhoeven's first big box-office bomb and subject to merciless ridicule.

Twenty years after the fact, one can now intuit the resting calm before the storm in Dennis Hensley's playful set of interviews with Verhoeven and Berkley in 1995, conducted directly before and after the *Showgirls* premiere. The article features one interview with Verhoeven and two with Elizabeth Berkley, who at the time was poised to follow through on her breakout role à la Sharon Stone in *Basic Instinct*. In spite of some of Hensley's startlingly perverted and inconsequential questions (i.e. to Verhoeven: "If the man doesn't climax, when does the lap dance end?" and to Berkley: "Did you go to craft services naked?"), both director and star project a confident optimism that is almost painful to read in retrospect. However, all of their answers and by extension, Hensley's questions, are in keeping with the revised consensus in view of the film today—that is, a lighthearted and less punitive approach to *Showgirls*, regardless of qualitative assumptions about the film's relative merits or shortcomings.

Showgirls swept the notorious Razzie Awards in 1995 with seven wins and thirteen nominations and in good humor, Verhoeven became the first person to accept his Razzie for Worst Director onstage at the awards ceremony, to a standing ovation. The public opinion of the film has evolved over the ensuing twenty years, from disgust and mockery to patronizing snark and finally, a rising undercurrent of measured appreciation. When I first interviewed Verhoeven in Los Angeles, he was proud to mention Adam Nayman's excellent book *It Doesn't Suck: Showgirls*, which ECW Press released in April of 2014 through their "Pop Classics" series of critical essays. For better or for worse, *Showgirls* has become one of the defining films in Verhoeven's oeuvre, as well as the one that has inspired the most debate.

It is in that spirit of active discourse that I am including an original text by Verhoeven that is not strictly an interview, though it does engage in the ongoing dialogue about the film. *Showgirls: Portrait of a Film* is a folio-sized photo book that has been orphaned by an obsolete publisher and is currently out of print. Paul Verhoeven has kindly granted me permission to reprint his introductory and closing essays for the book, along with the corresponding storyboard selection. Storyboarding is an integral component of Verhoeven's filmmaking process and I am thrilled to include over thirty of his sketches here, beginning with the *Showgirls* storyboards that accompany his essay, "Shooting the Script," and followed by storyboards for five of his other films.

Drawn on the fly each evening in preparation for the following day's shoot, the *Showgirls* sketches differ from other of Verhoeven's storyboards in that they were prepared during the film's production, as Verhoeven explains in "Shooting the Script." On a more visceral level, the crude drafts of figures representing Elizabeth Berkley, Gina Gershon, and Kyle MacLaughlan's characters engaged in a pivotal lap dance sequence, while informative in their precise blocking and technical detail, cannot help but inspire a chuckle with their haphazard puerility. The same can be said for the storyboards for the opening sex scene in *Basic Instinct*, which provide an informative supplement to the Laurent Bouzereau interview. The storyboards for both of these films are so finely mapped out, from the exact camera angles to the positioning of the actors, and with an eye toward later scenes that purposefully mimic the movement and staging of their predecessors. Verhoeven is a talented fine artist with a background in painting, and the more cartoonish renderings of erotic scenes in some of these storyboards betray his overwhelming attention to technical detail at the expense of anatomical accuracy. All of them offer a terrifically privileged view of the director's creative process.

In many ways a hallmark of Verhoeven's work since his debut feature *Business Is Business*, his casual, forthright portrayal of sexuality was also the focal point of the widespread ridicule later directed at *Showgirls*. Written prior to the film's excessive backlash, Verhoeven's introduction to the *Showgirls* photo book opens with the rhetorical question, "Is it all just tits and ass?" presciently acknowledging the smug reaction to come. Under the subheading "Sex, Cinema and *Showgirls*," his introductory essay provides fascinating insight into the genesis of the film, Verhoeven and Hungarian screenwriter Joe Eszterhas's love letter to Las Vegas's ersatz glitz and glamour, told in the style of an NC-17-rated MGM musical. Verhoeven and Eszterhas share an expat's obsession with the ideal of the American Dream and its dark-sided corollary: the ruthless pursuit of wealth and personal gain. Having collaborated before on *Basic Instinct*, the duo's blunt amplification of sexuality is a given, but Verhoeven provides an additional explanation for his provocative work that dates back, surprisingly, to his formal training as a mathematician, awarded with a doctorandus from the University of Leiden with a special concentration on the theory of relativity: "I think of myself as provocative in a different sense: as a director who explores the difference between reality and the way in which we usually see reality portrayed." Verhoeven goes on to argue that *Showgirls* in fact represents a very basic reality—of evolutionary science—offering the following explanation: "Most women like to show off their bodies in skirts that reveal their legs or blouses that emphasize their breasts because they like to use their sexual power—they know that dressing this way will attract men who will ultimately give them babies. (Of course, this is not a conscious process.) That's the simple biology lesson of it all." This is an argument that Verhoeven consistently defends, one that he often presents under the mantle of level-headed reasoning, yet is clearly problematic in its strict rationale for female desire—not to mention the fact that none of Verhoeven's female characters indicate even a subconscious desire to have children (Sharon Stone's "Hate rug rats" line in *Basic Instinct* seems par for his heroines . . .). All of Verhoeven's female leads do engage in sex primarily for gain (if not mere survival) while the men are blissfully susceptible and beholden to the women's considerable sexual prowess. The men get to reap the sexual benefits of this primal game even if they are ultimately handed the short end of the stick, trampled by their female counterparts. The bottom line, as I see it, is that these relationships fit perfectly into the microcosms of Verhoeven's films, which leave no room for nuance. These women exhibit a ruthless confidence that is effectively portrayed as admirable and intimidating—if not entirely realistic.

In her interview with Dennis Hensley, Elizabeth Berkley praises Verhoeven multiple times for his ability to portray his female leads "in their power," and the *Showgirls* storyboards seem to support that image, with Berkley vigorously performing the same calculated grinding movement on Kyle MacLachlan's character in two distinct scenes. As cold and domineering as Verhoeven's leading ladies are, they are also the characters for whom we root to survive and succeed. Regarding Verhoeven's somewhat reductive view of the human sex drive, it is nonetheless his wholehearted, discerning opinion, and less misogynist than what many of *Showgirls'* more contemptuous viewers likely have in mind. It is certainly one worth considering when watching Verhoeven's films and reading the other interviews in this book. Returning to the essay's initial question, "Is it all just tits and ass?" Verhoeven's response is thus: "Even if this perception were true, that's fine with me: Why shouldn't we enjoy the beauty of the human body? Like it or not, we are biologically destined to enjoy sexual attraction as the means by which we continue the species. However, the experience of making *Showgirls*, and the aesthetic, emotional, and thematic elements expressed in these photographs, mean considerably more to me."

Before *Showgirls* was even released Verhoeven was already hard at work on the script for *Starship Troopers* (1997). He and Ed Neumeier began work on the adaptation of Robert Heinlein's science fiction novel around the time of *Basic Instinct*, and Verhoeven saw the project as an opportunity to reunite with his *RoboCop* team of writer Neumeier, producer Jon Davison, and special effects guru Phil Tippett. Verhoeven has always acknowledged his talent for genre filmmaking and at first glance *Starship Troopers* appears to be a well executed generic hybrid of creature feature sci-fi meets WWII-era war movie, with giant bugs standing in for enemy troops. The film is a rousing, gruesome war fantasy with chiseled young soldiers who are disturbingly keen on annihilating the insect race or less specifically, "anything with more than two legs!" As Verhoeven explained to Bill Warren for *Starlog* magazine, "it's an American *Soldier of Orange*, where the enemy is not Germans, but giant insects. It has that idea . . . that feeling of innocence, of being a young kid and thinking the world is wonderful and everything will go well, that feeling that is then destroyed by the cruelty of war was the idea that attracted me." Verhoeven's interview for the sci-fi magazine is loaded with detail and focused intently on the upcoming film, with only a few qualms raised on behalf of Robert Heinlein purists. The film takes a minor stumble in November of 1997 with the publication of a few negative and plainly misguided reviews alleging that the film projected a fascist agenda. Rita Kempley's vituperative piece for the *Washington Post* was the first such review, referring to Verhoeven as the "lap dance maven (of *Showgirls* infamy)." Kempley could sense the satire in the film's glaringly propagandist (and comedic) newsreels, but complained obstinately that Verhoeven's denunciation of war-mongering wasn't clear-cut, maintaining that the director "seems more drawn to Nazi chic than Yankee gumption." Kempley's colleague Stephen Hunter wrote an even more vicious, tone-deaf review, claiming that the film was " . . . spiritually Nazi, psychologically Nazi. It comes directly out of the Nazi imagination, and is set in the Nazi universe." Olivier Guéret interviewed Verhoeven exactly one month later at a conference where the press was forewarned in light of the negative reviews to not ask the director any questions about the fascist interpretation of the film. This did not prevent Guéret from raising the topic in conversation, which didn't appear to faze Verhoeven. He clarified to Guéret: "It's true that fascism isn't dead and that it remains present in several countries around the world—but that isn't what the film is about. When you see the topics that I raise using the Federation's newsreels, I'm pointing out dysfunctions within the current American regime," wherein the tongue-in-cheek catchphrase repeated at the end of each newsreel, "Would you like to know more?" implicitly begs the question, "Do you want to dive even further into this system that already exists in America?"

Verhoeven postulated to Bill Warren in 1997 that there is an important difference between the sci-fi/war movie genre, which includes films like *Starship Troopers*, and sci-fi/horror, "where the enemy is invisible in the story, or just slightly visible . . . always spooky and not a substantial enemy you have in front of you for very long." Three years later, this description would apply to Verhoeven's next film, *Hollow Man* (2000), a loose interpretation of H.G. Wells' *The Invisible Man* with references to the second book of *The Republic*, in which Plato speculates that a man who acquires invisibility would inevitably commit evil acts. Even with a backbone in Platonic discourse, the most enduring feature of *Hollow Man* is the special effects, and Verhoeven indulges Douglas Eby with all of the gritty details: comprehensible descriptions of the mechanics of motion capture photography as well as a concise account of his collaboration with Phil Tippett and Sony Imageworks to create an accurate digitization of the human body. Free from controversy, *Hollow Man* performed well at the box office but came and went rather quietly, supporting Verhoeven's later confession to various interviewers that the project made him feel like a director for hire. Feeling hemmed in by an increasingly conservative studio system, Verhoeven left Hollywood after *Hollow Man*, never to return.

In between projects in 2003, Verhoeven was interviewed by the transgressive filmmaker, photographer, artist, and author Bruce LaBruce for *Interview* magazine. The two directors chatted freely during this in-between stage of Verhoeven's career on a wide range of topics from pornography to socialism, Christianity, Hitchcock, homosexuality, and DVD commentary tracks. Speaking out at one point against the strain of "liberal existentialist thinking" that fears and distrusts technology, Verhoeven argues that in fact, "science is the only religion you can really trust." Coming from a Fellow of the Westar Institute (a group of scholars who research early Christian history), this is more than just a sarcastic quip.

Verhoeven has long been an avowed atheist but has always harbored a profound interest in Christianity irrespective of his personal (dis)beliefs. His sole flirtation with the Christian faith was a dangerous one, when he briefly joined the Pentecostal church during a rough patch in his late twenties and nearly lost his mind. His bout of religious fervor came to an abrupt halt as soon as he and his wife-to-be decided to terminate her unwanted pregnancy, thus solving all of their immediate problems. No longer a fanatic, he appeared to cling to a remnant of religious belief as late as 1979, when he spoke to the *Leeuwarder Courant* to promote *Soldier of Orange*: "I'm very preoccupied with the fact of whether God exists or not. This has determined a large part of my life. I'm not sure if I believe in God . . . You could say that my films are about the fact that I do not know." Verhoeven's agnostic spate did not last very long but his academic interest in Jesus Christ evolved into a lifelong fascination. He became a Fellow of the Westar Institute soon after he moved to California, and the Christ allegory in *RoboCop* is one discernible indication of his contemporary research. Rüdiger Sturm's 2009 interview with Verhoeven delves headfirst into this sideline, and is devoted entirely to Verhoeven's thoughts on the historical Jesus and his book on the topic, published in English in 2010 by Seven Stories Press under the title *The Real Jesus of Nazareth*. Verhoeven explained to Mark Jacobson of *New York* magazine in 2010 that the scholarly tome started out as "a treatment for a film I have been thinking of making for the past thirty years." Verhoeven mentions this slippery project, *Christ the Man*, in interviews throughout this book, beginning with his 1984 interview with Mark

Valen, when Scorcese's *Last Temptation of Christ* was just a rumor in the making. James Hughes' 2007 interview for *Stop Smiling* also tackles Verhoeven's historical research and includes an insightful discussion of Pasolini's *The Gospel According to Matthew*.

Time and again, Verhoeven speaks assertively about the Christian religion in a dry, dismissive manner that would undoubtedly shock most conservative Americans. The same can be said of Verhoeven's various accounts of his childhood in The Hague during the last years of WWII. Growing up in German-occupied territory, in an area near a prominent bomb site, Verhoeven frequently witnessed gruesome scenes of carnage and death firsthand, stepping over dead bodies on his way home from school and watching a bomb strike his neighbor's house as his own windows were blown in from the explosion. Speaking with his (mostly American) interviewers, however, Verhoeven unapologetically describes the time period as "wonderful," a "great adventure," and a thrilling experience for a six-year-old similar to John Boorman's depiction of childhood during the war in *Hope and Glory*. He admitted to Chris Shea and Wade Jennings that childhood exposure to war atrocities could ostensibly activate "a very strong depression, which probably sinks into the subconscious later when it's all over and the war is over and peace starts," but denied that the war had such an effect on him. He later confided to Jay Holben in a 2000 interview for *American Cinematographer*: "saying, 'Oh, it has to do with my youth' makes it kind of understandable, but I really don't know if it's the truth. That was just a way to answer the question for journalists! (*Laughs*) I use violence because I *like* violence."

In 2006 Verhoeven returned to the wartime era of his childhood with *Black Book*, his first Dutch film in over twenty years. A thriller about a Jewish singer who goes undercover for the Dutch resistance, *Black Book* was hailed by the press as Verhoeven's return to form and an effective melding of propulsive, classical Hollywood-style narrative with complex characterization that acknowledged the latent anti-Semitism of many resistance fighters. The film was a success in the Netherlands, though some critics complained that it was aesthetically "superficial." *Black Book* received positive reviews in both the US and Europe, proving that Verhoeven could break out of the rut of science fiction.

Unable to latch onto a suitable project in the United States, he continued to work in the Netherlands after *Black Book* and even participated in an interview book penned by his biographer, Rob van Scheers, whose contribution to the scholarship on Verhoeven cannot be understated. His 1997 biography, *Paul Verhoeven*, is a core reference and the source of countless anecdotes that have been repeated in nearly all of the extant literature on Verhoeven, this introduction included. *Volgens Verhoeven* (*According to Verhoeven*) is a recent collection of interviews with Verhoeven that focus on some of his favorite films, transcribed into first-person essays. Van Scheers has granted me permission to print Julia van den Hout's new English translation of the chapter on *Vertigo*, one of Verhoeven's greatest influences, the film that he calls his "alpha and omega."

From 2011 to 2013 Verhoeven remained in the Netherlands and oversaw a crowdsourced television production for the Dutch cable network Ziggo called the *Entertainment Experience*. Riffing on an opening segment written by Kim van Kooten, thousands of contestants submitted fragments of a script to be pieced together into a television movie, the process of which was documented for a reality-style television series. Verhoeven was not satisfied with any of the thousands of scripts that were submitted, so he and Robert Alberdingk Thijm rewrote each segment and assembled it all into the 55-minute long film, *Steekspel* (or *Tricked*) in 2012. In 2013, the Dutch blogger Nostra spoke with Verhoeven about the complexities of the crowd-sourcing experiment and forwarded general questions from his readers to the director. I also questioned Verhoeven in Los Angeles in 2014 about the *Entertainment Experience* and about the new filmmaking techniques he adopted to direct *Tricked*, which he refers to as his "fourteen-and-a-half movie." Verhoeven explained to me how he and his co-writer completely overhauled the contestants' submissions: "I thought that I would be able to use at least one or two scripts for each segment as they were, or perhaps combine two or three together for a five-minute episode but even that turned out to be absolutely impossible. We had to bend, change, restructure, and invent whatever it took to keep [the script] going."

I found Verhoeven's intense commitment to quality control delightful, as well as a promising indication that he was ready to return to directing after a long hiatus. As it turned out, Verhoeven utilized *Tricked* as a low-pressure testing ground for new filmmaking techniques, such as a new "dialectic" camera style, in which two cameramen film different views of the same scene, and then went on to employ that very technique on the 2014 *Elle* shoot in Paris. When I interviewed him in Los Angeles, he was preparing to leave for Europe the next day to complete the casting, and one year later I spoke with him again over the phone just as he was about to enter into the post-production stage. The critical anticipation for the film was starting to accumulate based on the spare details of the film that had been made available to the public and as of late 2015, there is still little known about the film, other than the fact that it stars Isabelle Huppert and is an adaptation of the French novel *Oh . . . !* by Philippe Djian, who also wrote the source novel for the 1986 Jean-Jacques Beineix film *Betty Blue*. Huppert is one of the most daring actresses of her generation, Verhoeven has a provocative reputation of his own, and the word is that Djian's novel pivots on the familiar plot device of "rape and revenge." Many journalists have grasped at those details and used them to jump to the conclusion that Verhoeven has directed another "erotic thriller," although the translated premise of Djian's novel strikes me as too violent to be erotic.

Unsettled by the prospect of Verhoeven eroticizing rape (as he has come close to doing twice before, in *Flesh+Blood* and *Basic Instinct*, in respective scenes where the characters played by Jennifer Jason Leigh and Jeanne Trippelhorn fluctuate in their consent, both for the purposes of character development), I asked Verhoeven about the rumor in 2015. He assured me that "those people who think that this is an erotic film will be disillusioned. They are in for a strange confrontation with a movie that is . . . not ordinary."

We will know soon enough if Verhoeven's next film will warrant the hackneyed "comeback" label, but personally I was sold as soon as he took that weighted pause before opting to describe *Elle* as "not ordinary." There is something uncanny about all of Verhoeven's films that is akin to the perspective of an outsider looking in, something so unordinary that it rejects all potential labels. He observed during our first interview, "As I get older I've grown more interested in doing things that are beyond the norm . . . and I think that to a certain degree this return to Europe has to do with being able to make the kind of movies that I want to make." *Elle* represents an entirely new phase for him, as his first feature in a decade, his first French-language film, and his first collaboration with the inimitable Isabelle Huppert. Regardless of how the film plays out, its audience is surely in for a distinctly Verhoevian "strange confrontation," and I hope that the interviews in this book will provide an enlightening backdrop to the spectacle onscreen.

I want to thank Paul Verhoeven, Stacy Lumbrezer, and Mita DeGroot for their kind and generous assistance in my search for original content for this book. Many thanks also to Michael Chaiken, for convincing me to take on the project, and to Carrie Jones, for her invaluable friendship and editorial verve. This book would not have been possible without the patient advocacy of Leila Salisbury, Valerie Jones, and Lisa McMurtray at the University Press of Mississippi, and the brilliant translators Julia van den Hout and Alexandra Valentine Proulx. Thanks to all of the interviewers who made this book a pleasure to compile, and to Gilles Boulenger, Rüdiger Sturm, and Rob van Scheers for their exemplary books and long-distance support. Thanks also to Jim Allen, Nick Dawson, Nicolas Rapold, Violet Lucca, Andrew Repasky McElhinney, Gavin Smith, Dan Streible, and Jaap Verheul for their valuable help and backstage advice and finally, to Chris Millstein and my parents; Marty and Mimi, for their vital encouragement.

MBF

Chronology

1938	Born 18 July in Amsterdam to Wim Verhoeven, a primary school teacher and headmaster, and Nel Verhoeven.
1955	Studies art at L'Ecole de la Tour in Paris and learns to speak french, but misses the deadline to apply for film school.
1956	Attends the University of Leiden in the Netherlands, where he studies mathematics and physics for five years.
1959	Attends the Nederlandse Film Academy in Amsterdam. Directs his first film, the 35-minute short *One Lizard Too Many*.
1960	Premieres *One Lizard Too Many* in the presence of Crown Princess Beatrix on June 15th.
1962	Directs *The Hitchhikers* and *Nothing Special*.
1963	Directs his fourth short film, *Let's Have a Party* and meets Martine Tours, a violinist.
1964	Receives his doctorandus in mathematics and physics, with an emphasis on Einstein's Theory of Relativity in June. Is drafted to the military in July, where he directs his first color film for the Marine Film Service, the twenty-three-minute *The Marine Corps*.
1966	Completes his two-year term of military service. Goes through a Pentecostal phase and suffers a mental breakdown when his girlfriend becomes pregnant. They decide to abort the pregnancy and Verhoeven abandons his religious beliefs.
1967	Marries his girlfriend, Martine Tours, on April 7th.
1968	Shoots a documentary, *Portrait of Anton Adriaan Mussert*, about the leader of the NSB, the 1930's Dutch pro-fascist party. Begins shooting the television series *Floris*, starring Rutger Hauer, in July.
1969	The first episode of *Floris* airs on October 15th and the show is a huge success.
1970	Directs *The Wrestler*, a twenty-minute sex comedy filmed by cinematographer Jan de Bont. *Portrait of Anton Adriaan Mussert* finally broadcasts on April 16th with black bars added to obscure the identities of the interviewees.
1971	Directs his first feature length film, a sex comedy about the lives of

	prostitutes called *Business Is Business*. The film is a record-breaking success.
1973	*Turkish Delight* premieres on February 22nd and becomes the highest-grossing Dutch movie ever made.
1974	*Turkish Delight* is nominated for the Academy Award for Best Foreign Film.
1975	Verhoeven's third feature, *Katie Tippel*, premieres on March 6th.
1977	*Soldier of Orange*, based on the memoirs of Dutch Resistance fighter Eric Hazelhoff Roelfzema premieres on September 23rd to great acclaim.
1979	Begins shooting the controversial *Spetters* about young working-class motorcyclists in August. *Soldier of Orange* premieres successfully in the US.
1980	*Spetters* turns a good profit at the box-office but the Dutch press attacks the film and vilifies Verhoeven, instigating the formation of a protest group called the National Anti-*Spetters* Action Committee (or NASA). After winning the Los Angeles Film Critics' Award, *Soldier of Orange* is nominated for the Golden Globe for Best Foreign Film. Verhoeven makes his first trip to Hollywood at the invitation of Steven Spielberg.
1982	Verhoeven re-teams with his former producer Rob Houwer and shoots his first "art" film, *The Fourth Man*, in May.
1983	*The Fourth Man* premieres on March 24th. It is both a critical and financial success and Verhoeven's reputation in the Netherlands is redeemed after the *Spetters* fiasco.
1984	*The Fourth Man* wins the Los Angeles Film Critics' award for Best Foreign Film. Verhoeven shoots *Flesh+Blood* in Spain for Orion Pictures, ending his professional relationship with actor Rutger Hauer.
1985	*Flesh+Blood* premieres at the Venice Film Festival in August and the following month, Verhoeven moves to the United States to film *RoboCop*. In October he directs *The Last Scene*, a twenty-five-minute television episode for the HBO series *The Hitchhiker*.
1986	Verhoeven shoots *RoboCop* and joins the Jesus Seminar, a group of theologians and academics who meet biannually to discuss the historical accuracy of the gospels' portrayal of Jesus Christ.
1987	*RoboCop* premieres on July 17th and becomes the sleeper hit of the summer.
1989	Verhoeven spends 20 weeks shooting *Total Recall* in Mexico, where most of the cast and crew become violently ill. Verhoeven nearly collapses from exhaustion but continues to direct the film.

1990	*Total Recall* premieres on June 1st and becomes an even bigger hit than *RoboCop*.
1991	Verhoeven begins shooting *Basic Instinct*, with a script by Joe Eszterhas, in April. The Gay and Lesbian Alliance Against Defamation (GLAAD) protests the production, claiming the screenplay is homophobic. Eszterhas angers Verhoeven by trying to adjust the screenplay in response to GLAAD's accusations. Verhoeven breaks away from Eszterhas and begins to write the screenplay for *Christ the Man*, based on his research on the historical figure of Jesus Christ.
1992	*Basic Instinct* premieres on March 20th. The film grosses $118 million in box-office sales ($353 million worldwide).
1994	Begins shooting *Showgirls* in Las Vegas in November. Verhoeven forfeits seventy percent of his fee in order to get pre-approval from the studio to shoot the film with an NC-17 rating.
1995	Resumes work on *Starship Troopers* with screenwriter Ed Neumeier. *Showgirls* premieres on September 22nd and is a box-office failure. Verhoeven becomes the first director to attend the Golden Raspberry Award ceremony to accept his "Worst Director" award in person.
1996	Begins shooting *Starship Troopers* in May.
1997	*Starship Troopers* premieres on November 7th. The film turns a respectable profit at the box-office amid scathing reviews.
1999	Begins work on *Hollow Man* as *Turkish Delight* is voted Best Dutch Film of the Century at the Netherlands Film Festival.
2000	*Hollow Man* premieres on August 4th. It receives poor reviews from critics but debuts at the top of the box-office, eventually doubling its budget to become Verhoeven's biggest hit since *Basic Instinct*.
2005	Returns to filmmaking in Europe with the Dutch/German/British co-production *Black Book*, a WWII thriller based on an original script by Gerard Soeteman. Production commences in August and *Black Book* becomes the most expensive Dutch film ever made.
2006	*Black Book* premieres in September at the Venice International Film Festival where it is nominated for a Golden Lion. In the Netherlands, Verhoeven receives a hero's welcome as HRH the Prince of Orange and his wife HRH Princess Máxima attend the Dutch gala premiere.
2007	*Black Book* premieres in the United States in January at the Palm Springs International Film Festival. In March it is the opening film of the Miami International Film Festival. In April he is knighted in the Order of the Netherlands Lion.
2008	Co-written with his biographer Rob van Scheers, *The Real Jesus of Nazareth* is published in the Netherlands in September.

2010 An English-language translation of *The Real Jesus of Nazareth* is published in May by Seven Stories Press.

2011 The *Entertainment Experience* film project is launched in September. Verhoeven and writers Kim van Kooten and Robert Alberdingk Thijm supervise a large "crowd" of competitors who all contribute to the writing and production of a film in eight parts while the process is documented online and shown on Dutch television.

2012 Verhoeven's adaptation of the *Entertainment Experience* film, now titled *Tricked*, premieres in September in Amsterdam.

2013 *Tricked* screens at the Tribeca Film Festival in New York City. Originally intended for television, the film is medium-length with a fifty-five-minute running time.

2014 Verhoeven goes into production at the end of the year in Paris on *Elle*, his first feature film since *Black Book*. Written by David Birke (*13 Sins*), the film is an adaptation of the novel *Oh . . .* by Philippe Djian (*Betty Blue*) and stars French actress Isabelle Huppert.

2015 September marks the twentieth anniversary of the release of *Showgirls*. Verhoeven oversees the post-production of *Elle* in the Netherlands later in the fall, with an initial release tentatively slated for February 2016.

Filmography

ONE LIZARD TOO MANY (1960)
Eén Hagedis Teveel
The Netherlands Student Film Industry (Nederlandse Studenten Filmindustrie)
Director: **Paul Verhoeven**
Screenplay: Jan van Mastrigt
Cinematographer: Frits Boersma
Editor: Ernst Winar
Music: Aart Gisolf
Cast: Erik Bree, Marijke Jones, Hermine Menalda, Hans Schneider, P.A. Harteveld
B&W, 35 minutes

NOTHING SPECIAL (1961)
Niets Bijzonders
The Netherlands Student Film Industry (Nederlandse Studenten Filmindustrie)
Director: **Paul Verhoeven**
Screenplay: Jan van Mastrigt
Cinematographer: Frits Boersma
Cast: Jan van Mastrigt, Marina Shapers
35 mm, B&W, 9 minutes

THE HITCHHIKERS (1962)
De Lifters
The Netherlands Student Film Industry (Nederlandse Studenten Filmindustrie)
Director: **Paul Verhoeven**
Screenplay: Jan van Mastrigt
Cinematographer: Frits Boersma
Editor: Ernst Winar
Cast: Geerda Walma van der Molen, Jaap van Donselaar, Maarten Schutte, Jan van Mastrigt
B&W, 17 minutes

LET'S HAVE A PARTY (1963)
Feest
Ministerie van Buitenlandse Zaken
Director and Producer: **Paul Verhoeven**
Screenplay: Jan van Mastrigt
Cinematographer: Ferenc Kálmán-Gáll
Editor: Ernst Winar
Music: Dick Broeckaerts
Cast: Yvonne Blei-Weissmann, Dick de Brauw, Pieter Jelle Bouman, Wim Noordhoek
35 mm, B&W, 28 minutes

THE MARINE CORPS (1965)
Het Korps Mariniers
Multifilm
Director: **Paul Verhoeven**
Cinematographers: Peter Alsemgeest, Jan Kijser and Jos van Haarlem
Editor: Ernst Winar
Music: H. C. van Lijnschoten
Color, 23 minutes

PORTRAIT OF ANTON ADRIAAN MUSSERT (1968)
Portret van Anton Adriaan Mussert
Vrijzinnig Protestantse Radio Omroep (VPRO television)
Director: **Paul Verhoeven**
Compilers: **Paul Verhoeven**, Leo Kool and Hans Keller
Cinematographer: Jaap Buis
Commentary: Hans Keller
B&W, 50 minutes

FLORIS (1969)
(Television Series)
Cinécentrum N.V., Max Appelboom Producties
Producer: Max Appelboom
Director: **Paul Verhoeven**
Script: Gerard Soeteman
Cinematographer: Ton Buné
Art Director: Jan P. Koenraads
Editor: Jan Bosdriesz
Music: Julius Staffaro

Cast: Rutger Hauer (Floris van Rosemondt), Jos Bergman (Sindala), Ton Vos (Wolter van Odesteijn), Jacco van Renesse (Rogier), Tim Beekman (Sergeant), Hans Culeman (Maarten van Rossem), Diana Dobbelman (Ada), Ida Bons (Viola), Hans Boskamp (Lange Pier)
B&W, 12 episodes, 30 minutes each

THE WRESTLER (1970)
De Worstelaar
RNtv
Producer: Nico Crama
Director: **Paul Verhoeven**
Screenplay: **Paul Verhoeven** and Kees Holierhoek
Cinematographer: Jan de Bont
Editor: Jan Bosdriesz
Music: Jack Trombey (as J. Stoeckart)
Cast: Jon Bluming, Bernhard Droog, Peter Faber, Wim Zomer, Mariëlle Fiolet
Color, 20 minutes

BUSINESS IS BUSINESS (1971)
Any Special Way, Diary of a Hooker, Wat Zien Ik?
Rob Houwer Productions
Producer: Rob Houwer
Director: **Paul Verhoeven**
Screenplay: Gerard Soeteman (based on a collection of short stories by Albert Mol)
Cinematographer: Jan de Bont
Set Design: Massimo Götz and Henk Koster
Editor: Jan Bosdriesz
Music: Julius Steffaro, Jack Trombey
Cast: Ronny Bierman (Blonde Greet), Sylvia de Leur (Nel Muller), Piet Römer (Piet), Jules Hamel (Sjaak), Bernard Droog (Bob de Vries), Eric van Ingen (Albert), Henk Molenberg (Client, Cleaning Scenes), Albert Mol (Van Schaveren), Trudy Labij (Prostitute), Ton Lensink (Client, Witch Scene), Dini de Neef (Older Prostitute), Carry Tefsen (Prostitute), André van den Heuvel (Drunk), Allard van der Scheer (Client, School Scene), Helmet Woudenberg (Client, First One), Jan Verhoeven (Client, Chicken Scene)
Color, 93 minutes

TURKISH DELIGHT (1973)
Turks Fruit

Verenigde Nederlandsche Filmcompagnie (VNF), Rob Houwer Productions
Producer: Rob Houwer
Director: **Paul Verhoeven**
Screenplay: Gerard Soeteman, Jan Wolkers (novel)
Cinematographer: Jan de Bont
Editor: Jan Bosdriesz
Art Director: Ralf van de Elst
Music: Rogier van Otterloo
Cast: Monique van de Ven (Olga Stapels), Ruter Hauer (Erik Vonk), Tonny Huurdeman (Olga's Mother), Wim van den Brink (Olga's Father), Hans Boskamp (Shop Manager Winkelchef), Dolf de Vries (Paul), Manfred de Graaf (Henny), Dick Scheffer (Accountant), Marjol Flore (Tineke), Bert Dijkstra (Civil Servant), Marijke Frijlink (Moniek), Olga Zuiderhoek (Gonnie), Maartje Seyferth (Josje), Aime Mars (Indonesian Girl), Suzie Broks (Truus), Jaap van Donselaar and Jans Kemna (Eric's Friends)
35mm, Color, 112 minutes

KATIE TIPPEL (1975)
Keetje Tippel
Rob Houwer Productions
Producer: Rob Houwer
Director: **Paul Verhoeven**
Screenplay: Gerard Soeteman, Neel Doff (Memoirs)
Cinematographer: Jan de Bont
Editor: Jane Sperr
Art Director: Roland de Groot
Music: Rogier van Otterloo
Cast: Monique van de Ven (Keetje Tippel), Rutger Hauer (Hugo), Peter Faber (George), Eddy Brugman (Andre), Hannah de Leeuwe (Keetje's Sister Mina), Andrea Domburg (Keetje's Mother), Jan Blaaser (Keetje's Father), Huib Broos (Manager of Wax Factory), Theu Boermans (Doctor), Carry Tefsen (Woman in Wax Factory)
35mm, Color, 109 minutes

SOLDIER OF ORANGE (1977)
Soldaat van Oranje
Excelsior Films/Film Holland/The Rank Organization/Rob Houwer Productions
Producer: Rob Houwer, Gijs Versluys
Director: **Paul Verhoeven**

Screenplay: Gerard Soeteman, Kees Holierhoek, **Paul Verhoeven**, Erik Hazelhoff Roelfzema (Novel)
Cinematographer: Jost Vacano
Editor: Jane Sperr
Art Director: Roland de Groot
Music: Rogier van Otterloo
Cast: Rutger Hauer (Erik Lanshof), Jeroen Krabbé (Guus LeJeune), Susan Penhaligon (Susan), Edward Fox (Colonel Rafelli), Lex van Delden (Nico), Derek de Lint (Alex), Huib Rooymans (John Weinberg), Dolf de Vries (Jack Ten Brinck), Eddy Habbema (Robby Froost), Belinda Meuldijk (Esther), Peter Faber (Will Dostgaarde), Rijk de Gooyer (Gestapo-Man Breitner), Paul Brandenburg (SS Lt. Thelen), Ward de Ravet (Resistance Leader), Bert Struys (Resistance Leader), Reinhard Kolldehoff (Geisman), Andrea Domburg (Queen Wilhelmina), Guus Hermus (Van der Zanden)
35mm, Color and B&W, 155 minutes

GONE, GONE (1979 TV movie)
Voorbij, Voorbij
KRO Television
Producer: Joop van den Ende
Director: **Paul Verhoeven**
Script: Gerard Soeteman
Cinematographer: Mat van Hensbergen
Editor: Ine Schenkkan
Music: Hans Vermeulen
Cast: André van den Heuvel (Ab), Andrea Domburg (Dorien), Piet Römer (Gerben), Hans Veerman, Guus Oster (Ben), Jan Retel (Cees), Hidde Maas (Arie), Leontien Ceulemans (Tine), Riek Schagen (Niels' Wife), Maarten Spanjer (Jogger), Simone Kleinsma (Tour Guide),
Color, 58 minutes

SPETTERS (1980)
Endemol Entertainment/VSE Productions
Producer: Joop van den Ende
Director: **Paul Verhoeven**
Screenplay: Gerard Soeteman
Cinematographer: Jost Vacano
Editor: Ine Schenkkan
Art Director: Dick Schillemans
Music: Ton Scherpenzeel and Kayak

Cast: Hans van Tongeren (Rien), Renée Soutendijk (Fientje), Toon Agterberg (Eef), Maarten Spanjer (Hans), Marianne Boyer (Maya), Peter Tuinman (Fientje's Brother Jaap), Saskia Ten Batenburg (Truus), Yvonne Valkenburg (Annette), Ab Abspoel (Rien's Father), Rudi Falkenhagen (Hans' Father), Hans Veerman (Ed's Father Willem), Ben Aerden (Old Homosexual), Kitty Courbois (Doctor), Gees Linnebank (Homosexual), Hugo Metsers (Hell's Angel), Peter Oosthoek (Priest), Jeroen Krabbé (Frans Henkhof), Rutger Hauer (Gerrit Witkamp)
35mm, Color, 120 minutes

THE FOURTH MAN (1983)
De Vierde Man
Rob Houwer Productions/Verenigde Nederlansche Filmcompagnie (VNF)
Producer: Rob Houwer
Director: **Paul Verhoeven**
Screenplay: Gerard Soeteman, Gerard Reve (Novel)
Cinematographer: Jan de Bont
Editor: Ine Schenkkan
Art Direction: Roland de Groot
Music: Loek Dikker
Cast: Jeroen Krabbé (Gerard Reve), Renée Soutendijk (Christine Halsslag), Thom Hoffman (Herman), Dolf de Vries (Doctor de Vries), Geert de Jong (Ria), Hans Veerman (Undertaker), Hero Muller (Josefs), Caroline de Beus (Adrienne), Reinout Bussemaker (First Husband), Erik J. Meijer (Second Husband), Ursul de Geer (Third Husband), Filip Bolluyt (Surfer)
35mm, Color, 102 minutes

FLESH+BLOOD (1985)
The Rose and the Sword
Riverside Pictures/Orion/Impala
Producer: Gijs Versluys
Director: **Paul Verhoeven**
Screenplay: Gerard Soeteman, **Paul Verhoeven**
Story: Gerard Soeteman
Cinematographer: Jan de Bont
Editor: Ine Schenkkan
Art Director: Felix Murcia
Music: Basil Poledouris
Cast: Rutger Hauer (Martin), Jennifer Jason Leigh (Agnes), Tom Burlinson (Steven), Jack Thompson (Hawkwood), Fernando Hilbeck (Arnolfini), Susan Tyrrell (Celine), Ronald Lacey (Cardinal), Brion James (Karsthans), John Dennis

Johnston (Summer), Simón Andreu (Miel), Bruno Kirby (Orbec), Kitty Courbois (Anna), Marina Saura (Polly), Hans Veerman (Father George), Jake Wood (Little John)
35mm, Color, 126 minutes

THE HITCHHIKER, EPISODE 3.11: "LAST SCENE" (Mar. 25, 1986)
Markowitz/Chesler Producing/Quintina Productions
Producers: Jon Anderson, Lewis Chesler, Riff Markowitz
Director: **Paul Verhoeven**
Teleplay: Robert J. Avrech
Story: Richard Rothstein
Cinematographer: Reginald M. Morris
Editor: Stan Cole
Art Director: David Fischer
Music: Michel Rubini
Cast: Peter Coyote (Alex Nolan), LaGena Hart (Leda Bedell), Page Fletcher (The Hitchhiker), Tom Heaton (Paul), Garwin Sanford (Duncan)
35mm, Color, 29 minutes

ROBOCOP (1987)
Orion Pictures
Executive Producer: Jon Davison
Producers: Edward Neumeier, Arne Schmidt, Phil Tippett, Stephen Lim
Director: **Paul Verhoeven**
Screenplay: Edward Neumeier, Michael Miner
Cinematography: Jost Vacano, Sol Negrin (uncredited)
Editor: Frank J. Orioste
Art Direction: John Marshall, Gayle Simon William Sandell
Music: Basil Poledouris
Cast: Peter Weller (Officer Alex J. Murphy/RoboCop), Nancy Allen (Officer Anne Lewis), Dan O'Herlihy (The Old Man), Ronny Cox (Dick Jones), Kurtwood Smith (Clarence J. Boddicker), Miguel Ferrer (Bob Morton), Robert DoQui (Sergeant Warren Reed), Ray Wise (Leon C. Nash), Felton Perry (Johnson), Paul McCrane (Emil M. Antonowsky, Jesse D. Goins (Joe P. Cox), Del Zamora (Kaplan)
35mm (printed on 35mm and blown up to 70mm), Color, 103 mins

TOTAL RECALL (1990)
Carolco Pictures
Executive Producers: Mario Kassar, Andrew Vajna

Producers: Buzz Feitshans, Ronald Shusett, Robert Fentress, David Rodgers, Elliot Schick
Director: **Paul Verhoeven**
Screenplay: Ronald Shusett, Dan O'Bannon, Gary Goldman
Screen Story: Ronald Shusett, Dan O'Bannon, Jon Povill
Story: Philip K. Dick ("We Can Remember It For You Wholesale")
Cinematographer: Jost Vacano
Editing: Carlos Puente, Frank J. Urioste
Art Direction: José Rodriguez Granada, James E. Tocci
Music: Jerry Goldsmith
Cast: Arnold Schwarzenegger (Douglas Quaid/Hauser), Rachel Ticotin (Melina), Sharon Stone (Lori), Ronny Cox (Vilos Cohaagen), Michael Ironside (Richter), Marshall Bell (George/Kuato), Mel Johnson Jr. (Benny), Michael Champion (Helm), Roy Brocksmith (Dr. Edgemar), Ray Baker (Bob McClane), Rosemary Dunsmore (Dr. Lull), David Knell (Ernie), Alexia Robinson (Tiffany), Dean Norris (Tony)
35mm (printed on 35mm and blown up to 70mm), Color, 113 minutes

BASIC INSTINCT (1992)
Carolco Pictures/Canal+
Executive Producer: Mario Kassar
Producers: Alan Marshall, William S. Beasley, Louis D'Esposito
Director: **Paul Verhoeven**
Screenplay: Joe Eszterhas
Cinematographer: Jan de Bont
Editor: Frank J. Urioste
Production Designer: Terence Marsh
Music: Jerry Goldsmith
Cast: Michael Douglas (Detective Nick Curran), Sharon Stone (Catherine Tramell), George Dzundza (Gus), Jeanne Tripplehorn (Dr. Beth Garner), Dennis Arndt (Lieutenant Walker), Leilani Sarelle (Roxy), Bruce A. Young (Andrews), Chelcie Ross (Captain Talcott), Dorothy Malone (Hazel Dobkins), Wayne Knight (John Coreli), Daniel von Bargen (Lieutenant Nilsen), Stephen Tobolowsky (Dr. Lamott), Benjamin Mouton (Harrigan), Jack McGee (Sheriff), Bill Cable (Johnny Boz), Stephen Rowe (Internal Affairs Investigator), Mitch Pileggi (Internal Affairs Investigator), Mary Pat Gleason (Juvenile Officer), Freda Foh Shen (Berkeley Registrar), William Duff-Griffin (Dr. Myron), James Rebhorn (Dr. McElwaine)
Color, 35mm, 128 minutes

SHOWGIRLS (1995)
Carolco Pictures/Chargeurs/United Artists/Vegas Productions

Executive Producer: Mario Kassar
Producers: Charles Evans, Alan Marshall, Ben Myron, Lynn Ehrensperger
Director: **Paul Verhoeven**
Screenplay: Joe Eszterhas
Cinematographer: Jost Vacano
Editors: Mark Goldblatt, Mark Helfrich
Art Direction: William F. O'Brien Allan Cameron
Music: David A. Stewart
Cast: Elizabeth Berkley (Nomi Malone), Kyle MacLachlan (Zack Carey), Gina Gershon (Cristal Connors), Glenn Plummer (James Smith), Robert Davi (Al Torres), Alan Rachins (Tony Moss), Gina Ravera (Molly Abrams), Lin Tucci (Henrietta "Mama" Bazoom), Greg Travis (Phil Newkirk), Al Ruscio (Mr. Karlman), Patrick Bristow (Marty Jacobsen), William Shockley (Andrew Carver), Michelle Johnston (Gay Carpenter), Dewey Weber (Jeff), Rena Riffel (Penny/Hope)
35mm, Color, 131 minutes

STARSHIP TROOPERS (1997)
Sony/TriStar Pictures/Touchstone Pictures/Big Bug Pictures/Disney
Producers: Jon Davison, Alan Marshall
Co-Producers: Frances Doel, Stacy Lumbrezer, Edward Neumeier, Phil Tippett
Director: **Paul Verhoeven**
Screenplay: Edward Neumeier
Novel: Robert A. Heinlein
Cinematographer: Jost Vacano
Editors: Mark Goldblatt, Caroline Ross
Art Direction: Bruce Robert Hill, Steven Wolff Allan Cameron
Music: Basil Poledouris
Cast: Casper Van Dien (Johnny Rico), Dina Meyer (Dizzy Flores), Denise Richards (Lt. Carmen Ibanez), Jake Busey (Ace Levy), Neil Patrick Harris (Carl Jenkins), Clancy Brown (Sgt. Zim), Seth Gilliam (Sugar Watkins), Patrick Muldoon (Zander Barcalow), Michael Ironside (Jean Rasczak), Rue McClanahan (Biology Teacher), Marshall Bell (General Owen), Eric Bruskotter (Breckinridge), Matt Levin (Kitten Smith), Blake Lindsley (Katrina), Anthony Ruivivar (Shujimi), Brenda Stron (Captain Deladier), Dean Norris (Commanding Officer)
Color, 35mm, 129 minutes

HOLLOW MAN (2000)
Columbia Pictures Corporation/Global Entertainment Productions GmbH & Company Medien KG
Executive Producer: Marion Rosenberg

Producers: Alan Marshall, Douglas Wick, Stacy Lumbrezer, Kenneth J. Silverstein
Director: **Paul Verhoeven**
Screenplay: Andrew W. Marlowe
Story: Gary Scott Thompson, Andrew W. Marlowe
Cinematographer: Jost Vacano
Editors: Mark Goldblatt, Ron Vignone (extended version)
Art Direction: Dale Allen Pelton
Music: Jerry Goldsmith
Cast: Elizabeth Shue (Linda McKay), Kevin Bacon (Sebastian Caine), Josh Brolin (Matthew Kensington), Kim Dickens (Sarah Kennedy), Greg Grunberg (Carter Abbey), Joey Slotnick (Frank Chase), Mary Randle (Janice Walton), William Devane (Dr. Howard Kramer), Rhona Mitra (Sebastian's Neighbor), Pablo Espinosa (Ed, Warehouse Guard), Margot Rose (Mrs. Martha Kramer), Jimmie F. Skaggs (Wino)
Color, 35mm, 119 mins

BLACK BOOK (2006)
Zwartboek
Fu Works/Umedia/AVRO Television/VIP 4 Medienfonds
Executive Producers: Graham Begg, Jamie Carmichael, Sara Giles, Andreas Grosch, Henning Molfenter, Andreas Schmid, Marcus Schöfer, Charlie Woebcken
Producers: Jeroen Beker, Teun Hilte, San Fu Maltha, Jens Meurer, Frans van Gestel
Director: **Paul Verhoeven**
Screenplay: Gerard Soeteman, **Paul Verhoeven**
Cinematographer: Karl Walter Lindenlaub
Editors: Job ter Burg, James Herbert
Art Directors: Roland de Groot, Cornelia Ott (supervising art director), Maarten Piersma, Wilbert Van Dorp
Music: Anne Dudley
Cast: Carice van Houten (Rachel Stein/Ellis de Vries), Sebastian Koch (Ludwig Müntze), Thom Hoffman (Hans Akkermans), Halina Reijn (Ronnie), Waldemar Kobus (Günther Franken), Derek de Lint (Gerben Kulpers), Christian Berkel (General Käutner), Dolf de Vries (Notary Wim Smaal), Peter Blok (Van Gein), Michiel Huisman (Rob), Ronald Armbrust (Tim Kuipers), Frank Lammers (Kees), Matthias Schoenaerts (Joop), Johnny de Mol (Theo), Xander Straat (Maarten), Diana Dobbelman (Mrs. Smaal)
Color, 35mm, 145 mins

TRICKED (2012)
Steekspel

FCCE
Producers: René Mioch, Justus Verkerk, Mardou Jacobs (line producer)
Director: **Paul Verhoeven**
Writers: Kim van Kooten, **Paul Verhoeven**, Robert Alberdingk Thijm
Contributing Writers: Esther Schmidt, Renee Van Armerongen, Martijn Daamen, Fleur Jansen, Sander Blom
Cinematographers: Lennert Hillege, Richard Van Oosterhout
Editor: Job ter Burg
Art Director: Maarten Piersma
Music: Fons Merkies
Cast: Peter Blok (Remco), Robert de Hoog (Tobias), Sallie Harmsen (Nadja), Gaite Jansen (Merel), Ricky Koole (Ineke), Carolien Spoor (Lieke), Jochum ten Haaf (Wim), Pieter Tiddens (Fred), Ronald van Elderen (Gijs)
Color, 55 mins (85 mins including documentary)

ELLE (2016)
Entre Chien et Loup/SBS Productions
Producers: Saïd Ben Saïd, Michel Merkt, Manon Messiant, Oury Milshtein
Director: **Paul Verhoeven**
Screenplay: David Birke
Novel: Philippe Djian
Cinematographer: Stéphane Fontaine
Editor: Job ter Burg
Production Design: Laurent Ott
Cast: Isabelle Huppert (Michelle), Christian Berkel (Robert), Anne Consigny (Anna), Virginie Efira (Rebecca), Laurent Lafitte (Patrick), Lucas Prisor (Kurt), Charles Berling (Richard), Vimala Pons (Hélène), Jonas Bloquet (Vincent), Raphaël Lenglet (Ralph), Olivia Gotanègre (Nurse), Judith Magre (Irène), Clémence Chatagnon (Clerk)

Paul Verhoeven: Interviews

How Could He?

Ale Van Dijk / 1968

From *Het Vrije Volk*, October 22, 1968. Translated from the Dutch by Julia van den Hout.

Published as an op-ed with the questions omitted, this early "interview" with Verhoeven allowed the young director the opportunity to respond to the controversy surrounding his documentary about the 1930s leader of the NSB (the Dutch pro-fascist party), Anton Mussert. Dutch celebrity historian Professor Lou de Jong had already chronicled the history of the NSB in a twenty-one-part series that aired on television from 1960-65. Acting on the advice of Professor de Jong, the Dutch public broadcasting station (the VPRO) cancelled the scheduled broadcast of Verhoeven's documentary at the last minute, shortly before this interview was conducted. The VPRO officially cited "a lack of information value" as their reason for cancelling the broadcast, although the station was in fact concerned that Verhoeven's documentary was too provocative in its uncritical portrayal of Mussert. Portrait of Anton Adriaan Mussert would not air until April of 1970, following a change in personnel at the VPRO, with the addition of black bars masking the identities of the interviewees. —MBF

PAUL VERHOEVEN: Professor De Jong has already offered a lot of factual information about Mussert in his television series, and I didn't want to repeat that. Personally, what intrigued me about Mussert—I'm thirty, so I just turned seven at the end of the war—was how such an intelligent man could believe that "God sent Adolph Hitler to Earth to save Europe and the Netherlands." He actually said that once!

To Mussert, Hitler was a prophet, and though I never make that explicit in my movie, you can see it in the background and below the surface of the film. But from the moment that he first met the Fuhrer in 1936, he no longer believed in Hitler as a prophet. That is what I tried to bring out in my movie, because what he thought before that moment has already been presented by De Jong in his television series.

I never give my own opinion about Mussert once throughout the entire movie. Instead I allow others to speak for themselves: Professor Schermerhom (who knew

Mussert as a student and engineer), Mr. De Zaaijer (who was a member of the same student organization as Mussert and demanded after the war that he be subjected to the death penalty), Mrs. Rost van Tonningen (a ninety-year old teacher who once taught Mussert), former classmates, and fellow NSB members—I gave each of them a chance to speak. And so the focus of my movie is not so much on Mussert's betrayal of his country but rather asks the question, "How could such an intelligent man get to that point?"

I finished work on the movie in April and I started on a different project right away. Is it my fault that so much has changed at the VPRO in the meantime? What good is all this commotion? Why all of the fuss about the release of this movie?

For the next few weeks, director Verhoeven will be busy in and around the Castle De Doornenburg, where he is filming a thirteen-episode Ivan Hoe-type series for NTS, *Adventures of Young Floris the Fifth*.

Blonde Greet Emigrates: *Business Is Business* Travels to Germany and the United States

Ale Van Dijk / 1971

From *Het Vrije Volk*, December 22, 1971. Translated from the Dutch by Julia van den Hout.

Amsterdam—"Blonde Greet" and "Haar van Boven" (Nel Muller) will soon travel to theaters in West Germany and the United States. German and American actors have already overdubbed the dialogue in Munich where Rob Houwer, producer of the most successful Dutch film of all time (*Business Is Business*) lives.

"A sequel to *Business Is Business* will not likely happen," said director Paul Verhoeven (33) yesterday. "After so much success, a sequel will never measure up to the original. But on the other hand, it might be worth it if even half of the public that saw the first film would come to see the second."

Director Verhoeven made changes to the film at a few moments that seemed inappropriate for West German and American audiences. "Those were mostly scenes that I noticed in screenings and thought to myself, 'Hey that can be shortened' judging from the audience's reaction, or 'That seems particularly funny to them.' Or, 'If I do the scene this way, the audience will enjoy it more.'"

In fact, Verhoeven would like to make similar changes to the prints of the film that are currently screening in the Netherlands. "But the film is still playing in thirty-five Dutch theaters, so that isn't the easiest thing to do," he reassured us.

More than two million Dutch people went to see *Business Is Business*. However, Verhoeven has not become a millionaire overnight. He still lives in his apartment in Leiden. "For a house in the country, you're talking at least 100,000 (NLG), and I haven't earned anything near that amount," says Verhoeven. "While making the film, I got paid a normal salary, and of course now there are a few extras here and there. But the contract that I signed didn't stipulate a percentage of the profit. I mostly invested in my good name."

Business Is Business is Verhoeven's second big success, after the *Floris* television series, which was very well received by the public.

QUESTION: After *Business Is Business*, did any producers approach you about new feature films?
PAUL VERHOEVEN: They have indeed, but I've only made definite plans with Rob Houwer. In any case we're going to make another film in 1972.

Q: Will it be another comedy?
PV: There are a few projects. I am working on serious plans for three of them. But it may well be that Houwer will come up with a very different scenario. I'd rather not make another comedy. In fact I don't really like comedies, nor do I ever watch them. I only like Billy Wilder, and Stan and Oliver. Fernandel? I find him terribly annoying. Louis de Funes? I'll never watch that again. There are plans to make a film of Jan Wolkers' book *Turkish Delight* and I quite like that idea. I could only make a sequel to *Business Is Business* if the plot is brilliant. But I think we already got the best out of Albert Mol's book that we could, thanks to Gerard Soeteman, who wrote the screenplay. By the way, I also made *Floris* with Soeteman.

That was one of my demands in directing *Business Is Business*—I'd only do it with Soeteman. Of course Soeteman and Mol are discussing a sequel, but I'm more interested in *Turkish Delight*. It's a deeper story, still about love, but with humor as well. But I'd need a bigger budget to make it. Besides that, I have a script for an adventure film set in the Middle Ages that also appeals to me. In the Dutch Middle Ages, around 1510. That would also require a larger budget.

Q: What was the budget for *Business Is Business*?
PV: I have no idea. Houwer never told me. He only mentioned it when I asked for too much, or went over schedule. But let's say *Business Is Business* cost half a million, then a medieval thriller would cost at least 1.5 million. It would obviously depend on whether you'd hire a Dutch or international cast. If you want German investors, they'll want to bring in some German actors.

But I could picture an all Dutch cast, with Rutger Hauer (who played Floris) and Willeke van Ammelrooy in leading roles, for example. And there's a demand for it from the public. The Italian western is popular these days, and James Bond too. The Middle Ages, with all of the costumes, could do well. Then picture an action film set in the Middle Ages—that could really work. Look, you could make a contemporary action film, but in the Netherlands you woudn't get further than a lame Dutch James Bond. You also can't make a good gangster film in the Netherlands. No, I can picture it in a historical time period, like World War II or the French revolution. The thought of making a real thriller fascinates me, but you have to be realistic about the options here.

Q: Who's getting rich off of *Business Is Business*' success? The premiere was on September 9th, and it's still showing at a lot of theaters.

PV: Rob Houwer, the man who invested in the film also makes the most money off it, of course. That's why he can continue making films here. But the theaters and everyone who worked on the film are also earning a lot from its success. People are suddenly going to the theaters again. *Business Is Business* has been the biggest blockbuster we've ever had.

Q: When did you realize it was going to be such a success?

PV: Right before the premiere, I lost all confidence in the film. I didn't think it was any good. But after the premiere, everyone came up to me to shake my hand and to congratulate me, and it was then I realized that maybe the film does work. Even so, I wasn't really stunned until after it had been playing in theaters for three or four weeks. By the second week the sales were already improving, the third week was even better and suddenly it was overwhelming. I thought, "What did I do to deserve this?" But there's also the flipside: a director might make a successful movie like *Business Is Business* only once in a lifetime. I'm still young, I don't know what people expect from me next. Look at (Bert) Haanstra, he made four films; two were enormous successes and the others were less so. That level of success has its consequences. Even if only for that reason, I'd like to stay away from comedies for a while.

Q: You mentioned that you have plans for a third project—What is it?

PV: I'd prefer not to give details about that yet. It's a TV documentary set during World War II. But that's all I can say. There are certain aspects of the war that really fascinate me. That's also how the VPRO documentary about Mussert came about. I wasn't old enough to fully experience that time, so I look at it from a different perspective than the older generation. But all of those fears that threatened to come true, didn't amount to much in the end.

Q: Has the success of *Business Is Business* left you feeling pressured to direct your next project?

PV: Yes, I'm already starting to wonder what everyone will expect from me now. I'm not sure what exactly made *Business Is Business* so successful but clearly it was something that is impossible to repeat. I have no idea what would accomplish that. At the time I had no idea how the audience would react. Each time I came across a problem during production, I always resolved it in the way that made the most sense to me. And what could that be? I'm not sure, but apparently it worked. And don't forget about Gerard Soeteman's screenplay! Above all, it looks like people are ready to go out and see movies again. It's impossible to plan for success beforehand. Albert Mol's book flew off the shelves, of course, but you can never tell what it is about a book or a movie that will make it a hit.

Turkish Delight and The Hague

Nieuwsblad van het Noorden / 1973

From *Nieuwsblad van het Noorden*, February 17, 1973. Translated from the Dutch by Julia van den Hout.

"Though there is quite a bit of sex, I don't think that people will see this as a superficial sex film. Clearly this is a film about a love affair between two people. The focus is on the emotions of the young lovers: it is a drama that culminates with the tragic death of the woman. That elevates the movie above the level of a sex production."

Speaking here is Paul Verhoeven in *Televizier*. Our television magazine interviewed the filmmaker about his latest movie, *Turkish Delight*, based on the book by Jan Wolkers. Paul Verhoeven had this to say about the sex scenes in the movie: "I thought it would be foolish not to show the audience everything that happens in the book. The book is by no means pornographic but thoroughly human. I wasn't afraid to show a great deal of realism."

"The movie isn't a simple translation of the book onto the screen. The book and the movie are on equal footing, existing on parallel planes. I can say with certainty that seventy percent of the scenes in the movie are taken from the book," responded Paul Verhoeven to the question of how much of the book made it into the film unaltered.

"The movie has its own character. Visual expression simply works differently. All at once you see the characters come to life. If you read the book, most of the attention is paid to the female character; in the movie, the male character is central. He is the protagonist and is constantly on screen. So the focus in the film has shifted a bit. In fact, Jan Wolkers agreed that the movie should have its own life outside of the book."

Paul Verhoeven on making a movie out of *Turkish Delight*: "It was extremely difficult. The story is full of flashbacks. It's written from memory, interspersed with information about the past. It was difficult to make it clear to the audience why the narrator is so miserable. In order to make the story more comprehensible, we chose to take certain scenes from the past or present and either make them longer or combine them together. Moreover, the book is filled with symbolism that doesn't translate easily to the screen. At the least, I tried to prevent it from turning into an Antonioni-like movie, which I specifically wanted to stay away from. This movie was intentionally made for a mass audience. It is what I like to call a commercial film."

I Distrust Anyone Who Pursues an Ideal

Leeuwarder Courant / 1979

From The *Leeuwarder Courant*, January 20, 1979. Translated from the Dutch by Julia van den Hout.

In the Netherlands, the name Paul Verhoeven is synonymous with successful films. *Business Is Business*, *Turkish Delight*, *Katie Tippel*, and *Soldier of Orange* drew millions of people to theaters. Paul Verhoeven is rightfully the most commercially successful filmmaker in our country. His latest movie is now also being shown on television by the TROS network (the second episode airs this Saturday), less than a year after the end of its theatrical run. This is against the rules of the Nederlands(ch)e Bioscoopbond (NBB) and the national Production Fund for the film industry (Produktifonds voor Nederlandse Films). These two agencies are therefore quite angry about the "arrangement" that producer Rob Houwer negotiated with TROS and they have vowed to never fall for a "scam" like that again.

The Production Fund, which represents both the NBB and the Ministry of Culture, Recreation and Social Work (CRM), finances about sixty percent of most Dutch movies. However, the Fund requires that a movie cannot air on television sooner than forty-two months after it has left the theaters. Producer Rob Houwer slyly avoided this rule by selling *Soldier of Orange*, which was still in theaters last year, to the TROS. Houwer insists that he produced the series separately, in addition to filming the movie. The Production Fund is left powerless, as they never would have even considered such bending of the rules.

The TROS also plays an unusual role in all of this. Baay, the Director of Programming for TROS announced that plans for a television series based on *Soldier of Orange* have been in the works for years. That could mean that TROS offered the television rights to help finance a Dutch movie. Furthermore, Baay emphasized that TROS has not profited off of the movie's success. Apparently TROS prioritizes the demands of its audience by refusing to deny them a chance to see a movie like this.

The Production Fund has learned its lesson. It won't be so easy to break the rules in the future, as they have revised their movie contracts to include a new clause. Director Paul Verhoeven has nothing to do with this financial scheme. His only comment about *Soldier of Orange* is that the publicity for the project has been poor from the start: "The publicity was always focused on the 'Orange,' in other words, on the royal family, which discouraged a lot of young people from going to see the movie when in reality, it's just a good action movie. Now TROS has chosen another horrible subtitle, 'For Queen and Country.' It makes me want to throw up. It emphasizes heroism, which doesn't reflect the nature of the movie, which is in fact realism. If I heard that title, not knowing anything about the movie, it would just make me think of those Jan de Witt boys. Nevertheless, I like the fact that the film is now being shown on television."

Paul Verhoeven is one of the only Dutch directors whose movies have gained recognition abroad. For example, *Soldier of Orange* premiered in Seattle a week and a half ago. *Turkish Delight* played in Munich for two years in a row, and *Katie Tippel* played for as long in Milan. "That's why it's nonsense when people say that Dutch films are never picked up abroad. You just have to make sure that it is a commercial film and the set design looks good. That was the case with *Katie Tippel*. The script was weak and the dramaturgy wasn't very compelling—that's something we never resolved because we spent too much time working on the script. But the sets were beautiful and it portrayed the time period well. That's why the movie was successful abroad. Of course *Turkish Delight* was different—that was just a really good movie, even though I'd make it differently today, in 1979," said Verhoeven.

Business Is Business, based on the eponymous book by Albert Mol, acted as a springboard for Paul Verhoeven. That was in 1971, which according to Verhoeven was the year that Dutch cinema was reborn. 1971 was also the year of *Blue Movie*, which paved the way for many more films. It wasn't until after *Blue Movie* that Dutch investors were brave enough to take on *Turkish Delight*, even though the idea to make a movie based on Jan Wolkers's novel was raised a few years earlier.

MUSSERT

Paul Verhoeven's first official film was for VPRO television, for which he made a documentary about Mussert. The movie raised a great deal of controversy. Even Professor de Jong, Director of the Dutch Institute for War Documentation, advised the VPRO against airing the documentary, which he deemed too positive, stating that Mussert was portrayed too favorably. Verhoeven was the first to film members of the NSB [the Dutch National Socialist party during WWII] without a black bar over their eyes or distorted voices.

"De Jong said that the documentary was too subjective even though it was a very objective film. During my research for the film, I began to find Mussert more or less sympathetic, or rather, I began to feel sympathy for him. In a way I almost felt a connection with him. He was studious and what particularly appealed to me was the huge religious enthusiasm he had for Hitler. Clearly, the guy chose the wrong side, but he believed in Hitler. He saw Hitler as a messenger of God and himself as a prophet. He really believed that. That's also what he wrote in his diary."

"Listen, I respect it when someone fully commits to something. It doesn't matter what, as long as it is consistent. Anyone can choose the wrong thing. But anyone who makes a choice like that and stays loyal even when it does not turn out as he imagined, I find courageous. I never wanted to force an opinion on anyone with the film. Everyone must decide for themselves what they thought about it. After it aired, it turned out most people agreed with it."

"In *Soldier of Orange*, for example, I deliberately portrayed Alex Rooyaard, the young man who later joins the SS and dies in Russia, as a sympathetic character. The boy was a victim of his mother, who was German. And his friends wanted nothing to do with him following the outbreak of the war. The guy had to make a choice and the only thing he could choose was the German military. I respect a choice like that."

RELIGION

Religion plays a very important role in Paul Verhoeven's life. He even briefly considered becoming a "prophet" and going to preach the gospel in Africa. His movies often include religious symbolism. They are often quite hidden, but they are there. For example, in *Turkish Delight* Olga sleeps in a crimson red bed, surrounded by candles placed there by Erik. "She's lying there like a sacrifice on the altar. I'm very preoccupied with the fact of whether God exists or not. This has determined a large part of my life. I'm not sure if I believe in God. It's something that you know when you're ready. You could say that my films are about the fact that I do not know. When I was younger, I never even dared talk about the subject, I was so intensely preoccupied with it. I think I'm starting to get past that and I am beginning to use it in my films."

It is Paul Verhoeven's dream to make a movie about John of Leiden and his group of Anabaptists, who took over Münster in 1531 to establish the Kingdom of Heaven on Earth. He hopes it will help him work through his religious issues. With a grant from the CRM, Verhoeven wrote a thesis about John of Leiden, who began as a prophet and ended up a totalitarian dictator. That thesis is the basis for a potential screenplay. "The history of John of Leiden shows that religion is often nothing more than a smokescreen for power. God wants this, and God wants that. This is all nonsense of course, because God doesn't want anything at all. That is why I distrust anyone who holds an ideal and strives to achieve it."

"In the end those are the people who are only looking out for themselves. Hitler is another good example of a man who touted ideals but was only out for personal gain. A movie about John of Leiden should also be a takedown of idealism. Plus a movie based on a topic like John of Leiden should do well commercially, since it has all the makings of a good action movie."

COMMERCE

Paul Verhoeven is a commercial filmmaker. He believes that movies should be created to make money. He has proven that with *Business Is Business*, *Turkish Delight*, *Katie Tippel*, and *Soldier of Orange*. "The Dutch film industry is in danger of collapsing. Nine out of ten movies are art films. That is not a good policy. I have nothing against it, but they don't earn a penny. They are all flops. Eventually they won't be able to find investors anymore, and the Dutch film industry will go down the hole. I find this irresponsible. The situation is absurd. Film is a commercial business. They shouldn't have to stop making art films, of course, but more commercial films must be made."

"Take for example *Inheritance* (*Dag Dokter*, 1978). It's a good movie but the topic is elitist, so no one wants to go see it. The theme of *Turkish Delight* is more pedestrian, so it appeals to a wider group of people and consequently, the theaters are full. Commerce means a director is interested in what people want to see. But it's a hard thing to plan. You can never say beforehand: this movie is going to be a hit. The most important thing is that the director likes his own subject. Of course, another measure of success is funding: if you can't find anyone to fund your film then your idea probably isn't any good."

BREAK

For years, Verhoeven collaborated with producer Rob Houwer. They were the golden duo of the Dutch movie industry. But that came to an end last year. "Oh, it just got on my nerves that Houwer was shouting out to anyone who'd listen that he made those movies, which is utter nonsense. Gerard Soeteman and I made those movies and no one else. Houwer always claimed all of the publicity for himself. The three of us have made good movies together, so I think we should all share the praise and money. But Houwer has profited the most from the movies, by far."

"In all those years of collaborating with Houwer, I was rarely interviewed, for example. Since I've broken off from him, I get non-stop requests. I just started a production company with Gerard Soeteman and Joop van den Ende: VSE film. Once we get up and running we want to start working with other directors as well. Maybe we can even make a film collective one day. I think that would be great."

Their first project is already underway: a movie about young working people. "I think it's going to attract a wide audience. It addresses a lot of familiar problems so it's a very current movie."

Director Guido Peters is currently working on a movie based on Jan Wolkers' book *Kort Amerikaans*. Why isn't Verhoeven directing that, after his successful adaptation of Wolkers' *Turkish Delight*? "I didn't want to do it because it would be boring. You should never repeat yourself. Wolkers initially wanted me to adapt his book *De Walgvogel* but I just wasn't interested in his books anymore. I think it's exciting to go into unknown territory. I made *Turkish Delight* after *Business Is Business*—that was a big leap for me at the time and it paid off. Doing something completely different every time requires a lot of guts and inspiration. You run the risk of falling flat on your face but that doesn't matter, as long as you're not afraid."

Paul Verhoeven on Sex and Violence in *The Fourth Man*

Peter Slavenburg / 1983

From *Het Vrije Volk*, March 29, 1983. Translated from the Dutch by Julia van den Hout.

Paul Verhoeven, director of such films as *Spetters*, *Turkish Delight*, *Soldier of Orange*, *Business Is Business*, and *Katie Tippel*, may be our most successful dutch filmmaker. People have lined up to see each one of his movies and Verhoeven's latest film, *The Fourth Man*, premiered in the Netherlands last week. It is based on the book of the same name by Gerard Reve.

The Fourth Man is a somewhat mysterious movie, with a central focus on death. Following a lecture for a literary society, author Gerard Reve (played by Jeroen Krabbé) spends the night with the society's treasurer, Christine (Renée Soutendijk), who owns a beauty salon.

Reve soon learns that Christine has been married three times and that each of her husbands died in tragic accidents. Christine also has a boyfriend, Herman (Thom Hoffman), who works in Germany. Gerard sees a photo of the handsome Herman, and immediately falls in love. "I have to have him," the writer mumbles. Herman returns to Christine's place and the consequences are fatal. Who will be the fourth man in Christine's life to die in an accident?

On occasion of his new movie, Paul Verhoeven had a conversation with our reporter Peter Slavenburg about film, Jesus, sex, life, and death . . .

PETER SLAVENBURG: I think that *The Fourth Man* is a beautiful movie. Did you know that it would turn out that way? I read there was a lot of uncertainty surrounding the set.

PAUL VERHOEVEN: Yes that's true. I felt terribly insecure while shooting the movie, and even when I began the editing stage—more than ever before, actually. The movie has a style which I haven't used that often, at least not for the past seven or eight years. The camera movement is a bit threatening, it doesn't have the same sharpness as in *Spetters* or *Soldier of Orange*. Those movies had a much faster pace. There is a strange tension in this film.

Besides that, as we filmed each scene individually, they didn't amount to much. They didn't work until they became a part of the movie, where they attained meaning. For example, we'd shoot a scene with the characters sitting around the dinner table having a rather normal conversation, but in the context of the movie, it would all come across as very unusual. Everyone on the set felt uncertain because there was no sense of context and ultimately the scenes weren't reflecting what they were actually doing.

PS: I can imagine that must have been rather uncomfortable for the actors.
PV: Yes, absolutely, but that was also due to the occult character of the movie. Is Christine such an unhappy woman that she will seduce any man she can find, just so that she won't be alone anymore? Whether it's Gerard, whom she suspects doesn't really care for women or Herman, the flamboyant man who must be thinking: "This is pretty convenient, this big house with that rich lady." Or is Christine a dark, diabolical woman? A woman who walks hand-in-hand with destiny? Which is the truth? Which of those two is the reality?

PS: It's hard to figure that out, concerning each of the characters.
PV: Yes, and that was a problem for Renée Soutendijk. I told her: "You should play up that devilish, diabolical aspect of the character," but you know . . . yeah, of course that's difficult to pull off. But I think she did a splendid job.

PS: The editing also took quite a bit of time, didn't it?
PV: It was the longest time I have ever taken to edit a movie. We ran into crisis after crisis because we just lost sight of it all. When you're editing, you're dealing with only a small piece of the film. You work on just a minute each day, sometimes two minutes if you're lucky. It was often hard to maintain perspective. You're just sitting there messing around with one little section. Should it be like this, or like that? What are you supposed to do with this stupid little scene of a group of people chatting around a table? Is it interesting, or should it be cut out? That nags you; the fact that you don't have any concrete scenes. I've never dealt with that problem before.

PS: Aren't you afraid that after directing *Spetters* you'll be criticized for making another harsh, sexual movie with a lot of horror elements? I think you took quite a weak book and turned it into a very strong film, but I can imagine there are a lot of people who would say the opposite.
PV: I always thought it was an average book within a pretty nice oeuvre. It wasn't

difficult to spice it up. I'm surprised to hear people say that it's a harsh movie. I actually think it's a marvel of gentleness.

PS: You can't be serious . . .
PV: Well yeah, kind of. Take the sex scenes; they are much more subdued than in *Spetters* or *Turkish Delight*. Everything is shown in shadow and you can't actually see anything. I really tried to prevent the viewer from being distracted from the basic premise. In the background there is the idea that Christine is like a spider who eats her mate after fucking him. He is her prey.

I felt that if I included too many erotic scenes the audience would get distracted, like "Hey, I see a penis!" or "What do Renée Soutendijk's tits look like?" That's why I tried to keep everything very restrained while filming. It's erotically charged, of course, but not sexually exploitive. I really feel like I did the opposite of what I did in *Spetters*.

HORROR

PS: Alright, then let's talk about the horror scenes: the pierced eye. Isn't that harsh? I think the way you do it in your film is much scarier than in all those horror movies.
PV: That's because you are distanced from those movies. In my movie, you feel that something is about to happen that creates a sense of tension, and then it actually happens. And on top of that . . . the eye is such a frightening symbol, the piercing is almost a castration. And on top of that, my movie isn't like those horror movies where heads are being axed off every five minutes. In the opening sequence, for example, when that spider crawls across the crucifix: he stops on Jesus's eye. That's not necessarily scary, but it is an image that lingers and doesn't reveal its true meaning until later.

PS: When you first read Reve's book, did you envision the movie as it is now?
PV: No, not at all. I thought it was a good story, good enough for sixty minutes of television. Then Gerard Soeteman read it. He called me one night and said, "There is much more here than what is written in the book." He wrote the screenplay very quickly in about six or seven weeks, as if he were drawing from a vision. I hardly added anything, it was really amazing.

So I could see that the book was good, though not necessarily on the page. By the way, I haven't come up with the idea for any of my movies. I was actually quite taken aback when Gerard first described his version of the story to me.

PS: In comparison to the book, there is almost no homosexual interaction in the film.

PV: No. We thought it impossible not to introduce the boy, Herman, into the film, although he is only a minor character in the book. You know the movie, *The Bridge over the River Kwai*? At the end of that movie, they blow up the bridge—the whole movie leads up to that explosion. It doesn't happen in the book, but there wouldn't be much of a movie without it.

Here I thought: you can't make a whole movie about this guy Herman without showing him. Then find out later, like in the book, that something happened. But if you emphasize Herman, then you have to leave out the other boys that Reve sleeps with in the book.

It seemed unneccessary to have Gerard engage in all of these sexual situations with a guy who plays no further role, so it was one or the other: in order to prioritize Herman, the other guy had to disappear. It's about Herman—he is the one who Gerard Reve pursues. Even for people who didn't pick up on Reve's preference for men, it is clear in the movie that he's only vaguely interested in Christine. Even when he's fucking her, he's looking at a photo of Herman.

JAN BLOKKER

PS: In the film Jeroen Krabbé doesn't look much like the real Gerard Reve; he is slicker and much more harsh. Who did you model the movie-Gerard after?
PV: Ha, after Jan Blokker. I don't know what Blokker looks like now, but when he was a critic, he had that dark, greasy, combed back hair. He was also a heavier man. Jeroen Krabbé is obviously not a big guy, but we had him grow out his hair and gain a little weight. By adding some grease, Jeroen gained that dirtiness, the heaviness and cynicism that Blokker used to have. Also in his actions; he's an unpleasant man. In the movie, Gerard is a cross between Jan Blokker and Gerard Reve. It's faction: a cross between fact and fiction, the condensed truth.

PS: Did Gerard Reve offer any further input on the movie? He let it be known that he would be available for advice, if needed.
PV: No, he had nothing to do with it. He actually had no interest in being involved. He didn't read the script and he still hasn't seen the movie. He was supposed to come watch it a few weeks ago, but after that upheaval about his fascist ideas he fled home to France.

PS: Reve's book is structured as a framing narrative. He tells the story of the Fourth Man to a boyfriend in bed.
PV: We changed that a bit. We didn't think the outer framework was that interesting so we replaced that with the image of the spider at the beginning and end of the movie, like an overture and finale. The spider returns, and with it, the image of Jesus. The thought there is the statement by Jesus that was recently discovered to

be apocryphal: It's God's will that evil is done. That seems like a rather un-Christian idea. The Bible says that it's inevitable that evil exists. The other proclamation is much more to the point and so the whole movie is pretty much based around it. It's not necessary to understand that, but I do think many people are shocked by that image of the spider crawling across Jesus's head.

PS: I think that many people, especially religious people, will be much more shocked by the scenes where Gerard touches the crucifixion statue, and especially Jesus's crotch on the crucifix. You might run into some trouble for that.

PV: Yeah, I don't know. Gerard Soeteman said the same thing. It wasn't in the script, but during filming I felt like it was necessary. Look, I wasn't raised religious, but ever since childhood I've always wanted to take a peek behind that loin cloth.

Just look at De Sade: all sex and torture, not very different. A stretched out body just hanging there, naked, except for that cloth; I think that also has some sexual meaning. It's more than just suffering. It's not quite sex but close to it. Maybe it's a childish thought but I think many people feel that way even though they may not admit it.

LOTS OF MONEY

Over the last few years, Paul Verhoeven and Gerard Soeteman have been working on American projects. It isn't that Verhoeven is dying to make an American movie, but rather because he needs money that the Netherlands isn't able to offer—lots of money.

PV: Everyone has a few things they want to do in their lifetime. For me, there are two or three projects that would never secure financing in the Netherlands. So I can either limit myself to *The Fourth Man*, or at most a project like *Soldier of Orange*; or I can work on the projects that I want to do and wait for my big break. I prefer to work here. I'm bored in the US and I'm a little tired of the people there. *Soldier of Orange* cost three million, and that was already a huge gamble. Five million is the absolute maximum here. But the movies I want to make will cost, I think, about 15 million guilders. And in order to come up with that kind of money, it's necessary to get American investors.

PS: The projects you are referring to are mystical and take place in the Middle Ages. What is your interest in the Middle Ages?

PV: I think I've been fascinated by it since *Floris*. God, I don't know, I just think it's an incredibly interesting time period. You could also ask me about my obsession with the Second World War. It gives me the opportunity to frame things in a fast and extreme way. Matters of life and death. These days it's extremely difficult to do that in the Netherlands, where death is associated with illness. In other countries like Asia, Africa, even in the United States, death is associated with violence. It's very difficult to make a movie here in which people die. Not that it's necessary for people to die, but that threat—the kind that you feel in a city like New York—doesn't exist here.

Dramaturgically it's difficult. The worst that can happen in the Netherlands is that you lose your job or that you become seriously ill. The chance that you get your head bashed in while walking down the street is extremely small. It could happen tomorrow but that would be extreme, while in the United States, it happens all the time. But during the war, and in the Middle Ages, those situations were the same in the Netherlands as elsewhere in the world today. We live in a paradise in the Netherlands, and dramaturgically, that's annoying. There is more to be said about despair than there is about happiness. And I'm not talking about what I'd prefer in real life, but when it comes to dramaturgy, to working with tension and contrast—that is what holds onto people's attention. How long can you spend describing happiness? It's almost impossible to do. Okay, sometimes it works in music, but only for a minute. You can't get away with that in a movie. Just look at television series: they're all dependent on tension. They're crap shows—*Dallas* and *Dynasty*—but it's all conflict: he said this and she did that. Maybe that's not the best example, but it proves that you can do a lot more with conflict, unhappiness, and difficulty than you can do with happiness.

What do you see, then: two people hug for just a few seconds and nothing happens. The movie doesn't really begin until a bomb explodes and those people drop dead, right? It's like the question of whether the gospel would have been so successful if it didn't end with a stunning murder. That is drama. In that regard, Buddha had a much more difficult time.

PS: Hmm. It appears as if your interest in death extends beyond a mere professional interest.
PV: Absolutely. I'm fascinated by death. Especially because I'm scared of it. I am against death. It's nonsense to say that life has meaning and is beautiful because it has an end. Actually, I think that someday death will no longer be inevitable. Our science has only been in existence for a few thousand years. Add a few billion years on to that, and you'll see that death no longer exists. In my opinion, that would be a meaningful improvement on life.

Interview with Paul Verhoeven

Mark Valen / 1984

From *Films and Filming*, January 1984. Reprinted by permission of the author.

Dutch director Paul Verhoeven's films have had minimal exposure in the U.K. despite the fact that Holland is just across the Channel and in his homeland he's the top in his field, as at least the country's most popular and well known filmmaker. His films are known for their uncompromising reality and explicitness in exploding screen taboos. They're passionate, thought provoking films with free spirited, outgoing characters. Of the four that have been released outside Holland, *Turkish Delight*, *Katie Tippel*, *Soldier of Orange* and now *Spetters*, *Turkish Delight* was nominated for the Academy Award in the best foreign film category, and *Soldier of Orange* for the Golden Globe. His latest film *The Fourth Man*, a supernatural mystery, has been making the film festival rounds and is due for release next year.

All are based on material from books or true accounts. *Spetters* is the first original screenplay he and his constant screenwriter Gerard Soeteman have collaborated on. When I met him on a recent visit to England he proved to be in his mid-forties, slight, dark, greying and with a decided twinkle in his eye. I found him very friendly and open to talk at length about his work. Not very familiar with London, he had not formed much of an impression of the city, but admitted a fondness for British music, particularly Bryan Ferry. He's now preparing two big-budget, American financed films, one to be shot in Spain, the other in Africa.

MARK VALEN: *Spetters* is the first film you and Gerard Soeteman scripted from an original story. What inspired you to this story?
PAUL VERHOEVEN: We started the story in '72. It was about two boys and a girl. The gay guy wasn't in it then. Gerard wanted to write about a guy who is crippled, who is completely paralyzed and wants to die, and no one will help him.

I wondered what would I do myself in that situation. It expanded over six or seven years until we made it in '79. In the meantime I saw the play *Whose Life Is It Anyway?* It affected me because we were on the same subject. Then I interviewed a lot of working class guys, really tough guys around Rotterdam who don't care about education. The system in Holland is for working class guys at the age of sixteen or seventeen to have to enter into a profession and take supplementary courses. For four or five months I gave film lessons to find out what type of personal feelings there were, how they saw life.

After making *Soldier of Orange* about upper class people, university students and royalty, people who had their future laid out, I wanted to do a film about working class people. I wanted to prove I could make a film about younger people with no education, but still interesting enough to make a film about.

MV: You say your films are drawn from your own experiences. What personal experiences have you brought into *Spetters*?

PV: The boy who committed suicide was based on someone I knew at school. He was a scriptwriter. These boys have no experience, no education, only perhaps talent. The only way they can break out is if they're good at something. Rutger Hauer as Witkamp is based on an existing character. He even looks like Rutger. He is a symbol for the younger guys. He has everything through motorcycles.

MV: The character of Jeff the queer-basher has the tables turned on him and is raped by a gang of men. Afterwards he becomes gay. Do you really think someone would come out gay after a violent act such as a gang bang?

PV: That's one of the problems I see now in the film. I would have done it in a different way now. By attacking homosexuals he was attacking himself. I now think the character of Jeff was not completely successful. The character was so shocked by the rape that his mind was confused and he took the opportunity to accept to himself that there was certain feelings in himself he hadn't realized.

MV: In your new film *The Fourth Man* the central character is a gay author. There's no violence between him and the young man he seduces. Is *The Fourth Man* a more positive image of gays because they are older and more mature?

PV: I'm more mature! *Spetters* jumps from one situation to another. Jeff's character is a real problem, but the character of Maya (the virtuous, Indonesian girl) is not a problem, but she is also jumping. She goes into religion, then to being a nurse. Religion replaces her relationship with Ron, the same as I think religion can easily replace a lot of emotions, so for her it's a kind of escape. She realizes God can't help Ron, then she makes another jump and becomes a nurse. The film is made of character spotlights, these moments of their lives, and putting them in a kind of serial.

MV: You compared the suicide in *La Dolce Vita* to the suicide in *Spetters*.
PV: *La Dolce Vita* was at the back of my mind when I made *Spetters*. I wanted to make a film about blue collar people, and Fellini made one about the Roman high society, and that's of course the difference. But all of the elements in *La Dolce Vita* are also in *Spetters*. For example the religious and sexual things. The style of *Spetters* is much more cruel, rude, cynical, direct, and documentary-like, and *La Dolce Vita* is highly stylized.

MV: Your films tend to satirize religion. Did you have a strict upbringing?
PV: Not at all. But I'm always very interested in religion. The situation of Maya going to a religious group, I was close to becoming involved with that type of religious party when I was about twenty-six. I had a religious crisis and wondered whether I wanted to be a film director or a missionary. Maya's change comes when she realizes God is not going to come down and help Ron. If you want to do something you have to do it yourself. And that's my philosophy, that's why Maya is an autobiographical character.

MV: How did you and Gerard Soeteman begin to collaborate?
PV: We went to the same university without knowing each other. We met when he wrote a script for a television serial, in 1969. That was also the first time Rutger Hauer worked with us.

MV: What other directors besides Fellini influence you?
PV: Hitchcock. *North By Northwest* and *Vertigo* made a big impression on me. Also early Bergman. *The Fourth Man* was influenced a lot by Hitchcock. David Lean inspired me a lot too. Eisenstein's *Ivan The Terrible* is one of the only films I consider real art. It's beautiful. He's using linear movements that aren't used much by directors, but it always stuck in my mind. I used that for *Spetters*.

MV: Was *Spetters* difficult to make?
PV: Yes, particularly the motorcycle races. I had *Ben Hur* on my mind a lot when filming that. I don't try to copy them, but I use them in inspiration.

MV: Your films have a dark sense of humor and irony. Your characters' lives often seem ruled by fate. Do you believe fate controls our lives?
PV: It's more that I consider life to be very chaotic. Your doctor could examine you and say you haven't got long to live. These things happen. The scenes with

the orange peels causing an accident for instance. What are just orange peels to a family is fate to another. There's a song by Bryan Ferry where he says something like, "I like life around the corner." That can be a very pleasant surprise, but it can be unpleasant also. *Spetters* is based on that feeling. You can have everything going so well in your life, and suddenly a tragedy can wipe it all away. This happens to a lot of people, and it's a terrible fear I have.

MV: Which of your films is most personal to you?
PV: *Spetters*, it's the only one based on an original idea. My other films are based mostly on true stories or incidents. The film we are doing for Orion pictures now, *Flesh+Blood* is another original script. It's based on medieval facts, not a fairy tale at all. I'll use the same realistic approach as *Spetters*. It's to be filmed in Spain. After that I'll make *Harry's Tale* in Africa.

MV: Do you still consider yourself a Dutch filmmaker?
PV: Yes, but I want to try my hand at making American films. It's a big challenge. I'm taking as many precautions as possible against failure because I see what's happened to all the European directors that have gone to film in the States. Most have tried and failed because they have no first hand experience of America.

MV: You have a strong narrative style that could easily adapt to American films.
PV: Yes and I don't want to make a film about American lifestyles because that is more difficult as I don't know the country well. *Flesh+Blood* is a medieval tale and *Harry's Tale* is a seventeenth-century adventure story, subjects I have studied.

MV: What did *Spetters* cost to make?
PV: About one million dollars. *Soldier of Orange* was the most expensive at two million. But *The Fourth Man* only cost about 750,000.

MV: You usually work with the same stars over again. Do you plan to work with Monique van de Ven (from *Turkish Delight* and *Katie Tippel*) and Renée Soutendijk (from *Spetters* and *The Fourth Man*) again?
PV: I hope to if a suitable role comes along for them. Rutger Hauer, who has been in nearly all my films, is cast for *Flesh+Blood*.

MV: Your leading actresses play seducing, dominant, opportunist characters. Do you find women in general to be like this or are you just attracted to that type of woman?
PV: In my mind I think I am, but I'm married to a very kind, intelligent woman, not at all the type Monique and Renée play.

MV: Do you like that character?

PV: Absolutely like her. Not for family life. For love and affairs yes, but it's impossible to live with somebody like that. In *Spetters* you have two opposite kinds of women: the opportunist and the saintly Maya. In *Flesh+Blood* there are two similar types of women. One is a really medieval Scarlett O'Hara. The other is more like Maya, very soft. If you believe in the philosophy of Jung, every man has a female image of himself. You're looking for that image of yourself. Perhaps that's me split up into two different persons.

MV: Your female characters do have a masculine/feminine side to them. As does the male lead in *The Fourth Man*. But Rutger's roles are very macho.

PV: But in *Turkish Delight* he's very soft. I don't see myself as macho. I can be very feminine. Even in sex when I sleep with a woman I have both sides. It's not just Boom! Boom! Boom!

MV: Which of the three male leads in *Spetters* did you identify with most?

PV: I think Ron, but partly because I liked the actor who portrayed him (Hans Van Tongeren). He was extremely talented.

MV: Do you find the Dutch people to be more accepting of homosexuality than some other countries?

PV: Yes, there are no problems anymore in the past few years. There was a public opinion poll as to what the citizens thought of homosexuality. Seventy percent of the population didn't care anymore. They think, well this is life, it's acceptable.

MV: Jeff's father certainly didn't accept it.

PV: Well there are still these religious groups that think homosexuality is evil. If they have a gay neighbor they pray to God that he will take away their sickness. But there are only a small percentage of Dutch who feel that way now. The area where we shot *Spetters* is where a lot of these people live, very Calvinistic and extreme Protestants.

MV: What was your religious background?

PV: None at all. I wasn't even baptized.

MV: Were you raised around Amsterdam?

PV: In The Hague. My parents are Protestants. My interest in religion came when I was older. I hope to make a realistic portrayal of Christ someday. It would have to be an American movie because it would be expensive. I hear Scorsese is going to make a film about Christ, but I don't think it will be very realistic. I hope to be the first to make a definitive film about him.

MV: I read Universal pictures is going to make an American version of *Spetters*.
PV: Yes, but I don't have any involvement in it. But there are so many films coming out of America these days dealing with youth, especially high school.

MV: *Spetters* is more realistic than most of those. Do you think the American version would sanitize it, after all there are a lot of shocking things that happen in *Spetters*.
PV: I'm sure they'll make it more easy going.

MV: Do you like shocking people?
PV: Yes, but not in an exploitive way. For instance in *Turkish Delight* there's a lot of sex in it, but it's important from the point of view of human feelings. I wanted to prepare the audience from the beginning to expect a love story with nudity, which was told in a free way, with a lot of things you don't see.

MV: Do the actors get tense during the love scenes?
PV: Absolutely, every actor has that problem. With Renée I had problems during *The Fourth Man* shooting, because although she had done nude scenes before and not cared about it, criticism of *Spetters* was so awful and so mean, the actors were very depressed about it.

MV: I thought it was a big hit in Holland.
PV: From the point of view of the audience, but not from the critics. They hated it. But all the facts of *Spetters* came out of the papers. The robbing and raping is always reported in The Hague.

MV: How was *The Fourth Man* received?
PV: Much better. They considered it my first step to art because it's more stylized, which is ridiculous; the critics are so stupid in Holland that if they see a highly stylized film they begin to think about Fassbinder or Bertolucci and they think it's "art." If you make a film like *Spetters* that's completely open and not stylized for art but for realism, they look down on it.

MV: Will you make another film in Holland?
PV: Yes, but the American projects are a big challenge to me right now. Sometimes these big productions get delayed for so long. I was supposed to make *Flesh+Blood*

right after *Spetters*. The Ladd company was to produce it. They liked the script but kept saying they wanted little things changed here and there, and finally decided it wasn't a commercial enough project for them. Then United Artists were going to do it, but the whole blow-up with David Begelman and MGM/UA's financial crisis wiped it off their schedule, in the meantime I made *The Fourth Man* in Holland. Now Orion are committed to making *Flesh+Blood*. If there becomes a long gap between *Flesh+Blood* and *Harry's Tale* I may have to make another Dutch film in the meantime.

Paul Verhoeven on the Violence in His Films

Ariejan Korteweg and Bart Jungmann / 1985

From *Nieuwsblad van het Noorden*, September 13, 1985. Translated from the Dutch by Julia van den Hout.

"More fairy tale than Grimm, tougher than a samurai and louder than an opera." Screenwriter Gerard Soeteman came up with this tagline for the movie *Flesh+Blood*, directed by Paul Verhoeven. The director himself prefers to emphasize the "lightness" of the film: "It has the airiness of an operetta, but regardless of its 'entertainment' value as a medieval adventure spectacle, it is full of cruelty and violence." This was the topic of conversation between the director and two of our writers for the newspaper—but first Verhoeven told us about his experience filming in Spain, where conditions were so harsh it's a miracle that the movie was even made—and as of yesterday, showing in theaters in the Netherlands.

Filming *Flesh+Blood* in rural Spain was not the happiest experience of Verhoeven's career. He looks back on it reluctantly and responds to our questions with short answers: "The shoot was extremely tough. It was a fourteen week battle. A permanent crisis situation. On the razor's edge. It was a battlefield. Complete misery, frustration, and discouragement, and it left a bad taste in my mouth. If I compare it to *Spetters*, for example—that was a nice experience. I look back on that with joy, even though it was later overshadowed by the boy's suicide." (He is referring to the actor Hans van Tongeren).

With the experience behind him, Verhoeven is proud to have withstood the perilous "rain in Spain." "It was like an initiation but I managed to survive. It forced me to grow as both a director and a human being."

Initially he hesitated to revisit the experience. "So much has been written about this already." But Verhoeven is not the type to stay quiet. "I quickly realized I would have to do things that aren't usually expected of a director. There was a Spanish co-producer—his name is on all of the posters—and he provided zero help whatsoever. You don't really think about all of the money that goes into these productions. *Soldier of Orange* was also a big production but I think that it would have been even more expensive if we had made it like an American movie."

Verhoeven added: "A good collaboration developed between the Dutch and the Spanish, so that at least went well. I hardly noticed that I was working with such a large crew. Everyone had their own job so it all worked out."

ONGOING FEUD

"I've always worked with the same group of people and this was the first time I had to work with a whole new crew, which certainly added to the conflict. Here in the Netherlands they've always given me the benefit of the doubt. They could think what they wanted about Verhoeven and his sexual aberrations, but at least they all agreed that it made for interesting cinema."

Apparently that was not the case in Spain: "I had an ongoing feud with most of the foreign actors, who didn't know me at all. Only Jennifer Jason Leigh, who plays Agnes, showed some solidarity. The majority didn't trust me. There was a mood, like 'What is he trying to get us to do now?' I wanted to create a sort of baroque atmosphere and that demanded an expressive style of acting. The foreign actors weren't familiar with that and they had a hard time with it. They thought they were over-acting, and that was uncomfortable for the Americans. Don't be mistaken, they may be B-actors, but they do have some skill. They master their craft."

RUTGER HAUER

"I was certainly taken aback when Rutger Hauer joined the argument and challenged me as well." Paul Verhoeven arrives at what must have been his biggest disappointment in Spain: the attitude of his leading man Rutger Hauer, with whom he's often collaborated since the television show *Floris*. Hauer, who has since made a name for himself in Hollywood, sided with the Americans in questioning Verhoeven's working methods.

"Rutger could have tempered the situation, but he didn't even try. If only he could have worked like he did on *Soldier of Orange*, then the three of us—together with cameraman Jan de Bont—could have controlled the set. I think that was very significant. Hauer and I have made several movies together and for him of all people to start acting difficult—that was a big signal for the others. Rutger's attitude was, 'I've already made a career for myself, now let's see you do it. Now that you have the opportunity, let's see what you can do.' Rutger feels like he's already made it in America, and he's right. *Blade Runner* is on its way to becoming a real cult hit. But he is forgetting that his career is partially based on my work."

A KIND OF FLORIS

"Hauer was more or less simultaneously working on *Ladyhawke*, and I think that also influenced his behavior—*Ladyhawke* is also a Medieval movie and he was nervous that two would be too many. I believe that he outdid himself in my movie, because he has a great role in *Flesh+Blood*."

Paul Verhoeven can think of another reason for his star's attitude. "Perhaps it is partly my fault. I gave him some literature on John of Leiden for inspiration before the shoot and because of that he wanted to make the character of Martin darker. 'He has to burn at the end,' he told me. Whereas I wanted to give the character a sense of lightness—like a kind of Floris, actually."

"There is a sort of pseudo-realism in the movie. You can't play a serious role in a movie where people fall through chimneys and erect a siege tower to storm a castle. In retrospect, maybe I described the role to him incorrectly. Added on to that, this is my first English language movie and my English isn't perfect. So I wasn't able to help him with his diction and that gave him a sense of insecurity."

THE END OF YEARS OF COLLABORATION?

"Well, I'm not going to rush into another movie with Rutger. This of course hit me pretty hard. But hey, if the movie has a decent run my perspective could change. I already went through the same thing with Jan de Bont. We fought constantly while filming *Katie Tippel*, to the point that afterwards I told myself that I'd never work with him ever again. We developed a deep hatred for each other and now seven years later on *Flesh+Blood*, we became each other's support."

"This project was just as uncertain for me as it was for Rutger. I was already on edge and couldn't take this on top of everything else. But ever since *Floris* I've fallen for his charm. I recognize some of myself in him and I will always have a soft spot for him, although that is definitely affected now. Neither of us is eager to work together again."

PAINFUL DETAILS

Those who have heard Verhoeven's horror stories about his experiences on set will be surprised to discover that *Flesh+Blood* has even made it to theaters. The heated atmosphere on set, albeit unintentional (Verhoeven: "I would never intentionally manipulate my actors. I hate that type of direction.") nonetheless seems to have had an impact on the movie itself. Sex and violence are unmistakably the twin pillars that support *Flesh+Blood*—and Verhoeven doesn't shy away from showing both in detail. Violent deaths are prolonged and heavily charged with symbolism, Verhoeven portrays the horrors of the plague with extensive detail, and in one scene a woman appears to enjoy being raped.

Verhoeven's direction of the rape scene abruptly summons our attention. Agnes is kidnapped and raped by the gangleader Martin (played by Hauer). Soon she begins to tolerate it and even appears to enjoy herself "but she is only pretending," says Verhoeven. "She knows that Martin is the only one she can count on and she manipulates him. She pretends to like it, but that is a lie."

ROLE REVERSAL

When Agnes takes the reigns and pretends to enjoy herself the other bandits notice and cry out 'Hey look, Martin is getting fucked.' "In principle I don't think it is possible to start a romantic relationship with your rapist, as it happens in the movie, but hypothetically anything you can imagine is possible in real life. They're both victims of their situation and so they are thrown together. In a movie, it's possible that Martin and Agnes will eventually grow closer to each other."

When we question the logic of some of the characters' actions in the film Verhoeven replies, "It's not Dostoyevsky. You have to keep the movie going forward. With an art film, you have different criteria but this is an adventure, it's entertainment." At the same time Verhoeven stresses that *Flesh+Blood* isn't your average adventure movie. Halfway through the conversation he tells us, "The characters are different from what we're used to seeing in adventure films. Every character is a secret opportunist and actually, all human action in this film is based on self-interest. It is a compromise just to stay alive."

"I didn't want to make this into a movie about heroes and villains. I like to show that no one is capable of being just one or the other. No one can be a dauntless hero—like Agnes, for instance, who finds a common cause with her kidnappers. We've seen that a lot lately in the papers, with the Patricia Hearst kidnapping" (the daughter of the American newspaper magnate who committed robberies with her kidnappers but later claimed she only did it out of sheer necessity).

So do all individuals use each other in order to survive?
"Yes. And now you're probably going to ask me why I have such a negative view of mankind?"

Not negative, rather cynical.
"That would be the case if this were a serious movie—but it isn't."

JAN DE QUAY

"It's interesting to show that people aren't solely attracted to good. Think of the Dutch during the occupation—take someone like Jan de Quay, who led the Dutch Union and tried to collaborate with the German occupation. It was just like Philippe Pétain and the Vichy regime in Paris, right? And yet De Quay was still elected Prime Minister a few years later. What good is our integrity then?"

That same cynicism—we'll call it that for now—also lurked in the background in *Spetters*. Certain characteristics in the role of Fientje (Renée Soutendijk) can also be found in Agnes in *Flesh+Blood*. Both characters are tough, ruthless, and businesslike.

THE MODERN WOMAN

"Why do I give such roles to women? Yeah, I like women who make their own decisions and are a bit business minded. You don't see that too often in movies, and that's what I find interesting in female roles. Agnes is in fact a prototype of the modern woman who thinks men are replaceable. She even says it to her suitors in the film: you or him, it doesn't matter. That plays very strongly in the scene where she's standing there holding two pieces of jewelry, trying to decide which one to take. She takes both, because that's what she wants."

CENSORSHIP AND RAMBO

At the end of *Flesh+Blood* the major supporting characters suffer the bloodiest deaths. The scenes were so horrific that the American censors had them cut. No matter how much Verhoeven argued that the cruelty was necessary, the American censors would not allow the film to be go uncut.

"I compared it to *Rambo*. How many people survive in that movie? Yes, they said, but the characters who die in *Rambo* are unknown to the audience. If you know someone, their death comes as a harsh blow and that is exactly what I wanted to show in my film. Once you follow a character throughout the film you should also see how they die. I will never turn the camera away. I think that death is horrific and that is why I prefer to show it so explicitly. That is not sensationalism."

"You shouldn't distort death or aestheticize it. Geysers of blood gushing in slow motion—all of that fake gore is hypocritical. It's a moral issue because if you don't show it clearly then you're just glossing over and whitewashing it. That is my complaint about that style of filmmaking. Whenever I watch scenes like that I think to myself, 'That isn't what it looks like. That isn't death.'"

But you're directing a film, not reality. Why then do you go for that plastic realism? "I'm still a part of this world, and so is my movie. Films may not be real but I still want to send out a warning: Don't think these are just puppets falling down. This touches on something very emotional that is deep within me. Of course sometimes I overshoot the target. If you have a problem with a specific scene, okay—then I'll admit that maybe I went a bit too far."

SCIENCE

The violence in *Flesh+Blood* is also functional in another respect, says Verhoeven. In the character of Steven, an engineer who develops plans for modern weaponry, there is a resounding protest against the subjugation of science to warfare through the ages. "Da Vinci and all those other scholars at that time were already working for the weapons industry." He references a scene in which poisoned meat is thrown into a well: "That was essentially an early attempt at biological warfare."

How do you feel about the movie now? Your first international film, despite all of its problems—is it a masterwork?
"No, definitely not. And I never intended it to be. I certainly didn't put my heart and soul into it. But neither is it a transitional film, it's too big for that. It is a beginning. My first film in English, my first international production. That opens doors, and now I want to move forward."

He sums up a few of his current projects for us: *Gangreen* (the book by Belgian writer Jef Geeraerts), another project based on the Batavia shipwreck, and a film about John of Leiden, the sixteenth-century leader of the Anabaptists who provided a partial inspiration for *Flesh+Blood*.

Flesh and Blood

Bertrand Borie / 1985

From *L'Ecran Fantastique*, October 1985. Reprinted by permission of the publisher. Translated from the French by Alexandra Valentine Proulx.

BERTRAND BORIE: After shooting documentaries for television, your first fiction production was *Floris*, a television series set during the Middle Ages. Was it around this time that *Flesh+Blood* was born?

PAUL VERHOEVEN: Yes, that was a bit of a happy coincidence. After seeing *Floris*, which was a show intended for children, the producer asked to meet with me. He wanted to make a film about the same period, but for an adult audience. So in 1971 my scriptwriter, Gerard Soeteman, who is also a historian, came up with the story. The final scenario was completed in 1980. However, it wasn't conceivable for a Dutch producer because of the budget; it was too risky. You know, in Holland the cinema is more of a hobby than an industry. At that time we made three, maybe four films a year. Nowadays, no more than ten . . . not even enough to maintain standing crews of basic technicians.

BB: What was the budget?
PV: Not that huge—$7.5 million. Even still, that was unimaginable for a Dutch film. We had to make it an international production and find money elsewhere. The project resurfaced in 1980, when I first went to the US. For them, the project was plausible because its budget was relatively small. An average budget over there can easily eclipse $12 million! As a matter of fact, they financed $6.5 million and the additional million was split between Holland and Spain, where the film was shot.

BB: Considering the final product, the budget is still surprisingly low . . .
PV: Absolutely, and I think I can objectively say that in *Flesh+Blood* you can see all of that money on the screen. We had the chance to work with extremely professional Spanish technicians. In a way, it's better that we worked with them instead of with the Americans. Since many of their films are shot in Spain, they have the

same level of experience. I also found the crew to be more intuitive and able to adapt to any situation.

BB: Presumably the screenplay went through a lot of changes as you worked on it for such a long period of time?
PV: Yes of course, but only in some respects. The essence of it was already in the first draft, most importantly the trio of Stephen and Agnes, who were already a couple in the initial draft, and Martin, whose intervention tears them apart. Also the fact that Stephen likes Agnes at first, but no more than that—it's she who tries to win him over. Her abduction serves as a catalyst for Stephen to take action. The two significant changes to the original script concerned the character of Stephen, and the relationship between Martin and Hawkwood, the leader of the mercenaries. In the first version, Stephen was more negative and cynical, maybe even more of a realist. Everything was a joke to him; he chased after girls and prostitutes, which was common at the time. It's later on that he became more serious, studious, and romantic, doubling as an aspiring young scientist. There is a faint echo of Leonardo da Vinci in his character; a somewhat academic da Vinci who progressively becomes a warrior. And it's with this in mind that we are introduced to the "metaphor" of scientific advancement. It's all very elliptical, of course, but what we see emerge with Stephen is a very modern problem: the good and the bad applications of science. We made this adjustment to the character while working on the script with the Americans, but also through historical research; studying men such as da Vinci and their research into weapons of war. We based everything on reality, synthesizing two or three sketches of the era. In a sense, we can say that Stephen is the hinge between the Middle Ages; he represents physically, mentally, and intellectually the awakening of the Renaissance.

BB: And for Martin and Hawkwood?
PV: Well, at first their relationship constituted a sort of counterpoint to the Stephen-Agnes-Martin triangle. They start out as friends, then Hawkwood betrays them. . . . In the original script, the relationship between the two men represented a pretty significant part of the plot, but that faded little by little until it almost disappeared. Their conflict has nothing to do with the possible consequences of Hawkwood's betrayal, strictly regarding their personal relationship. It's a very typical relationship in Westerns, the type you find in Peckinpah's *Ride the High Country* and *The Wild Bunch*.

BB: Why did you remove this aspect from the script?
PV: That type of development is always difficult to express. Essentially, as the relationships among the trio grew richer, the one between Hawkwood and Martin

began to weigh down the plot, making it confusing. As a matter of fact, we weren't able to fit it all into the script. That's not to say that another screenwriter couldn't have found a way to carry out both relationships simultaneously . . .

BB: Is Hawkwood's strong personality a consequence of this?
PV: It's very likely. Isolated, his character had to develop on his own. But that all happened gradually. That's the nature of the writing process.

BB: The story of John of Leiden also comes up . . .
PV: Exactly. That was also a bit of an accident. During my research, around 1978 or '79, I began to look into a very specific period out of pure curiosity. That's when I discovered the events that occured in Münster, Germany in 1534. John of Leiden was a Baptist pastor who established himself in Münster: the city was Catholic and he rendered it Baptist, ushering in a sort of pre-Protestantism. As such he introduced something akin to communism by abolishing private property and organizing social security for everyone. Paradoxically, he ended up a dictator, killing those who didn't agree with him in the city where he had become king in only two months. It seemed to me a representative paradox of the era. And all of that exists in the film, as a watermark.

There are other things that affected the evolution of the script. Primarily Stephen, the Hawkwood-Martin relationship and the Münster affair, particularly the political dimension of it. Then of course there was the very difficult task of evaluating all of the information that resulted from many years of dedicated study of the era. If you were to read the 1971 version, I think you'd find it to be completely different but at the same time, everything is essentially still there. Especially the characters.

BB: The ending was also the same?
PV: No, that's right, I forgot . . . initially, Hawkwood and Martin died. And Stephen got back together with Agnes but she no longer loved him. She hated him. Basically, Stephen was the only survivor . . . overall, the first script was pretty negative and cynical.

BB: Concerning the characters, Martin gives off the impression of being almost immortal. He has a supernatural quality . . .
PV: Rutger Hauer had been playing that role since the time of *Floris*, fifteen years ago . . . at that stage, the character was "cleaner"; more human. The rape scene, for example, didn't exist. In our minds, he was a survivor type: someone who knows how to use everything, including religion, to their advantage. And at the same time there are those elements that, as you mentioned, are supernatural—like how

he enters and exits through the chimney—that was actually inspired by the life of the French bandit Cartouche. On top of that, he's a man for whom the good and the bad are almost supernaturally combined. He sometimes has very human emotions, but that doesn't stop him from commiting horrible acts. However, he commits them with poise and a certain elegance.

BB: In your opinion, does he possess mythical qualities?
PV: Yes, a little bit, but unexaggerated. Maybe because he isn't quite the hero in the traditional sense . . . he's like El Cid!

BB: And how did you choose Jennifer Jason Leigh?
PV: I watched *Fast Times at Ridgemont High*, in which Jennifer had a small role. I was actually watching it for another actress, but happily discovered that it was Jennifer who was made for the role of Agnes. So it was partly by chance that she got the role. I wanted an actress capable of a lot of nuance . . .

BB: Because Agnes is a little bit of a troubled character . . .
PV: Yes. Her attitude regarding the two men is complex, ambiguous. Moreover, she doesn't fit into the typical American image.

BB: Did you want to portray her with a somewhat diabolical femininity?
PV: Diabolical . . . maybe, but in the psychological sense. In any case, with a femininity that, as a man, certainly scares me a little! At the same time, it attracts and fascinates me. She is at once feminine and does things that go far beyond what ordinary women do. During the rape, for example, she does something that she saw her servant do earlier, revealing her acute intuition. This may also be why there is something diabolical about her. But I also think that in a way, that could be true for every character in the film. Certain things are never explained, which serves to amplify some of the films' more realistic elements. And we could also say that in a psychological sense, Stephen and Martin represent for Agnes two complementary facets that we all posses: with Stephen, it is the romanticism and the magic of first love. And with Martin, it is the flesh, sex, temptation . . . a little like Fournier's *Le Grand Meaulnes*. Uniting Stephen and Agnes is a rape that, as a result of her consent, turns into a seduction . . .

BB: There is this mandrake root, this magical element, that introduces us to the fantastic . . .
PV: Yes, but at the time, these things weren't considered fantastic; they were based on a certain kind of reality. Everyone believed in the virtues of the mandrake back then. In some part, Agnes is responding to Stephen with a "scientific"

challenge. She pushes the affair to its limits as if to say: "Let's see if it's true!" And we allow it to remain unclear . . . . Our attitude is the same regarding the history of the statue of St. Martin, that also provides a bit of a comic relief. But magic often presents the paradox of double vision: we both accept it and know that it's a complete illusion. Our mind is split between a reaction of prosaic rejection and an opening up to that which is beyond our understanding.

BB: You did a lot of research to find the filming locations. Why did you finally pick Spain?
PV: It's true: My assistant travelled throughout Europe, but of all the most beautiful sites, the most practical were in Spain. The locations were much closer to each other, more isolated from roads and modern life in general.

BB: The scenes filmed at the Belmonte castle are reminiscent of certain scenes in Anthony Mann's *El Cid*. For example, when Sancho besieges Alfonso and Urraca . . .
PV: That's very true. I'm glad because *El Cid* is a film that I admire a lot—I've studied it very closely! You know, we are all subconsciously influenced by scenes in films; it's an acquired visual language that we all share in common.

BB: Despite your admiration for a film like *El Cid*, do you think that *Flesh+Blood* runs counter to the way that Hollywood usually approaches history?
PV: Absolutely. Even though it's not my style, I've always been interested in Hollywood filmmaking, but our starting points are different. Hollywood films often rely on a literary version of history, on popular heroes surrounded by legend, which is never the case with my characters. With regards to *Flesh+Blood*, although it is an adventure story, the approach is still very realistic. There is hardly a detail that cannot be found in some historical document, be it the costumes or the scenery. The distance separating us from the courtly traditions of Arthurian legends is vast. But that also helps to give the film weight, it portrays a cruel, dirty era of the Middle Ages—where killing is almost pleasurable. But that's how it was back then. Cutting up an animal contaminated with a sickness, plague or cholera, and launching it at the besieged was commonplace during that pitiless era. They had discovered biological warfare, which we now consider to be some kind of very sophisticated form of warfare, but it existed back then. We should not forget that this was also an era where a sword, a piece of armor, or a horse had its price. In this respect, the film takes you behind the scenes of a traditional epic.

BB: The "realism" therefore consists of portraying those details as they were?
PV: Not at all. A film like *Flesh+Blood* does not claim to be a documentary. It simply claims to be true. As a type of fiction, realism must synthesize authentic elements,

but with its own style. We spent more than a year researching the precise scenery, the costumes, etc. Of course you won't find the entire costume of such and such a character in a specific document. But, on the other hand, there is not a detail that you won't find somewhere in the historical record. Realism isn't an attitude that can be studied or calculated: it can only come from an observation of the facts. But I have to insist: *Flesh+Blood* is an entirely made-up story and consequently, all of the realistic elements have been transmuted in order to integrate them into this type of narrative.

BB: Neither does historical realism refer to an absolute in terms of the image. For example, the way you show violence and eroticism . . .
PV: Right. Some of the sex and violence happens to be accurate, but it's devoid of sadism or voyeurism. Actually, when I show people being hit with weapons, the injuries are consistent with the epic literary tradition. It also corresponds to the idea that in those times, things like death and violence were both gratuitous and pervasive. Adopting that way of showing things is a kind of realism. It's something the critics forget when they say that my goal is to shock. You know, the problem with "authenticity" is that everyone's perception of it is relative and subject to moral and aesthetic considerations that often have nothing to do with the matter at hand. So, you accurately show the costumes and technology of that era—that's authenticity. You show the cruelty with which people confronted each other— that's violence! Where is the logic? I don't know, I think it's complete nonsense . . .

BB: However, you use violence and eroticism throughout the film, though all within limits. Generally speaking, what attitude do you have towards those two components of cinema?
PV: Concerning violence, I think we are all marked by certain things that we have seen. When I show violence, it most often appears in one form or another as visions that I am unable to escape. But I'm not a moralist, nor do I want to be one. I think we should be objective and admit that it is part of our nature to be fascinated by violence. In movies, the usual trick is to lure the spectator over to the hero's side so that he will like him and support his use of violence—just look at Rambo! That's something that I wanted to avoid. I tried to be true to the era. I wanted to show people for whom violence is gratuitous, who kill instinctively, on a whim, for no reason. That's the kind of violence I wanted to show—something that comes out of nowhere. Maybe that's what makes it so horrible. It's dangerous to rationalize violence, so instead the movies too often make it enjoyable.

BB: And as for eroticism?
PV: That's completely different. In my eyes, eroticism and love are both beautiful.

I'm only showing acts that, in my opinion, represent something beautiful, in part because it reflects a profound exchange between two beings.

BB: Don't you think that by opening with strong scenes—the siege and later, the rape—you took a risk in order to maintain the spectator's attention?

PV: No. It isn't easy, but essentially it's a question of the script and the direction. You can express strength and power—even the spectacular—with something other than battle scenes. It's important to keep the spectator focused on the narrative. It is much more difficult to capture their attention with characters who are hard to identify with; who are acting in service to a different logic. And sometimes, as we know, they do things that appear completely illogical. With Hawkwood for example, he is consumed with pity during the siege, exhibiting a very human reflex to care for the nun that he injures. But this ultimately leads him to betray his men. . . . At this point, he becomes a different character. Martin and Agnes change as well, especially after the rape. That's the real difficulty: getting the audience to identify with the characters.

BB: Concerning the photography, one gets the sense sometimes that you are trying to imitate the style of Dutch painting . . .

PV: Indeed. The director of photography, Jan de Bont, has been living in Los Angeles for many years, but he is originally from Holland. And don't forget all of the research that we did on the time period—those documents also influenced us on a visual level. What we tried to do—even with the costumes—was to use dramatic colors. For example, the entire beginning of the film is grey. Overall, we tried to minimize the colors. Green, red, yellow are colors that in my opinion should be handled with caution. But think of the paintings of that era: they're often dark. The problem is that you also have to compose the images with the audience in mind . . .

BB: The opening scenes must have required a lot of work?

PV: Yes, but they were shot in only three-and-a-half days! And without storyboards! The shoot, which was scheduled for thirteen weeks, went on for fourteen weeks and two days. We shot the battle scenes last since we were pressed for time. But we made up for that in other ways: we had very good equipment—specifically a crane—and an efficient team. We were able to pick up the pace because I had a particular vision for what I wanted in terms of the angles, the framing . . .

BB: Why does the camera move so much during those scenes?

PV: For two reasons, I think: first, I had to introduce a number of characters while establishing a certain ambiance. I didn't want to do a series of separate shots, so linking everything into long shots seemed a better option. Also, because of the time constraint I allowed myself to follow my instincts more. I think this introduced a kind of spontaneous lyricism to the imagery. When you are working in the moment like that, sometimes you don't even realize how far away you've drifted from your original plans. I glide over the characters and objects more than I introduce them.

BB: You also employed a number of special effects, most notably in the final scene when the set burns down. How were you able to do that without damaging the premises?

PV: Shooting on real locations poses a lot of problems. For example, in Avila there were colonies of birds perched on the walls and the committee protecting the city did not want us to shoot any scenes with explosions—they didn't want us to scare the birds away. When we see a man impaled by a sword in the film, we had to find the same materials used in aeronautics in order to give the weapon both substance and natural thickness while, at the same time, having it contour halfway out of the actor's body! Regarding the final scenes, we had to meticulously protect everything. We had an excellent Spanish special effects team, backed by an American crew, all trained to deal with problems posed by fire.

BB: Wouldn't it have been safer to build a set?

PV: Yes, of course. Safer and more practical, but also a lot more expensive! We had already spent a lot on backgrounds and costumes.

We were especially lucky that the local authorities respected our special effects technicians. Normally, no insurance company would have agreed to cover something so risky. Thank god everything went well.

BB: And why did you choose Basil Poledouris for the music?

PV: Originally I had three composers in mind: Jerry Goldsmith, but he was too expensive; James Horner, who is a charming man, but didn't really like the film; and Poledouris, who, in my opinion, is a remarkable composer. Maybe because of his Latin background, he was the most appropriate choice. Of course, when it came to composing the music, he also studied compositions from that era. Even with the score, I wanted the film to have an air of authenticity . . .

Man of Iron

Brian Cronenworth / 1987

From *American Film*, October 1987. Reprinted courtesy of the American Film Institute (AFI).

Paul Verhoeven's *RoboCop* was the summer's flashiest, smartest action movie—a futuristic nerve grinder with a devilish streak of anti-corporate satire. The grimy wasteland of Old Detroit (actually Dallas) in the Nineties isn't just a backdrop for the exploits of Murphy, the Cop of Steel (Peter Weller), a staunch patrolman who is gruesomely blown apart and then reconstituted as a law-and-order "terminator." The urban environment is an integral part of *RoboCop*'s volatile mixture of graphic violence, comic book dynamism, and unexpected poignancy, as Murphy's purged memories of hearth and home begin to seep back into his cyborg consciousness.

At first blush, Verhoeven seems a mite overqualified for a robot-vigilante film. In the past, the forty-eight-year-old Dutch director has been associated with imported art movies: the sardonic, sexy love story *Turkish Delight* (1973), Verhoeven's first project with favored actor Rutger Hauer, and historical epics like *Katie Tippel* (1975) and *Soldier of Orange* (1979). Although his work always exhibited a sharply ironic edge, it seemed to be settling into a worthy, turgid rut.

But *Spetters* (1980), an abrasive teen picture about sex, death, and motorcycles, and *The Fourth Man* (1984), a hallucinatory thriller about a bisexual writer's descent into psychosis, boosted the energy level quite a bit. So Verhoeven's switch to English-language moviemaking, in the 1985 US/Dutch coproduction *Flesh+Blood* (a gruesomely realistic epic about the warriors of the Middle Ages), wasn't such a drastic turnaround; it just brought different aptitudes to the surface.

Now that he's one of Hollywood's hottest directors and has moved his base of operations to Los Angeles, Verhoeven seems to have shed much of his lingering European gloom. Sprawled on a couch in his publicist's Beverly Hills office, he admits that he's become a rapt student of American culture.

PAUL VERHOEVEN: I spent every minute I could spare watching those Iran-Contra hearings. I am fascinated by these people—the change in mood when

Oliver North testified and how the senators tried to get some of that wonderful charismatic quality to rub off on them. I also closely followed the aftermath of the Challenger disaster—the same spectacle of people reproaching each other and lying and cheating. It was wonderful!

BRIAN CRONENWORTH: You put a lot of emphasis on the future of American society in *RoboCop*—with snippets of TV news coverage, especially.
PV: That is one of the things I found most interesting in the story. I don't think I am extremely inspired by a scene with twenty people shooting at each other. The other layers are much more interesting to me.

BC: Do people find it surprising that a director of your background would want to make a picture like *RoboCop*?
PV: A friend overheard somebody who was looking at the *RoboCop* poster say, "Paul Verhoeven? Why is he doing this piece of shit?" An admirer of *The Fourth Man*, I suppose. But I think if he saw the new film, he wouldn't have that problem anymore. I don't think *The Fourth Man* is any better or more important or more artistic. You can do a comic book movie and still put your soul into it.

BC: Nevertheless, a typical career pattern for an American director—Spielberg is a perfect example—is to start out making movies in popular genres, and then to "graduate" to serious period epics or to films based on distinguished novels—
PV: And I am going the other way? To this silliness? (Laughs) Now I feel I have opened something that I kept covered for fifteen to twenty years.

I think my ultimate goal would be combining the European kind of movie and the American, something like what David Lean has done: interesting characters, plus some action and spectacle. But that's not something you can do right away. You have to build up to it.

I hope all my films have a kind of rough energy and don't pretend too much that they are art. I always had a problem with arty European pictures; I thought they were dull. From American movies I got a sense that movement is more essential than dialogue or character.

BC: By American standards, you're juggling a lot of elements in *RoboCop*. There are three or four layers of imagery, and it's all very fast paced.
PV: Perhaps that is a result of my mathematical training? Could be. I studied painting in Paris when I was sixteen, but then switched to mathematics for several years before I sort of stumbled into film. I have always been very much concerned with precision, with clarity.

I like to be able to see everything that is there. I hate shots where a person is sitting there and you can't tell whether there's a chair or a tree behind him because it's been shot with a telephoto lens. We always used 16mm and 25mm lenses, which give you deep perspectives and sharpness all the way back.

Also, I've studied Hitchcock for a long time, and he is a director who is always balancing things. There is no confusion in his shots. For audiences nowadays you have to have more clutter, more realism, to disguise that kind of stylization. But it is the same principle.

BC: *RoboCop* has a rather sweet undercurrent—Peter Weller seems innocent, almost fragile. But the film is also quite savage at times.

PV: Only in a couple of sequences, I think. Especially when Murphy is killed. From the beginning, I wanted his death to be extremely cruel; it was necessary from both a philosophical and dramatic point of view. The character has not done enough memorable stuff before he dies that you could root for him, so his death has to be memorable.

I don't think the Christian religion would have had the impact it has had if the death of Christ had not been so excruciating. I won't compare Christ to Murphy, but of course there were parallels in my mind. The basic idea was to do something about a human soul that is destroyed and resurrected. And for a real resurrection, we needed a real crucifixion.

BC: Do you share executive producer Jon Davison's feeling that before the MPAA forced you to trim scenes to avoid an X rating, the violence was actually less wrenching, because it was more cartoonish?

PV: Yes. Not so much Murphy's death scene, because that was intentionally disturbing, but it's true of the other two scenes that they had problems with [rival robot ED 209's kill, and a bad guy getting it in the neck]. When those scenes went "over the top," they were easier to accept and seemed to work better as a strange form of comic relief. They were shot to be more than real, to go much further than people's imaginations.

BC: Apparently one element that took a long time to develop was the robot suit itself.

PV: With robots, everything has a tendency to get silly. By looking at the dailies, we found what was working and what was not—which angles would sell him and which had to be avoided at any price. [RoboCop designer Rob] Bottin followed the shapes of human muscles very closely in his design. Most robots look strong but stupid. This one is strong but elegant.

BC: Murphy looks like the robot Maria in *Metropolis*.
PV: Exactly. *Metropolis* was quite important for us, actually. We screened it for the production designer and the matte—painting people before production started.

The politics of *Metropolis* now seem very old fashioned, of course. Although by modern standards you would describe the old man character, the leader, as a fascist capitalist, he is more or less saved in the movie because his son does something wonderful for the blue collar people. *RoboCop*, though, has the same kind of guy at the top [Daniel O'Herlihy]. At one point I said to the writers, "You portray the top guy as benevolent, but we all know that the top guy is the worst of all." And [co-writer] Ed Neumeier said, "You are right, but we should leave people some hope at the end." So the Old Man is good and Jones [Ronny Cox] is bad—much like the old Christian conception that God is good and Satan bad, although he has less power than God.

BC: We're harking back to the Catholic imagery of *The Fourth Man* and *Flesh+Blood*.
PV: It is one of my favorite fields of thought. Religion is a hobby for me.

BC: When I saw *The Name of the Rose*, I thought it was a shame that you didn't get to do it.
PV: Me, too! (Laughs) I tried to get it, but Jean-Jacques Annaud was at work on the movie before I had even read the book.

BC: There's a wonderful moment in *RoboCop* when Murphy finally remembers his own name.
PV: It's an acceptance of what he has become, of having less and having more. He has taken control of what they have done to him, becoming Murphy again, but in a new way.

For me, the central scene of the movie is when Murphy takes off his mask to tell Nancy Allen his story, and accepts the loss of his humanity. I wanted the feeling of a lost paradise. We all have this thought in the back of our minds, that there is a lost paradise somewhere, although we are cut off from it. If I remember my childhood in occupied Holland, the events of that time seem to still be there, but I can't touch them anymore. That was one of the most important feelings behind the picture.

Paul Verhoeven Tackles Science Fiction

Indra Bhose / 1988

From L'Ecran Fantastique, January 1988. Reprinted by permission of the publisher. Translated from the French by Alexandra Valentine Proulx.

Paul Verhoeven has captured the attention of cinephiles with the realism, violence, and corrosive humor of his films. *RoboCop* is his first American production, and his first attempt at science fiction.

Born in Amsterdam in 1938, Verhoeven's childhood was marked by war and American cinema. He studied painting and later pursued a doctorandus in physics and mathematics at Leiden University. He directed a handful of short films before working as a documentarian for the Royal Netherlands Navy. When he returned to civilian life he attained critical success with his socio-cultural documentaries and found fame in 1969 as the director of the Dutch television action series *Floris*.

In 1971, he tackled feature filmmaking with *Wat zien ik (Business Is Business)*. The following year, he was nominated for an Academy Award for *Turkish Delight* and, in 1977, was nominated for a Golden Globe for *Soldier of Orange*, a film about the Dutch resistance. Followed by *Spetters* (1980), a film about social violence steeped in rock culture, *The Fourth Man* (1983), and *Flesh+Blood* (1985), one of the most challenging historical films of the past few years. Paul Verhoeven made his American debut on television with an excellent episode of *The Hitchhiker* titled "The Last Scene" starring Peter Coyote.

INDRA BHOSE: You've always shot films in Europe. What brought you to the United States to make a film like *RoboCop*?
PAUL VERHOEVEN: I'd already made a film for Orion in 1985. An old project I had in the back of my mind since the '70s that finally came to life under the title *Flesh+Blood*.

I guess Orion liked what I was doing. In any case, they called to ask if I was interested in a film called *RoboCop*, a film tons of directors had already turned down, some after an hour, some after a couple of weeks.

IB: Why did you take on a project that nobody wanted?
PV: It's all because of my wife. I was away working on the post-production of *Flesh+Blood* and she read the script. When I got back, she told me that it was fun and that I had to make the movie.

IB: How did you choose your collaborators?
PV: I was lucky enough to work with the cinematographer Jost Vacano. We had already worked together and he understood what it meant to make a film in America. He helped me a lot during the shooting. I trust him. I don't even need to look into the viewfinder, I just tell him what I want and he does it for me. At times I spent three or four days away from the camera! (*Laughs*)

He invented a shoulder camera, which was really practical. It has nothing to do with the Steadicam that attaches to one's body; this is a camera that we hold in our hand. It's the hands and the wrists that move it. There are gyroscopes underneath it to keep it balanced. We could do anything with it; it was great. It gave a very particular style to the entire movie; something very seductive, yet very fast.

IB: And it probably also helped you work faster?
PV: Yes, absolutely.

IB: You practically shot the entire film on location?
PV: Yes, we shot everything on location during the entire fourteen or fifteen days of shooting with the exception of a week in the studio.

IB: Was the police station also on location or was it a set?
PV: It was a real police station, but not a neighborhood one. I think it might have been a discotheque at some point, before being transformed into a police station. It was an old and very spacious building with a dance floor. A wonderful place.

IB: The film is supposed to take place in the near future. The script says 2020?
PV: No. That might have been written in the script, but it's not accurate. The year was never specified and the writers themselves always refused to say where the action took place. It was always supposed to be about Detroit in the near future.

"2020" could have been what was written on the first page of the script, but Ed Neumeier—one of the writers who was always by my side during the shooting, because he was also an associate producer—insisted that we remain vague. We couldn't give an exact date. I know that in the ad campaign they indicated 1991 or something like that. Financially, we couldn't have gone too far into the future anyway. We had budget problems: we had to create a universe with very little money.

Creating sets like in *Blade Runner* was out of the question. It would have cost us four, five, or six million dollars more. We didn't have that kind of money and what started off as a financial decision turned into an advantageous aesthetic decision. We decided not to try to build a futuristic universe with sophisticated phones or cars. Everything stayed completely normal. The policeman's car was a new, completely black Ford. As for the rest, the buildings and the elevators, we used mattes, about seven or eight altogether. Other than that, we used the existing scenery. I have to give credit to the producer: he knew how to stretch the money, spending only when it was impossible not to, that is to say on specific shots and locations.

IB: . . . and on the outstanding sets?
PV: Yes. The money went toward creating sets whenever it was impossible to shoot on location. It also went to financing the large robot, the one that doesn't move. The moving robot was a small scale model. The large one cost half a million alone, whereas the smaller one cost six or seven thousand dollars. RoboCop's "vision" cut into our budget by about 100,000 dollars or something to that effect. Same with the matte paintings.

WHO IS ROBOCOP?

IB: How would you describe the character of RoboCop to someone who hasn't seen the film?
PV: He's a cop who gets killed on the job while trying to stop criminals, thieves, and cop-killers. They kill him by shooting him and destroying part of his brain. A corporation experimenting with the creation of a robot police force sees a potential in this tragedy. They decide to take the cop's remains and create a new creature. His arms and legs are replaced with mechanical limbs, a computer replaces his half-destroyed brain and his body is protected by armor. He more or less keeps his heart, his lungs and the majority of his organs, but we don't see any of that. He still has his own mouth and jaw. This automaton is the ideal policeman, capable of resolving all criminal problems. The robot, however, has a personal problem: it seems that what's left of his brain is regaining consciousness and begins sending messages to the computer. Something's going on here: he had a life, a home. He starts to feel that he's lost his paradise and tries to find his previous incarnation. He understands that he used to be a real live policeman called Murphy and that he was murdered by a gang of criminals. He can't feel relief until he locates them and avenges his death. At the end of the film, we see him accept his new identity. He is physically different, but inside he's more or less the same Murphy. Anyway, he accepts his new situation, which may be the next phase of our evolution. The end is rather optimistic.

IB: When you made the film, did you have a particular audience in mind?

PV: Not really, no. I always try to aim for the widest possible audience while not limiting myself. I've never tried to make artistic films or films for any specific audience. I'd rather risk being too general or superficial if it means a larger number of people will see my films. I don't try to be sophisticated by addressing myself to anyone in particular. I have a large base of general knowledge: a doctorandus in physics, plus I've done a lot of math and know intellectuals like the palm of my hand. I've had it up to here with them! (*Laughs*) I have no reason to try to communicate any more with them through cinema. I'd rather address myself to a population that may be a little less cultured, but fun. It's another type of challenge.

IB: The message of the film scares me a little. You seem to suggest that the only way to resolve certain problems is with the help of robots. As if humans were incapable . . .

PV: No . . . and this film doesn't have a message. It's a fantasy, a complete fantasy; a real comic book scenario. I don't think it would be possible to create a creature like RoboCop. I think people will learn how to fix the problems of the world, sooner or later. If there's a message in the film, it is to accept oneself, or the immortality of the soul. I hope the soul is indestructible, but no one has come back to tell us yet. . . . In any case, I didn't want to make this film to be about any particular message or theme. Let's just say that the theme of the film is this: that no matter what we do to the soul, if the body remains it will find a way to transcend it.

IB: The film might have a comic book moral, but it's completely credible; even the leader of the gang is believable.

PV: It's true. The comic book aspect is mostly stylistic. The screenwriter carefully studied the comic book. One of the writers used to be the director at Universal, where he would spend his time reading comic books to see if they had the potential to be made into movies. Something from that experience stuck with him. When I started on this project, in September of '85, the first thing I read was a pile of comic books!

IB: Which ones did you enjoy most?

PV: I read so many . . . Spiderman, Roboman, Ironman, etc. . . . I read only comic books for months. I studied the pictures, the points of view, and the style. It all came back to me during the shooting. I also made the cinematographer, the technicians and all of my collaborators read them. That being said, the film isn't a movie adaptation of a comic book. We created a work that stands on its own. That is the movie's strength; it was conceived directly from that mode of expression. It isn't an adaptation.

AN EXHAUSTING SHOOT

IB: This was your first time shooting in the US. How did that go?

PV: Horrible! I came out of it totally exhausted! However, I don't think there's a significant difference between shooting in the US or in Europe. This type of film is obviously associated with technical problems: mock-ups, blue screens, mattes . . . a whole lot of things I wasn't really aware of before. I knew about these things, but I didn't really understand what they were all about. Action films are always very tiring to shoot because of the chases, the explosions, the fights, and on top of all that we had special effects! We had to be careful with every explosion because there's always the risk of an accident. Everyone always thinks of *The Twilight Zone* . . . there were moments where I thought I was going to quit because of how difficult it all was. I think the reason I carried on was because of the actors. I had a wonderful relationship with them. They were all wonderful and very creative and I had a lot of fun working with them. It was very enjoyable. They were always very cooperative, even in situations that could have been dangerous. They were always willing to give it a try and always had clever suggestions. It was a democratic shoot! I always had one of the two dialogists with me in case we needed to change a line. And that was wonderful too. It brings me back to your first question: I chose the cameraman, a German, but the others were Rob Bottin who designed the robot's costume, Phil Tippett who made the scale models, and Rocco Gioffre who made the mattes—they were all chosen by the producer. He told me they were the best in their fields but he could get them because he'd already worked with them and they all liked one another. They would do it for cheap, just to work on the movie! He was right—they were the best out there! Another producer might not have known who was the best in each field. And there's no way to know if we could have gotten them for the same rates. I think they'd also seen my movies and wanted to work with a director of "artistic" films. I don't think anyone regretted it. Everyone seemed happy. Phil Tippett, who worked on *Star Wars*, was very satisfied with my storyboards. He found them very dynamic, very interesting, and new. They were challenging for him. I think they all had a lot of fun, but it's the producer to whom I owe the film's success. He's the one that selected the crew for me. I didn't know these people. Without his help, the film wouldn't have been as good.

IB: Do you always draw storyboards for your films?

PV: This was the first time I made storyboards for the entire film. Usually, we only make storyboards for 60 or 70 percent of the film, but with all the models and special effects I felt that it was the only way to be sure everything went as planned. There were too many technical problems to deal with. With the storyboards I was able to draw out the sets, the camera movement, and the framing. All Phil had to do was place the models in the desired locations. The film was shot in strict accordance with the storyboards. At least 95 percent of it was.

IB: I suppose this includes the scene with the robot ED 209?
PV: Yes, absolutely. The only flexibility we had was with the speed of its movements. Phil Tippett was always nearby to help us make decisions about it. It's important to note that the actors were speaking to a wall in that scene. The big robot was added in later. Phil was really helpful when it came to making decisions about whether to shoot an extra take or not, or in telling the actors they should move quicker, etc. He was incredible at incorporating the characters into the sets. For example, we never see the junction line between the mattes and the sets. It really looks as though the robot is walking on the same ground as the actors.

IB: Wouldn't it have been possible to use a life-sized robot and to shoot everything at once?
PV: We thought about it for a second, but then we calculated the expense and the film would have cost five, six, maybe even ten million dollars more. It just wasn't doable. We would have needed complex hydraulic systems. It would have worked out, but it would have been incredibly complicated and we wouldn't have been able to bring the robot up to the fiftieth floor of the building. Also, it probably wouldn't have been capable of doing everything we needed it to: run towards a door, open it, and so on. Anyway, we were limited by the budget . . . and also we were able to go from the miniature model to the full-scale model without any transitions.

IB: What can you say about the television news sequences that serve as transitions between the different segments of the movie?
PV: I think it was a great idea and we never questioned it. They weren't included in the original version of the script, but they were in the draft I was given when I signed onto the project. I hadn't seen any other version of the script. To me, it seemed like a very original, personal, and artistic device to help move the story forward. It goes over really well with audiences. It's an original narrative technique. We can witness the action without having to sit through transitions.

IB: How did you film those scenes?
PV: Those sequences were shot digitally after the "filmed" scenes were completed. Except for the television interviews, which were done during the shooting. The commercials and the debate between the man and the woman were shot in January while the shooting wrapped up in November. The advantage of digital is that, besides being cheap and quick, it also brings an electronic feel to the image. The

difference in style between the digital and the filmic image is what made shooting those sequences digitally appealing.

IB: The producer Jon Davison told us about censorship problems . . .
PV: We had to edit the movie five or six times. The censors mostly had an issue with the scene of Murphy's death at the start of the movie. It was bloodier and more violent in the first edit. Now, all we see are his hands exploding. I wonder if that's not more horrifying! (*Laughs*) We had to cut out a lot of the brain splattering. Alas, there are only a few glimpses of that left. That scene is a lot less visceral now. However, the only scene I regret cutting is when Kinney dies in the washroom. It was also very bloody, but fun. It was so outrageous that it couldn't have been taken seriously. It really felt like it had the tone of a comic book. Now it's been cut to look more realistic. In the end, I think that was the wrong decision.

IB: The way that you tell it, it seems like the movie was meant to be a comedy . . .
PV: Absolutely! At least in the way some scenes were shot. I'm not saying that murder is a fun topic! However, some scenes really reminded me of comic books. Everything is so exaggerated that there is no possibility of confusion. The viewers weren't wrong when they first saw it (and laughed). They reacted wonderfully. Like at the end of the movie, when the guy's head explodes! But I don't want to give away too many details. I want your readers to enjoy the film! The cuts in Murphy's death scene are justified; it was realistic at first, but it clashed with the rest of the film's style. But let's be clear: the cuts represent only a few seconds in total!

IB: Is the version being released in Europe the same as the US version?
PV: Yes. We discussed this a lot. There were two versions of *Flesh+Blood*. The European one was more sexual and aggressive than the American one. We could have done the same thing with *RoboCop*. But it seemed to us that apart from Kinney's death scene, which I mentioned before, the American version was the better one. Everyone agreed, including the censors, and we didn't see any reason why we should modify it.

IB: Let's remind our readers that in the US a film rated "R" can't be advertised in the press or on TV, which practically sentences it to death.
PV: Exactly, that's the problem that Alan Parker ran into with *Angel Heart*. He had to cut it if he wanted it to be released.

IB: One more question, will there be a *RoboCop 2* as the end of the film suggests?
PV: Yes, but the ending has nothing to do with it. I don't think the studio would make the mistake of transforming Nancy Allen into a robot. We actually shot a

scene that we later cut where a journalist comes to interview her at the hospital during her recovery. No one expected to see her come back in the robot armor. We cut it because we realized in the preview that no one wanted to see anything more after RoboCop shouts: "My name is Murphy!" Orion already signed on two screenwriters for *RoboCop 2*. They're supposed to have their first reading in January of '88. I heard about their ideas, but I think it'll be difficult to top what we've already done.

Total Recall: Director Paul Verhoeven on His Mars Vacation with Arnold Schwarzenegger

Bill Florence / 1990

From *Cinefantastique*, December 1990. Reprinted with permission by Bill Florence.

Ask Paul Verhoeven what was most memorable about directing *Total Recall* and his reply will have nothing to do with the tremendous freedom given him by Carolco Pictures, or his colossal budget. He does not cite his film crew, part of which had worked with him before on *RoboCop*. Nor did the Academy Award-winning Dream Quest Images, or the script written by Ron Shusett, Dan O'Bannon and Gary Goldman prove to be the greatest attraction for Verhoeven.

The answer he *does* supply is given without hesitation. Said Verhoeven, "Working with Arnold [Schwarzenegger] was the most pleasant part of the whole production. Arnold is such a supportive guy, and he's so concerned with getting the best. He has a very pleasant temperament, always very balanced and always in a good mood . . . and that is in contrast to the whole production, which was very difficult."

"I'm not even talking about his acting; I'm talking about him as a human being," said Verhoeven. "His social abilities formed a support system which was probably the most pleasant aspect of the whole movie. I've never met an actor that is so easy to work with and is smart, makes good judgments, and is so supportive of the director."

Contrary to what some may think, Schwarzenegger has, according to Verhoeven, no ego. "You can say to him, 'That looks ridiculous, Arnold! You cannot do that!' And he'll say, 'Oh, really? Well, what about this?' or 'Can we do it this way?' or 'If that doesn't look good, what do you think I should do?' You can tell Arnold anything about acting or about his hair, the color of his jacket, or whatever—he will never take it personally. And if he's not good, if he makes a mistake or mispronounces something, then he will change it."

Schwarzenegger's own mild temperament is in direct contrast to that of Verhoeven, whose reputation as an excitable director was confirmed by the cast of *Total Recall*. "I'm much less in control than Arnold," said Verhoeven. "He doesn't have to raise his voice to get what he wants. He has a lot of power. If Arnold says, 'Yes,' it's yes. If he says 'No,' it's no. It is that easy. He has more power than anybody else I've known in my life, and he's probably even-tempered in part *because* he has that power. I'm much more emotional, much more directly confrontational."

Such an unassuming nature in an actor has not been common in Verhoeven's experience. "With many actors, you have to be very careful. A lot of them, if you criticize them—and I don't mean criticize in a mean way, like 'This is completely stupid!'—if I say, 'no, that should be different,' a lot of actors will lose confidence or start being nervous. But Arnold is so self-confident. He doesn't have an ego. You can just put that aside and talk about what's necessary."

Such praise would be meaningless if Schwarzenegger's performance in front of the camera wasn't up to snuff, but Verhoeven felt Schwarzenegger excelled in his role as Quaid. "His performance was great. This is still an action movie, of course, but there is much of what you would call 'normal' stuff, where [Arnold] is with his wife or the woman he loves, in bed, at the breakfast table."

Verhoeven wanted to break the mold for his leading actor as *Twins* had done. "In most of his movies, they have made Arnold into a kind of superhero. In *Twins*, they made him something different, they used comedy. But there is only one movie I know, the first one he ever did, where they used him as Arnold, and that was *Stay Hungry*. What I wanted to portray was Arnold as I know him, where he is just a pleasant guy to be with."

Summed up Verhoeven, "Many see Arnold only as this big muscle man, and that's not true. Muscle means no brains, right? To the contrary! Arnold has big muscles *and* big brains! He's very smart, and a very gifted man on a lot of levels."

The Vitality of Existence

George Hickenlooper / 1991

Excerpted from *Reel Conversations: Candid Interviews with Film's Foremost Directors and Critics,* Citadel 1991. Reprinted with permission by the publisher. All rights reserved. Reprinted by arrangement with Kensington Publishing Corp. www.kensingtonbooks.com.

After the phenomenal success of his two latest American films, *RoboCop* (1987) and *Total Recall* (1990), Paul Verhoeven sits comfortably in his modest West Hollywood office. As he signals his assistant to "boot up" the office espresso machine, I notice that his commanding gestures and thick accent give him that touch of savoir-faire characteristic of many European filmmakers. "See how far Tower Records is?" he says pointing to the building directly across Sunset Boulevard. "That's the distance my house was from where the Germans launched their V1 and V2 rockets," he continues, his eyes wide with anticipation as if it were still 1943 . . .

HICKENLOOPER: Your films are highly physical and emotional, often blatantly filled with symbolism. Are you conscious of this in your treatment of religion, war, whatever it may be in your work?
VERHOEVEN: As a director, my goal is to be completely open. Just look at how I portray sex in my films. They're considered shocking and obscene because I like to carefully examine human sexuality. It has to be realistic, otherwise it is bullshit. I really like documentaries; therefore, reality is important to me when I do fiction. It is often related to my own life, my Dutch background.

The art scene in Holland has always attempted to be realistic. The Dutch painters of four hundred years ago were meticulously realistic. The example I always like to use is a marvelous painting by Hieronymus Bosch titled *The Prodigal Son.* It is a painting of a brothel, and in the corner is a man pissing against a wall. You would never, never find something like that in an Italian, French or English painting of that epoch. The Dutch have always been more scientific, interested in detail, certainly less idealistic and more realistic. The sex scenes in *The Fourth Man* and *Turkish Delight* were based on real experiences I had or a friend had. It's very personal. Of course, I must admit that I love to shock audiences.

GH: Was that your intention in *The Fourth Man*?
PV: No, that film had more to do with my vision of religion. In my opinion Christianity is nothing more than one of many interpretations of reality, neither more nor less. Ideally, it would be nice to believe that there is a God somewhere out there, but it looks to me as if the whole Christian religion is a major symptom of schizophrenia in half the world's population: civilizations scrambling to rationalize their chaotic existence. Subsequently, Christianity has a tendency to look like magic or the occult. And I liked that ambiguity, because I wanted my audience to wonder, "What is religion really?"

GH: In *The Fourth Man*, as in many of your films, you often have a cavalier, if not black comic, approach to violence.
PV: Well, with respect to *The Fourth Man* and its religious theme, you have to remember that Christianity is a religion grounded in one of the most violent acts of murder—the crucifixion. Otherwise, religion wouldn't have had any kind of impact. With regards to the irony of the violence, much of that probably comes from my childhood experiences during and immediately following the Second World War.

GH: You lived through the German occupation?
PV: Very much so. In fact, if it hadn't been for the German occupation and then the American occupation I would have never been a filmmaker.

GH: How so?
PV: Well, during the bombings, going to the movies was not all that convenient, so when you did go you really loved it, even if the film was German propagandistic shit. Then in 1945 we were liberated by the Americans, and in the years afterwards the only thing you could see were American movies—these action, horror, and science fiction movies. And because there was no cinema industry in Holland, it seemed like another world. I wanted to do nothing but see movies. So by coincidence, when I was seventeen or eighteen, I was given a 16mm camera from an uncle. As a hobby I started experimenting, but then I became more interested in painting. However, here I was studying at a university for mathematics. It was a very confusing situation because I was doing mathematics, I wanted to be a painter and I started filmmaking as a hobby. But then I got involved with a film group at the university, so from a little hobby it became a real hobby where I was spending a lot of time doing it.

In 1964 I finished my studies as a mathematician, but then had to go into the military service for two years, and although they wanted to send me to study rocket science in Germany, I started to find out if there were other possibilities.

I got myself moved into the film department in the Navy, then for two years I started becoming more professional as a film director. I did documentaries for both the Navy and the Marines, so when I came out of the service I decided to become a real film director. It took me a couple of years before a television producer, who was impressed with all the action in my films, gave me a children's television series in 1968 called *Floris*—something like Ivanhoe or Robin Hood in Holland. That was really the first time I became a film director, and that series was seen by a German/Dutch film producer in 1970, and he gave me my first picture in 1971.

GH: As you first began to direct, did you ever find yourself applying your background in mathematics or painting?
PV: Whatever you study in the university, whether it is psychology, sociology, philosophy, it really programs your brain for solving problems. And in film you can find that very useful. For me, because I'm such an organized guy, by concentrating on mathematics for six or seven years, I think that I improved my proficiency considerably. You know, Eisenstein also had a degree in mathematics, or chemistry, and Pudovkin even . . . all coming from the university. And I'm sure that my style and Eisenstein's have a lot in common. It's not really on the surface, but if you study it shot by shot, you'll see where I took my clues from Eisenstein really.

GH: And like Eisenstein, you seem to have strong political views in your work, no matter how iconoclastic.
PV: Politics are of no interest to me. I have no real political beliefs. I find everything fascinating, especially the political beliefs of the United States. I find the fact that media and government made such a big deal out of Jim and Tammy Bakker and the flag-burning issue interesting. What interests me in exploring religion and politics is how easily a person can fall or break under tension. You get a very sharp focus on someone; it's like looking at someone under a microscope. They will react.

GH: When did you first get recognized for your work?
PV: In 1974 I made *Turkish Delight*, as I said, a very open, sexual, audacious film. It got an Oscar nomination for Best Foreign Film, and immediately afterwards I got phone calls from the American film industry. But I was afraid to go to the United States at that point. I was thirty-three or thirty-four, and I thought that I was doing perfectly well in Holland. *Soldier of Orange* was the last film that was made without really big problems—that was 1978.

GH: How did you get involved with that project?
PV: I got a book, an autobiography by Erik Hazelhoff Roelfzema, who had lived through that war period. It was his real account of what happened at that time.

My regular producer, Rob Houwer, thought it was too big of a project to do as a feature, and thought it would be too expensive. After having had three enormous successes in Holland, we made contact with the prince of the Netherlands—Prince Bernard—consort to Queen Juliana. He wanted to get the film . . . what do you call it in English? He became the honorary advisor to the film—honorary protector of the film.

GH: A kind of honorary executive producer?
PV: No, it's a very interesting thing. For example, the KLM is also under the royal protection of the Queen and the Prince—it doesn't mean anything really—it's just an honorary title. So when the Prince thought it was an interesting film, he gave it his honorary protection title. From that moment on, all the doors in Holland opened, more or less, to do this film because at the same time, the Prince was the General, head of the Netherland's defense forces (the army). He could make a phone call to all the military and say, help these people. So the producer had enough money, and the doors opened because the Prince was backing the picture. The film was made for two million dollars, but would have cost four or five if we had done it the regular way.

GH: Did your own experience, or your parents' experience with the German occupation have any influence on . . . ?
PV: I was seven or eight when the war finished, so I have a very vivid memory of it—walking along the street, seeing the burning houses, sitting at the table, and the house opposite you is bombed, and the windows blast into your room, and being forced to walk on the bellies of dead people because there was tear gas in your eyes. I mean, The Hague was the center of the German occupation, so I have an extremely vivid memory of the war.

I went to Leiden as a university student where I lived on the same street that the author of *Soldier of Orange* lived on, but he had lived there twenty years earlier. And I went through the same initiation process that the main character goes through—the hair cutting, the humiliation. It was a big, fun war. I love war. I mean, not as an adult, or as a father of children, but as a kid. It was like living in an amazing movie. I didn't know anything. You see people thrown out in the street, into cars. You don't realize that they're taking away four or five million people, and children. If I'd been Jewish my experience would have been quite different.

So for me the feeling that is conveyed in *Soldier of Orange* is that war is an adventure. It's not a heavy film. I think it's even a kind of humanistic film, because it makes all these statements based on the fact that the main guy is somebody who is not antifascist in the first place. He hates the Germans, but he has no political statement to make. He just says, you shouldn't be here. A lot of the resistance people in Holland liked it. It was, okay, let's kill the Germans, let's throw them out. A lot of people were like that. When you were in the resistance, you had all these wonderful women couriers who brought letters around; so you fucked them, and next you went with the gun and killed Germans. And that normally isn't spoken about that much.

GH: Rutger Hauer plays the protagonist in your film. When did you two start working together?
PV: I met Rutger in 1968. He was the hero of my "Ivanhoe" series. I found him in a small theater group in northern Holland. We went to him, or he came to us, and he was this blond Nordic guy who was excellent for the part.

We worked a year on this series, and then he did the male lead in *Turkish Delight*. By the time we began *Soldier of Orange*, I had known Rutger already for ten years, so we were very close, and I think he was the only guy in Holland who could have done this. Still, we did test him very profoundly because the character of the writer is much more of an aristocratic guy. The writer himself is an aristocratic man, and Rutger is much more of a . . . coming from the mud, you might say.

GH: Rustic?
PV: That's the word. So it wasn't clear that he would be able to do it, but then we started testing, and he transformed so well that there was no doubt that he should do that part.

GH: Your last project together was your American debut *Flesh+Blood*. Do you have plans to work together in the future?
PV: Well, yes but we had a terrible fight on *Flesh+Blood*. And our relationship and friendship was ruined during that picture. We hated each other so much by the end of the picture that it's going to take a couple of years to bring us together, but I would certainly like to work with him.

GH: Critically, it would seem that his best work has been with you.
PV: Right. And I think we can do great work together again, but I think that making the transition to the American cinema put too much stress on both of us. Deep in my heart . . . I dream about Rutger once per month, I think. And it's not always a nice dream. Last I remember, a couple of weeks ago, I dreamt that I blasted his head off, so I'm sure there are some feelings of revenge or whatever you want to call it—friendship, deep involvement with somebody who you work with fifteen, seventeen years. It's really stupid, after all this time, to have all this animosity between us, and I really would like it to be resolved at a certain moment in our lives when we're both more adult, perhaps.

GH: When you deal with actors on the set, do you ever want to evoke something specific from their performances?
PV: No, because I'm not coming from the theater at all. I never go to the theater. I hate it. I think it's boring, so my direction of actors is really based on what I think it should look like. And I don't use any psychology, manipulation methods. I just say what I want, and although I am not an actor, I certainly indicate by exaggerating what I want. It works pretty well.

GH: Do you rehearse with your actors?
PV: Sometimes, yes. I did some rehearsing on *RoboCop* because of Peter Weller's strange Robo-movements and stuff, but not dialogue rehearsal. If it's an adventure story with a lot of movement, then I think the actor and the director should go into physical training for a couple of months. That's a better preparation than working through the dialogue. I'm not that kind of a director.

GH: Did you have more creative freedom in Holland?
PV: I didn't feel that. *RoboCop* was Orion, and Orion gave me a lot of freedom. There really is much more diversity here. In casting, for example, there are more people to choose from. The whole world is here. In Holland they quickly grew intolerant of my work. The critics started calling me a decadent pervert who misrepresented Dutch culture. *Spetters* had the worst response I ever got. I attempted to make a serious film about human behavior and I got crucified. An anti-*Spetters* committee was formed, which said the film was antifeminist, antigay, and anti-invalid. It wasn't true. I was simply trying to be honest in portraying the way people act, and often it is antigay, antifeminist, anti-invalid. Of course, this is outrageous, unethical behavior, but it is behavior, so I portrayed it, and certainly at no one's expense. So, the answer to your question is no, I didn't feel that I had more creative freedom in Holland. Perhaps I was not politically correct enough.

GH: I understand that the original novelist of *The Fourth Man* based the story on real incidents, and then romanticized some of them.
PV: That is true. However, we significantly changed the book for the better. Most of it, though, does have something to do with the author, Gerard Reve, his attitudes, his character. He is an alcoholic, he is a homosexual. And we talked to him frequently about the details in his life. He really did meet a woman like the Christine character. In fact, when we were shooting in a local bar, she was there. She has a beauty salon. She was in her mid-forties when we were making the film, and looked very good.

GH: Would you ever return to Holland to direct a picture?
PV: I think there are one or two things I could do there, and which I can't do here because I could never get the money—either too personal or too specific. But, generally, I think I'm better off in the United States for the time being.

Paul Verhoeven: An Interview

Chris Shea and Wade Jennings / 1992

Excerpted from *Post Script: Essays in Film and the Humanities* 12.3 (Summer 1993): 3-24. Reprinted with permission by *Post Script*.

Paul Verhoeven appeared twice on Ball State University campus, in November 1990, in conjunction with the University's opening of an exchange with Groningen University in the Netherlands, and in September 1992, to join Millard Fuller, Bette Bao Lord, Terry Waite, Dennis Weaver, James Burke, et al., as a "UniverCitizen" in the award- winning UniverCity project. In 1990 he had just returned from the European and Japanese openings of *Total Recall* and was three days into the casting for *Basic Instinct*; in 1992, he was fresh from a worldwide promotion tour for *Basic Instinct* and reading scripts for his next project. (After development stints on several promising projects, e.g., *Mistress of the Seas*, Joe Eszterhas's *Showgirls*, the new biography of De Sade, Verhoeven has finally settled on *Crusade*, with Arnold Schwarzenegger, to begin filming in August, 1994.)

BACKGROUND

POST SCRIPT: What was your childhood like?

PAUL VERHOEVEN: I was born in '38 in Amsterdam and, as you know, the Germans occupied Holland in '40. So from when I was three until seven or eight, until '45, I was living in an occupied country. The first couple of years of the occupation were pretty mild, but the last couple of years were very violent, and I was living in The Hague, which was the center of the German government and also, even more important, the launching pads of the rockets, the V1s and V2s, which were invented by Wernher von Braun, who later was head of the NASA program here. He'd invented these armed rockets which were being made in Peenemünde, in Germany, then sent over to The Hague, and the launching pads were about one mile from our house. So these rockets were always sent to London. And, because of that, the English and the Americans were continuously bombing the area. That was in fact the area around our house, because they wanted to get rid of these rockets and these launching pads to prevent the rockets from going to London.

So when I was living there, especially the last couple of years—it was '44 when they started sending these rockets around—it was an extremely violent situation because of the bombs that were falling down. And as a child I think I saw so much violence there, so many dead bodies . . . There was a lot of blood, and, strangely enough, the whole area around our house was completely bombed out because the English squadron leader at a certain moment reversed the map in his cockpit and so they bombed the wrong area, which was a civilian area, and 20–30,000 people were killed. And that was just, let's say, 100 yards from my house. The whole area beyond the back of the house was completely destroyed, and so that part of The Hague was completely in flames.

PS: Did this help shape your view of violence?

PV: It's very astonishing when you are a child and your perception of the daily routine is dead people, violence, bombing, fire, day in, day out. I think that gives you a very strong depression, which probably sinks into the subconscious later when it's all over and the war is over and peace starts. For me . . . to be honest, the war was a great time. I mean I was a child and I loved it. I don't know if you've ever seen the movie by John Boorman, *Hope and Glory*; it was exactly like that but worse. I mean that was not so violent because there was not that much happening in London. There was bombing, but not like in The Hague, which was absolutely, extremely violent. But for a child it was kind of . . . *fun*. It's amazing to say so, but that's what I felt. It was like every day was a big adventure. Of course, if your brothers and sisters or parents are killed, that's a different situation, but in my family nobody was killed. So as a child you don't look much further around you—you're not aware of the 100,000 Jewish people who are sent away and never come back—you realize that after the war, but during the war I never realized it. For me, it was like the most fantastic special effects you've ever seen. Every night when you look up at the sky you would see burning planes coming down. And the next day my father would bring me for a walk, about half a mile, and we would look at the plane that came down. I remember, for example, that the Germans were picking up pieces of meat, which was the English pilot, and putting them in a little box. These things are so strange, in fact, but so normal for me at the time that I think that's responsible for a lot of the violence in my movies, my feeling that violence is normal, and that peace is a-normal, that war is the natural state, and that peace is an a-natural state—which of course is not true, and of course I'm not making propaganda for war—to the contrary.

PS: Has your attitude changed?

PV: When you get older and you have your own kids, it's the worst thing that can happen to you. But there are things which can be learned in an intellectual way from bad or good, moral or not moral—you are a child and you are open to everything and that. And you accept it as it is. And I think that's basically why my defense system against violence is very limited. When I make a violent scene in a movie, all these images of the war or similar images come to my mind, and I portray them as I saw them as a child, without any moral standards probably, because as a child you don't have them. You just look and see and think, "Oh, this is it." Well, you see a hand here, and a leg there. So I think in images like those in *Soldier of Orange*, when they're walking in the military complex and they see part of a leg on the ground. That's basically based on those images that I saw when this English pilot was downed. And so that's what I feel is the ultimate background of the violence that is in my movies.

EUROPEAN MOVIES

PV: The movies that I made [in the Netherlands] together with the same producer, that was Rob Houwer, and the same screenwriter, Gerard Soeteman, and whoever has seen *Soldier of Orange* or *The Fourth Man* can see that these are the same people who are throughout all my movies. We were a group of three people who always worked together for twelve, thirteen years, and we made seven movies together, which were all, by Dutch standards, extremely successful. In fact there was no reason at all to leave Holland until the beginning of the '80s. I mean after I made a movie in '73 or '74 which was called *Turkish Delight* and which got an Oscar nomination in Los Angeles, I was invited several times to come to the United States. Especially after I did *Soldier of Orange*. I got a lot of calls, even from Spielberg, who said, "I saw your movie. What are you doing in Holland? Come to the United States because it's much better here." And I doubted that in fact. I thought, "Well, I'm very happy in my country, why should I leave Holland? I can make the movies that I want to make, and I'm happy doing so, and there's a lot of talent there, especially really good actors and actresses." And it was only at the beginning of the '80s that it started to change and something very strange happened in Holland.

I mean you have to understand the system in Holland. Films are made for 50, 60 percent with government subsidy. There are only 14 million Dutch people, and to make a film successful, to recuperate the money you've put into the movie, there's this kind of language barrier, of course, which limits your audience pretty much to these 14 million in Holland, and a couple million in Belgium who also speak Dutch, and perhaps some people in South Africa, but that's really limited. But altogether movies are so expensive that if you don't have this government money, it's impossible to make a movie. Now, in fact, this nowadays applies to the whole European community. All European movies are made with government subsidy, because otherwise the European film industry by now would be completely dead. Now it's already pretty dead, although there's still something going on. But, without that money, it wouldn't work any more. So the situation we have to face is to get that money.

Of course you have to submit your script to a committee, and in the '70s this was a committee that was kind of right-wing, I would even say, but, being kind of right-wing, it was extremely liberal and accepted everything, more or less. If you did a good job, if you worked hard, if your films were more or less successful, you got the money for the next movie. You could go on.

And at the end of the '70s, beginning of the '80s, this committee became switched politically, I would say, to the left. And strangely enough, or perhaps not strangely, this left-wing committee, like a lot of left-wing organizations, was extremely, I would say, dictatorial or another word, would be probably close to fascistic—dogmatic probably is a better word, not so mean—but dogmatic in the way that they wanted a movie to be relevant. Now just entertainment was not enough, it had to be politically or sociologically or culturally relevant. And in the eyes of the committee the pictures I made in the '70s were not relevant; they were considered to be decadent and amoral, and they also thought that my pictures, especially a picture I made in '80 which was *Spetters*, were not presenting Dutch society in a good way. It was cynical, negative and downbeat. And they felt that I should not get any money any more. So at the beginning of the '80s it became very difficult to finance my movies. The last one I got financed, after a lot of rejections, was *The Fourth Man*, which was also, of course, considered extremely decadent because of the homosexual content. And that was the moment that I started to think that probably I should not stay longer in Holland.

PS: Which of your films do you like the least?
PV: I think that would be probably a film I made just before I came, before *Soldier of Orange*; it's called *Katie Tippel*. This is a movie that was situated at the end of the nineteenth century in Holland and Brussels, and I felt that we never were able to solve the problems of the middle part of the movie. So dramatically it fell apart halfway.

I think it's an interesting movie, with nice production design and nice parts—Rutger Hauer plays one of the parts—but basically it's the only movie that I would like to redo, because I felt that we never got to the level that we should have reached in the first place.

I still feel that the first English movie I did—in Europe, for an American company, just before *RoboCop*; was called *Flesh+Blood*, and it's a medieval movie that is very American because it has adventure and action and was kind of romantic.

Of course, it was very cynical and downbeat, but I didn't realize that, so for the American audience it didn't work at all—it worked okay in France, but here it didn't work at all. I have the feeling that after that movie I would like to do another medieval movie, and try to do *Flesh+Blood* in a kind of an American way. In fact, we are just developing a project for Arnold Schwarzenegger, which is a movie that is situated during the Crusades. So, it's the twelfth century, 1115 or something like that. So that's kind of a plan of mine to improve on *Flesh+Blood*. So these are the two movies, *Katie Tippel* and *Flesh+Blood* that I don't like.

PS: When you approach a movie, how much does your view affect the project?

PV: Well, that depends of course on what stage you get the script. On a lot of the scripts I did in Europe for movies like *Soldier of Orange* and *The Fourth Man*, I worked very closely with the scriptwriter. *Soldier of Orange* is based on a book, it's an autobiography by a Dutch war-hero; in fact he is the main guy in the movie. When we bought the book, I worked through the book with my scriptwriter to find out what were the most interesting scenes and to put them together and structure them, so that would be something that I would do in very close collaboration with my scriptwriter. And then he would write a first draft, I would write a second one, he would write a third draft. So we would work very closely together. And on the movie he'd be the writer, I'd be the co-writer.

There's a long story to *Total Recall*. The first script was written in '79 by Ron Shusett and Dan O'Bannon, the writers of the first *Alien*, and then in the ten years that passed between the first draft and when I started to work on the movie, which was '88 or something, they wrote together with some other writers twenty-five drafts of the same screenplay. There were seven directors involved, and I think several producers and co-producers, and they started the movie several times, and it always fell apart. And so when I got the script I had twenty-five drafts to go through and to select from—then filming you found out that first of all you have to select out what you've got for Arnold. There was never an Arnold Schwarzenegger role in the movie—it was about a very normal guy, physically, I mean.

Arnold is very normal, but he has this kind of physique that is bigger than life, isn't it? But this was written for somebody who looked like Woody Allen, somebody like that, and so we had to rewrite the script completely, and alter the third act completely. I think in both movies the structure and essential elements of the script were pretty much given to me, and mostly what I did was to build the building based on the blueprints, and with the European movies I think I was more a part of the blueprints.

PS: The Dutch film industry gives filmmakers about fifty percent of the money to fund the films. One might think this is helpful because you don't have to go looking for funds, but you've conveyed a negative feeling that it may be otherwise. Why such hard feelings?

PV: Well, the problem with the system like that is that it is a pre-censorship situation, as you understand. Let's make it a bit more clear. The censorship is not after the movie is done, the censorship starts before the movie is done. You have to give your scripts to a committee, and they judge if they want to give you the money or not. And so a certain genre of scripts is not admitted, for certain reasons, and these reasons are kind of film-political, I would say. And in my case the problem was that they felt that the scripts that I was giving to them, that I wanted to be financed, they thought were too . . . let's use the words "decadent" and "immoral," and that they were portraying that society in the wrong way. And so it got to be very difficult to convince them to give me money, and every year it got more difficult. And so, what is bad about the system is that you start to censor yourself. You think, OK, I want to do this, but I won't get that through, so let's do this. And so, it's really a bad situation, for a creative person that you start to change your scripts even, to get them through this committee. And when I felt that I was close to starting to do that, then I thought it was better to get out and go to the United States.

I mean, I think there are a lot of advantages to a subsidy system. This is one of the big disadvantages. If the people that are in the committee—and you're always talking about two, three people—there's a committee of, probably, ten people or something, but you know as well as I do, that there are always two or three people who decide what's happening in the committee, isn't it? Always the strong people. Now if these people dislike your work, you're in problems. And that's what happened to me. In '80 or '81, the presidency of the Dutch committee was given to a film critic who had hated my work ever since I started to do short movies in I think, '62, when he was a critic for a newspaper; it was a short film of twenty minutes . . . He started already to write extremely negative things about me, and throughout the years he has done so. So when he became the president of the committee, it got very difficult, and instead of compromising I felt it was better to change gears and move to the United States.

PS: What similarities do you see between the films you made in Holland and the ones you made in the US?

PV: I think my movies are mostly well thought-out, and I spend a lot of time in preproduction to make the movies as compressed and as fast as possible. Of course, the themes of the movies that I did in Europe are so different from the themes that I did here that it's difficult—even for a lot of people probably amazing—after seeing the American movies to go back to the Dutch ones and look at them. It's kind of amazing that the same person did that. I think there is always some things that will stay personal like some feeling for humor, if it's normal humor or a kind of black humor, and interest in people, but . . . It's very difficult for the person himself who makes these movies to see the similarities really. I mean, basically I think there's a big difference between *RoboCop* and *Total Recall* on one side and the Dutch ones on the other side. I see more dissimilarity, in the way that I think all my European work was based on reality. I mean *Soldier of Orange* is an autobiographical book, *Katie Tippel* was autobiographical, *Turkish Delight* was, *Spetters* was based on newspaper articles and all taken from magazines—all real things. Even *The Fourth Man*, even though it looks like a fantasy, was for eighty percent an autobiographical novel. And so everything was based on reality, and when I went to the United States, *RoboCop* and *Total Recall*, of course, are based on non-reality. There is nothing real there—it's all fantasy. So I think there's a big difference in approach. I feel a little bit like . . . when I went to the United States and started to do these movies, for certain reasons, that I was going back to my childhood. It's something like . . . I always liked special-effect movies when I was a kid. *The War of the Worlds*, produced by George Pal, was one of my favorite movies when I was twelve or something like that. And I even, when I was younger, I started to make a comic book based on that. I mean I loved that stuff, but then I started to work in Europe as a film director myself and I went much more to a realistic approach. And it's like I forgot about comic books and science fiction and all these childhood dreams that I had. And, strangely enough, when I came to the United States, that came back. It was offered to me, and I jumped at the occasion because probably I had repressed it for twelve or fifteen years. I mean, I've always been working with the same scriptwriter in Holland, Gerard Soeteman, and he's an historian and an extremely realistic person. And he dislikes fantasy, he dislikes science fiction; he thinks it's all nonsense, and he doesn't want to deal with it. Now, if you work together with somebody like that, then what you do are the things that you have in common; you don't do the things that are different. So what was activated when I was working with him was my sense of reality and realism, and I think when I lost that connection with him, when I went to the United States and started to work with other people, other scriptwriters, then these other things came up. And I think at a certain moment probably I'll switch back to reality, and I think—hopefully when I can continue to work here and everything goes well—I'm sure that in the next five years I'll be more into realism, back to realism, than I am now. I think even *Basic Instinct* is now already a much more normal movie than *Total Recall*.

ROBOCOP AND TOTAL RECALL

PS: Why did Orion pick you to direct *RoboCop*? What do you have over other directors?

PV: I didn't have anything over other directors. It was just that nobody else wanted to do it. It's absolutely true, and I'm not making a joke . . . I mean when I came to the movie, when they sent me the script, the project was really dead. It was just that Jon Davison, the producer, who knew my work, my European work, thought, "Well, perhaps we can . . . perhaps this Dutch director wants to do it, because we cannot find an American one." That was basically the whole idea. And it was not that I was a favorite person there, it was just the last chance, probably.

PS: How would you compare *RoboCop* and *Total Recall* to your earlier work?
PV: Deliberately, I think, these two movies are pretty far away from the work I did in Holland. They are action-oriented, they're very much science fiction, there's not that much dialogue, and they're probably less personal . . . I realized that so many European directors have failed in the United States, they have tried for one or two years to do personal movies in the United States, and then of course when they are not so successful, they have to go back.

I felt that it would take me about five, six years to learn about the United States, to learn the language better, to learn the cultural situation, to find out what American audiences are like, not only what they prefer, but what their perception of movies really is. And so I set out to do two movies, *RoboCop* and *Total Recall* that would not have too much dialogue in fact. I just tried to avoid any script that was based on dialogue, because, you can guess, I mean, it was certainly not my favorite thing—dialogue. It cannot be your favorite thing when you go to a country where you know the language only partially. And so I avoided that and concentrated on films that have strong visual impact. And because I was interested in science fiction and special effects, with my background in mathematics and physics, I thought it was interesting to learn how to do special effects movies.

And so that's what I did for the last five years, and it's only now in '90-'91 that I'm slowly starting out to go in different directions and trying to make movies that are more based on normal things than on special effects. In fact, *Basic Instinct*, with Michael Douglas, I would say is a kind of erotic thriller and is much more based on dialogue than anything I've ever done before.

PS: How important is the score in your movies?
PV: Very. I spend a lot of time with the composer to go through all the different cues and find the most effective music. Now of course I'm not writing the music, but you can help the composer a lot by saying, "OK, I want a rhythmic situation here, then I want to be changing the rhythm to a different mood." When you work very closely with the composer; I think you can really improve the score. And especially with movies like *RoboCop* and *Total Recall*, which are all action, I think a

good score helps to make it more pleasant for the audience to look at the movie. So I think it's very important. And I like music. I like it, basically because when I read a novel or look at films or whatever I always have the feeling that I have to see if I can do something with it.

PS: You've done two movies, and they've had to be cut because of the ratings system in America. How do you feel about that and about your artistic expression and how that affects your use of film?
PV: Well, in both cases, especially in the case of *RoboCop*, but also with *Total Recall*, when we gave the film to the MPAA, the ratings system board, we got an X rating. And, in fact, after cutting *RoboCop* seven times, we got seven times an X rating. And it was only the eighth time that we got the R. It was easier on *Total Recall*. I think we had to go there twice to get an R rating. The committee was much more appreciative. They liked it much more than *RoboCop*. They said that they liked the movie, even that they were pleased, but that they felt it was little bit too strong, and please could I soften or tone down a couple of scenes. Then they said, "This scene, this scene, and that scene." And so we did and then we presented and they said, "Oh, it's fine." It was very easy.

PS: How do you feel about the large amounts of violence that have been in a lot of the films lately?
PV: I like it.

PS: Do you feel that it affects the audience in a negative way . . . the children who see it . . .
PV: No. No, I don't think so. I've never felt that. I mean I've seen a lot of violent movies, and I never came out of a movie thinking that I should do something violent, really. Basically I don't think that people are violent because they see a movie, I think people are violent in the first place. I think people have a violent genetic structure, and I think that, if you look at the bad things that happened in the world, with or without movies, the bad things that happened, the evil things that happened in Europe in the '30s, '40s, I don't think that any movie pushed Hitler to do the things he did. I don't think that bad things come out of movies. I think movies are just a reflection of what society is about. There are two theories, of course, and what you're saying is the first theory, that violence in movies adds violence to society. The other theory is, of course, that violence in movies reduces violence in society, that people get enough violence in the theater that they are not violent anymore when they get out. I don't believe both theories, in fact I think it doesn't affect society at all. I think society is violent and it always will be.

PS: What was the total budget or cost on *Total Recall*?
PV: Well, we started out with a budget of $43 million, and then I went over budget, so it added up to $57 or $58 million, I think—which is an enormous amount of money, especially when you realize that then we have to add about $20 million for publicity, for spots on television and other promotional items, and there's another $5 million for prints to send to the theaters, of course, and there's probably another $8–$10 million for losing the interest during the couple of years the film is in production. Altogether the real costs are around $90 million, I would say. It's amazing, but it still works, you know. Because besides what the film will make in the United States around the world it will earn another $120–$130 million, so altogether the grosses of the movie will be around $240–250 million. And half of that, a little bit less than that, let's say, would be coming back to the studio, which is around, say, $110–120 million.

So basically you make such small profits on the theatrical release here and overseas that, of course, it's not worth doing, because that's too small a profit, isn't it?—about $10–20 million, which is an enormous risk on a movie of $90 million. But where they really make the profits nowadays is in the video sales and on television, and that's basically why you can do a movie like that, because then there is an additional $40 million coming back to the company, immediately after, let's say, one or two years, and then for the next ten years, there's every year $5 or 10 million dribbling in. So, although it seems to be outrageous to make a movie for $60 million, and ultimately for $90 million, from an economic point of view, it's still a healthy situation. Whether it's healthy from an artistic point of view, that's probably up to you to decide. But commercially, economically, it's OK—if the film works well, of course. If the film doesn't work, then . . .

Somebody asked me how I felt about *Ghost* doing better than *Total Recall*. The grosses of *Ghost* will end up close to $290–300 million, which is about $60–$70 million more than *Total Recall*. Now when you realize that the movie *Ghost* was made probably for half the price—say, $25–30 million—half the price of *Total Recall*, of course it's clear that a movie like *Ghost* is to the people that make it, still talking economically, more interesting than *Total Recall*. On the other hand, nobody in Hollywood realized when *Ghost* was finished that it would do something like that. They released it in a limited number of prints—which is an indication of the belief in the movie—they released it in about seven hundred or eight hundred prints. If you compare that with movies like *Total Recall* or others like the *48 Hrs.* sequel, which are released in 2,300 prints, that's where you see what the industry was really expecting was going to happen. And then they found out that *Ghost* was doing extremely well and they added prints and prints. But then it's difficult to foresee a success like *Ghost* or *Pretty Woman*, even. It's easier to foresee and to structure a film like *Total Recall*. And that's why we still make these movies, and if a movie does well like *Die Hard 2* or like *Total Recall* then it's a good investment. It's not the sensational investment that you get out of *Ghost* or *Pretty Woman*, but *Pretty Woman* and *Ghost* are really things that nobody could foresee.

PS: Is *Total Recall* real or a dream?

PV: Both. To be honest, that's what I want. I made the movie in a way that it would be true on both levels, and I spent a lot of time to get that. If you want a scientific explanation, you know, of course, in quantum mechanics there is a very interesting principle, the principle of uncertainty, Heisenberg's principle. If you have a big object and if you try to measure the place of the object and the velocity of the object at the same time, the more precisely you measure velocity the less precise place gets. So that's the principle. That means, of course, that there are different realities possible at the same moment. What I wanted to do in *Total Recall* is to do a movie where both levels are true. I mean for me, of course, the film anyhow has to do with two realities, one being the reality of going as a secret agent to Mars and discovering that there is a problem, and solving the problem, which is starting the nuclear reactor and helping the guerrillas and destroying Cohaagen.

The second level of the movie, of course, is that from the moment that he goes into the Rekall chair 'til the end it's a dream, and I tried to make that second level work throughout the whole movie.

So there's the dream level which starts when he gets into the chair and the thing is in his neck, and that would go throughout the whole movie, so in the next scene where they say, Oh, there's a problem, there's a big glitch here, that would be already the dream, of course. That's where the dream starts. And the next scene where they are fighting and stuff would be part of his dream, convincing him that it is real, because there is a glitch but that would be part of the program. It would be built into the program to make him accept the fact that it's real, but it's a dream.

If you look at the movie, if you haven't seen it, or for the second time, you'll see that the whole program that's set up at the beginning when he goes to the Rekall office and he talks to this guy who sells him the program on Mars, you'll see that he gets everything that he wants: he gets the trip to Mars, he gets the girl, the exotic girl, he kills the bad guys, and he saves the entire planet. That's what he does. And that's basically the dream. Even halfway through the movie, you may remember, this other guy comes in, Dr. Edgemar, and tells him that he's in a dream, that he's still in the Rekall chair, and then Arnold says, "If I'm there, I can kill you." And he puts a gun to his head and the guy says, "Sure, no problem for me, big problem for you, because you will be psychotic from now on because the walls of reality will fall apart. One moment you will be the savior of the rebel cause, the next moment you'll be Cohaagen's bosom buddy, but in the end—you will even have these strange fantasies about alien civilizations—but at the end you will be lobotomized." And then if you see the movie, you realize that all these things happen. I mean he is lobotomized at the end. That's why at the last shot, when they are so happy and kissing each other, it slowly fades to white, which for me meant, "OK, there he goes. That's the end-that's the dream—they lobotomized him." And all the other things happened, he finds the alien civilization, he rescues the planet, he finds the good girl, he kills the bad guys, but it's a dream. Now, of course you can see it as a reality, too. So at the end of the movie, getting to white means either it's a happy ending or he loses his brains . . . which is probably also a happy ending, I don't know.

That was basically what l wanted—that at the end there would be two possibilities, and they would be *both* true—for me they are both true—it's not either one or the other. It's not that *either* it's a dream *or* it is a reality. It is a dream *and* it is a reality. And I think they're both there.

PS: What made you choose *Basic Instinct*?
PV: Well, first of all, I wanted to do something different. I wanted to move away from the action/science fiction genre, because you get so typecast. Everybody thinks that the only thing you can do is science fiction-action stuff. And I think I can do something different, and I did a lot of different things in Europe, but then in Los Angeles after doing *RoboCop* all the scripts I got were kind of about robots and action and all that. *Total Recall* was a little bit in the same line, but I did it because it was the best script that I could really find after reading 150–200 other scripts. I wanted to do something light and something normal without science fiction, without special effects, and I couldn't find it. And then *Total Recall* was the best thing I could get in my hands, and so, after half a year of looking, I said, "OK, I don't want to do special effects, but in this case I like the script so much, let's do it again." So now, after *Total Recall*, I really want to move away from science fiction/action, and *Basic Instinct* is much more a Hitchcockian thriller. It's much more about people, in a kind of a tense situation, where a couple of murders are committed, and there are two or three possible suspects—they are all women, in fact. And the story is about Michael Douglas, who is the main character, a cop, a homicide cop, and he's investigating this murder stuff, and in the meantime he falls in love with a woman who could be the murderess. So that's the story a little bit.

FUTURE PROJECTS

PS: When are you going to make a comedy?
PV: Well, I've been trying to find a comedy in Los Angeles. But it's very . . . One of my favorite movies of the last couple of years was *A Fish Called Wanda*, and these scripts are really not very much available in the United States, and then, secondly,

they wouldn't send them to me immediately. So I have typecast myself into the wrong direction, doing these two movies, *Total Recall* and *RoboCop*, because normally what I get on my table in my office are all kinds of similar movies—like action, science fiction, adventure. When they see a comedy probably it would go to Danny DeVito or John Landis. So they wouldn't send that script to me. So I think to make a comedy you probably have to develop your own material which is what I'm trying to do. I'm setting up kind of a black comedy about two women that are married to men who are not . . . pleasant . . . and they decide to get rid of them. So that's what I'm planning to do. But that's if it's made, because it's kind of a dangerous subject for Los Angeles, for Hollywood. It might be too dark for them, although it's kind of a comedy. So I don't know really if it will be made. It will be ready probably in a couple of months, and then it's still to be seen if you can get the financing for a movie like that, that ultimately will be much less expensive than *Total Recall*, probably will be around, say, at the maximum 20 million dollars. But, like Spielberg said, when he wanted for years to do *E.T.*, he said it's much more difficult to get money for a small movie than to get it for a big one.

PS: Are you returning to reality with your upcoming movie *Christ the Man*, and what role does the Westar Institute play in that?

PV: I became aware of Westar about four years ago. I read in the *Los Angeles Times* an article about the Westar Institute and I was intrigued. I always wanted to do a movie about Jesus; I don't know why. I mean I was always intrigued by Jesus, I was always reading about him. And then I realized that it was always so difficult, because you read in the Bible . . . you read about all these things in the Gospels, and you never can figure out on your own what you think is true and authentic or what is probably something that was invented by the early Church or even the later Church. Mark was written in 65 or something, and probably the Gospel of John, which is the last one, about 90 or 100, so that's about thirty to eighty years after the death of Jesus. A lot of things can change in thirty years, especially in seventy years . . . And so there's a lot of things as in the Gospels that are probably more reflection, ideas of the early Church than things that really happened to Jesus, but they projected these events onto Jesus because Jesus was the hero, of course. And so, when you want to do a picture about Jesus, I think it's essential to realize what probably happened, what things are authentic and not. The Westar Institute is preparing the Gospels in four colors, which means from red, pink, gray, and black—red being highly authentic and black being non-authentic. That's what Robert Funk, the head of the Westar Institute, set out to do, and he brought all these scholars together—now already for five years or six years—that every half year come together. They take a part of the Gospels and they try to figure out if these things should be printed in red or pink or gray or black. And so, I think the

Gospel of Mark will be soon ready, in four colors. Nothing is decisive, and this is just scholars, and it might be people have different ideas in fifty years. The fifth Gospel, the Gospel of Thomas, was found in 1945 or '50, something like that. They might find a new gospel, and there might be new things in that new gospel that might change everybody's ideas again. But for the moment this is what a majority of American scholars think is authentic and not. And I think a big part of the Markan Gospel will be printed in black, meaning that about sixty, seventy percent of the Gospel by these scholars is considered to be non-authentic. And that's what I want to know—what scholars think at this moment is authentic, and I want to make a movie that's based on the red and the pink and not on the gray and the black. That was why I went to the Westar Institute—it's my interest in realism, in fact, isn't it? I want the picture about Jesus to be realistic. It should not be a fantasy like *The Last Temptation*. It should be as authentic as possible. But, of course, nobody of our age, nobody nowadays has been there—it's all reconstruction, it's all historical stuff. But it should be trying to find the historical values, and not the theological ones.

PS: With the reaction to *The Last Temptation of Christ*, are you worried about how your film about Christ might be received?
PV: Yeah. I'm sure there will be controversy, but . . . I don't see any sexual issues really there. I mean I strongly believe that, in the last part of his life—and that's the one that we are using in the movie, the last two, three years—I don't think that Jesus was really highly interested in sex. I think he was interested in the Kingdom of God, and he was expecting anyhow something to be happening very soon. A quite dramatic change of events he was expecting I think, and they didn't happen, of course. Nothing happened—well, he died—but I mean there was no major event, nothing, no intervention of God or something. Israel didn't change, and the people didn't change, and the Romans stayed there. And so he was expecting something radical, but it didn't happen, but I think his attention was really to the nearby and approaching Kingdom of God.

PS: Why all of a sudden are you making something as controversial as a film about Jesus?
PV: Well, I mean this picture about Jesus I wanted to do for a long time, and of course we have to realize that the situation in the first century in Israel was extremely violent in the first place. It's not a movie about peace. The Crucifixion was done every day or every second week, something like that. People were crucified by the thousands by the Roman governors. And Jesus's life was anyhow in constant danger. If we read the Gospels, we see he was trying to get out or he has to get out every time again because people are trying to stop him. He has to go to the hills—I

mean there's an element of constant danger in the first place. His foregoer, John the Baptist, of course, was killed by Herod Antipas because he was informed that John was preaching insurrection. And I think that you cannot see Jesus without seeing a little bit the issues that were there. In fact I think Jesus was crucified, the people that were crucified, the Jewish people who were crucified were mostly insurrectionists; in fact the charge that Jesus had to face was insurrection, being on the title on the cross, the accusation "King of the Jews," meaning a political issue, as having political power. And I think that the situation of Jesus and the way he died indicate that, at least in the eyes of the Romans, Jesus was a guerilla fighter. I don't think that's true; of course I don't believe that he was a guerilla fighter, but he was close enough to that for the Romans to perceive him like that.

PS: What is your goal in making the new Jesus movie, just to present Christ as an historical figure or to give people a new point of view on him?
PV: Yes, I have the feeling . . . I'm not baptized, I'm nothing in fact. I started to be interested in Jesus when I was twenty or something like that when I was studying him because he intrigued me. There's no doubt about that, as a hero, he's a pretty good guy, I think. There are other heroes, but he's also a good one. So, from the normal human point of view, he's worth studying, I would think. But then I felt that in the last twenty centuries, from the beginning 'til now, from the year that he died, which is about thirty, 'til now that there were brought in by the Church, by the churches, so many layers of—to use a strong word—nonsense, that I thought it would be important to peel off those layers and try to go back to the original and say, "What exactly happened? What did he really want? What did he really say?" Taking away things like, of course, the Virgin Birth, Mary being a virgin and how do you call that? Getting a child, which is, of course, mythology . . . Well, I say "of course," for me it is of course mythology, a lot of other people might feel differently. Not that I'm going to say anything about whether or not Mary is a virgin, that's not the issue, what I will do, just to give an example, is to show, in the first couple of scenes of the movie, Jesus with his brothers and sisters. And mother. Probably his father was dead by then, because there's not much mention of Joseph in the Gospels, anyhow, he seems not to play any important part, so probably he was dead. But in the Gospel of Mark and Matthew the names of his brothers are all mentioned—there are four brothers and a couple of sisters. So to see a Jewish family with the mother there and four brothers and a couple of sisters sitting around the table discussing the issues of the day, problems, political issues, that will be the set-up to counter the idea that Mary was a virgin. She could still be a virgin, with Jesus, but if I don't make him the oldest brother, then she will not be a Virgin anyhow. So that's basically what I want to do. Which is not provoking because I want to provoke, it's provoking because a lot of people,

especially Catholic people, are not aware that Jesus had four brothers, and seeing Jesus with his brothers sitting around is kind of, "Wow! I didn't know that was happening. How people here didn't know Jesus had four brothers?" A couple of months ago I was in Spain, when I was doing promotion for *Total Recall*, and during the interview I asked all of the people who interviewed me if they knew about Jesus' brothers and none of them knew. This is a Catholic Country. I had to pick up the New Testament that was in my room—you get it in your room always—I brought it down and I pointed it out and I said, "OK, read this, read this chapter," and they couldn't believe it. In the Catholic Church there is a strong resistance to accept that Jesus had four brothers. Now this is a minor item, I would say. But like the things I said before, emphasizing that he was killed by the Romans as a political insurrectionist, emphasizing that when he was arrested there was a real fight with swords, these kind of things will all be in the movie.

PS: Any other projects?
PV: I'm preparing another movie with Arnold Schwarzenegger which is situated in the time of the Crusades.

Beyond Flesh and Blood

Jean-Marc Bouineau / 1994

© Jean-Marc Bouineau/Le Cinephage. Excerpted from *Beyond Flesh and Blood*, Le Cinephage, 2001. Reprinted by permission of the publisher.

Published in 2001 by Le Cinephage, Jean-Marc Bouineau's Beyond Flesh and Blood *is an eclectic compilation of interviews with Verhoeven that were conducted from 1994 to 2000, the majority of which took place between 1994 and 1996. Bouineau and publisher Gilles Boulenger developed the book over the course of a six-year period, breaking down and organizing the interviews into chapter-length themes. The following excerpt consists of questions and answers that were conducted at the beginning of the interview series, approximately two years after the 1992 release of* Basic Instinct.*—MBF*

JEAN-MARC BOUINEAU: How do you feel about women?
PAUL VERHOEVEN: I think I have a high respect for women. I think they're really strong, intelligent and a lot of fun to work with. In my personal life, I don't look for love relationships that are extremely antagonistic. The relationships with the women in my life have always been pleasant. I'm really looking for a certain partnership in love and some equality. I don't need the fight at all. I have enough fights in my work life. I want to find people that can accept me so I can accept myself. I wouldn't go with a woman who is dangerous. Artistically I can understand that, but my work is not my life.

J-MB: How influential is your wife, Martine Tours, when you try to make up your mind?
PV: I decided to do *RoboCop*, which I first rejected finding it stupid, because of her. Martine convinced me to do *Basic Instinct* and to work with Schwarzenegger too. We really discuss everything. I have a real partnership with her.

J-MB: How influential was Sergei Eisenstein on your style?
PV: A lot of my editing techniques are based on Eisenstein's technique: cutting on movement, always keeping the movement floating around, fast movements

of the head looking in one direction shot from a reverse angle and vice-versa and then cut in the middle of the movement to give a double switch . . . I used that technique during the fight sequence between Melina (Rachel Ticotin) and Lori (Sharon Stone) in *Total Recall*. I still think that there are a lot of techniques that were invented in the '20s and '30s by Russian directors and others that I have yet to fully use, especially in the case of Eisenstein. They have to be rediscovered.

J-MB: It is obvious that *Basic Instinct* was influenced by *Vertigo*.
PV: When I was eighteen, I studied *Vertigo*. I must have seen it at least fifteen times. I know every shot of the movie by heart and entire scenes from *Vertigo* came back to me while I was shooting *Basic Instinct*. I didn't plan to do so, but as I was shooting in San Francisco I used a bridge, and it was geographically the one next to the bridge Hitchcock used in *Vertigo*. And I did the same for the car chase although I shot it in a different way. There are a lot of parallels, of course. When Catherine Tramell (Sharon Stone) goes to visit her friend, and Nick Curran (Michael Douglas) follows her, I asked my crew to find a church near Hazel Dobkin's house (played by Dorothy Malone) because I wanted to establish her as a peaceful person, even if we realize later that she is also a murderer. What I didn't realize at the time is that there is a similar sequence in *Vertigo* with a church in the background. It was a completely unconscious gesture on my part, but it's also true that I always liked those kind of religious symbols. However *Basic Instinct* is more about a man's obsession with a woman and how he is sexually addicted to her. It's not a romantic obsession.

J-MB: Your sex scenes are devoid of any carnal excitement. You can even sense danger during them.
PV: The sex scenes between Catherine and Nick in *Basic Instinct* were never supposed to get exciting. They are in fact thriller scenes. They are disguised as erotic scenes but it's basically a killer-walking-into-your-house-at-night kind of scene. It doesn't mean however that I think sex is dangerous. It's just that I find it interesting to use this soul-surrendering moment, this moment of ultimate confidence and acceptance, and corrupt it with danger. It's like the ultimate betrayal. It's just a dramatic effect, basically. It makes the contrast much stronger. I think it's fun. Most of the time when directors shoot sex scenes they don't mean anything. You have two people on a bed, and they are starting to do something that everyone knows everything about. Most of the sex scenes in American movies are used to show fucking and showing fucking is extremely boring. That's why I prefer to show sex for other reasons. I use sex for communication or hate or to express danger or to give a new piece of information. My sex scenes are always loaded with something else. I have used sex a lot of times as a counterpoint to trust.

J-MB: How would you describe your relationship with Sharon Stone?

PV: The only person that I ever had a strong love/hate relationship with is Sharon Stone because we really love each other but we also really hate each other. We can be really mean to each other and we can also be very caring and wonderful to each other. When I see her it's always the same feeling and I don't want to get into that—because then I would be the victim. I feel that ultimately she would come out the stronger one because I think that she's pretty devilish herself. She would destroy me. That's why I keep a certain distance, but the attraction and the rejection are very strong. I think that having her take the lead in *Basic Instinct* was commercially an extremely powerful choice although I was not aware of that when I did it. Nobody wanted Sharon because she was unknown, but I wanted her because I knew her from *Total Recall* and I thought that she could do it. So I pushed her for a long time. It was the best stroke of luck that I had because I think that she added something to the movie that I think no one else would have given me. And the fact that she basically showed whatever I asked her to show when it came time to show it made the movie what it is. She never complained, though she was resistant. In fact she had ultimate trust in that I was doing a good job. I don't think that I would have found many actresses that would have dared to do what she did. A lot of people would have backed out, you know. I think nearly everyone would have, but she didn't. She trusted me because she felt that I was giving her the chance of her life. I brought out things in her that no one had seen. It's the fact that no one knew this woman that made her so extremely convincing. I think that her presence in the movie was a sensation. You can see the effect that it had on her career. With only one movie she became a star. Now she has to find good directors. If she can fight with the director she will be fine. If the director doesn't fight with her I think she will have problems. Anyhow, in a year and a half, she went from being a nobody to being the most well known actress in the United States.

J-MB: You had a pretty rough ride with Joe Eszterhas on *Basic Instinct*?

PV: The first meeting I had with Eszterhas and Michael Douglas wasn't successful, although I thought it had been. There are a couple of pretty open sex scenes in the script and I told Eszterhas that with my Dutch background in realism I would probably show a bit more than he was expecting. And he didn't like that. So when Michael and I both went away for the holidays, Joe went behind our back to Carolco and said that he was convinced that I would make a pornographic movie out of it and that he didn't want to work in that direction. He told them that he wanted his script back. Carolco refused and Joe walked away from the movie. I have worked in the film industry for years and I've always been very happy to work with writers. On both *RoboCop* and *Total Recall* I had the writers always with me on the set. I'm really a believer in working together with the original writer, but in this case and at that time, because of his maneuvering, he just made it impossible.

J-MB: You're very faithful to your editors . . .
PV: Once I've finished shooting I give the editor everything and I pretty much stay behind. I don't look at dailies much, either. I like to see what the editor will do with it first. On the set you lose your perspective indeed. There may be takes that I prefer but generally his cut will be the one that I use. It's rare that I'll interfere and ask for something totally different. And this is how I work with everyone in postproduction. I've always felt that the postproduction process should be as collaborative as possible.

J-MB: Do you enjoy fighting with actors?
PV: I don't think that confrontation is a good way to be artistic. I don't believe that at all. It's just that I want the movie to be acted my way. I want the actors to follow my vision. I have a vision of how they should look, how they should behave, how they should talk, how they should walk. And *Basic Instinct* is a very strong example of that. The movie was so stylized that the actors were not immediately willing to go my way. I had to force them. I had to fight with them. I mean, I'm sitting there trying to get what I want and I try to do whatever is necessary. I'm not a manipulator, however. I won't say this in order to achieve that. I just say, "This is what I want." It's very Hitchcockian, you know.

J-MB: Does that mean that no one on the set can interfere with your vision of the movie?
PV: The clearer my vision of the movie is, the more fanatically I'm trying to get it. I want everything exactly like I have it in mind and if the cameraman doesn't do it the way I want, then I'll be upset and I will fight to get what I want.

J-MB: The more you make movies, the more linear they get.
PV: At the beginning of my career, it was difficult for me to have in mind more than twenty to thirty minutes of my movie. But now that I'm older I can foresee the whole structure and I'm much more able to make complex movies. I'm building complete symphonies. I'm able to play the piano, do a quartet and use counterpoint at the same time. And I achieved that with *Basic Instinct*. I even made a graphic representation of the different lines and the different levels of tensions. It was like a score.

J-MB: How different and/or similar are Christine Halslaag (Renée Soutendijk's character in *The Fourth Man*) and Catherine Tramell?

PV: They're basically the same character. *Basic Instinct* is an americanization of *The Fourth Man*.

J-MB: Though Dr. Garner (Jeanne Tripplehorn) is one of the most intense and feverish female characters portrayed in your movies, she was completely overshadowed by the character of Catherine Tramell. Can you talk a bit about her?

PV: When I shot the movie, the part of Jeanne Tripplehorn was as important as the part of Sharon Stone. But because of the public opinion and all the attention afterwards, all of the emphasis was placed on the performance of Sharon Stone. I really think that Dr. Garner is a pretty fascinating character. I spent a lot of time trying to make her as interesting as possible and I worked very hard with Jeanne on it. She is the only one that seems to have really consistent feelings for Nick Curran even if she knows that it is stupid to do so. Though she is not a shadowy character like Nick Curran or a perfidious female like Catherine Tramell, Dr. Garner is not free of any flaws. She does things that ethically deserve blame—she gives away Nick Curran's file to the internal affairs guy. She makes mistakes, but she is of course not the killer and neither is she a villain or an inhuman person that doesn't care about people. She is one of the most normal people in the movie, in fact. It's just because of her bisexuality and its impact that she becomes involved in all of this.

Basic Cutting: Paul Verhoeven's *Basic Instinct*

Laurent Bouzereau / 1994

Excerpted from *The Cutting Room Floor,* Citadel 1994. Reprinted by permission of the publisher. All rights reserved. Reprinted by arrangement with Kensington Publishing Corp. www .kensingtonbooks.com.

LAURENT BOUZEREAU: You come from Europe and have directed several films in Holland. Did you ever encounter any form of censorship over there?
PAUL VERHOEVEN: I know that the producer of *Spetters* was a little bit concerned by my explicit images. He tried to influence me to tone it down. I think he was a bit afraid about the homosexual violence, the homosexual rape, and also because you saw erections in the Dutch version.

LB: That's not in the American version I saw.
PV: No, that was all cut out. You know *Spetters* only came out in France for the first time after the success of *Basic Instinct* even though they released *The Fourth Man* in France a couple of months before *Basic* came out. It took *Spetters* about eleven years to come out, and I don't think it has anything to do with the fact that the film was not important enough, because they release everything over there. I think that even for France, the directness of that film was too explicit.

LB: What was so explicit about it?
PV: You see an erection when the young boy, who is a bit unclear about his sexuality, follows two guys in the underground tunnel and sees one giving a blow job to the other. You have a close-up of the prick of one of the guys, and you see the other one actually giving a blow job. Later, you see a guy holding his prick and raping another guy. It was really hard, hard sex. I had never seen that in movies with perhaps the exception of a couple of films Pasolini did toward the end of his life. But still, *Spetters* was extremely harsh, and it was a big scandal in Holland.

People said it was anti-homosexuals, anti-women, anti-invalids, that it was a fascist movie. In the film, an invalid kills himself, and people said it promoted the fact that invalids should commit suicide. For months all the press on the film was 300 percent negative.

LB: When you shot the film, did you find it offensive?
PV: Oh yeah. Absolutely.

LB: Did you think you were being anti-gay, anti-women, anti-invalids?
PV: No. But I thought it was extremely provocative. In fact, about two years ago there was an article in a film magazine readdressing the issues of *Spetters*, and now, after twelve years, people have a different opinion, and it's seen as an interesting portrayal of the eighties. I wanted to go beyond what was normal, to show things that are true and real but that are normally omitted. I'm not going to be elliptic or shoot it in a way you don't see it, I'll shoot it straight. This is how people give a blow job, and this is how they rape, this is how they masturbate, this is how you jerk off somebody, and you see it all. That's just the reality of life. I wanted it to be provocative.

LB: Do you feel that, as an artist, you always have to go a step further?
PV: Yes, as an artist and as a person. I always like to push the edges in every direction, in a moral way, in a sexual way, in a way of action and violence. Because if you see someone who is wounded or loses an arm in battle, for instance, and what it does to somebody, well, that's never been portrayed on the screen. I mean, if you portrayed this as a reality of life, it would probably be intolerable. It is always my ambition to use the depth of reality, the scope of reality, as much as possible and still try to integrate it in what I would call a vision . . . that's the ultimate goal.

LB: I must admit that the lovemaking sequences in *Basic Instinct* are extremely well choreographed.
PV: It's all extremely stylized, of course, and heavily storyboarded and extremely precisely edited. It's kind of a funny analogy, but if you look at the horse race in *Ben Hur*, it's done the same way. But in American movies, lovemaking sequences are not scenes; they are what we call a montage. Joe Eszterhas at least writes different things that are happening, but what you normally get is "They make passionate love" and that's it. It's almost like love scenes are on the divine level and you should not be intruding too much. It's like a fear of analyzing, a fear of destroying, a fear of even being explicit about it.

LB: Do you think American directors are too self-conscious about what can happen with the MPAA?
PV: Not exactly. I want to be clear that I don't feel that the MPAA is crazy or something, I have done four movies in America, and I had to deal with the MPAA on all of them. *Flesh+Blood* got an X, *RoboCop* got an X, *Total Recall* got an X, and *Basic Instinct* got an X, only now it's called NC-17.

LB: Why were those movies rated X?
PV: *Flesh+Blood* and *Basic Instinct* because of sex and violence, *RoboCop* and *Total Recall* because of violence. On *Flesh+Blood* and *Total Recall*, I think I had to go back to the MPAA three or four times, on *RoboCop* seven times, and on *Basic Instinct* ten times before they accepted it. Of course, I protected myself with a lot of other shots. All the sex scenes in *Basic Instinct* were shot from a lot of different angles. We realized during the shooting that some of the angles, especially the one when Michael is between Sharon's legs and licking her vagina would not be acceptable. Even when we looked at it in the replay because we were shooting simultaneously with video, we were all really laughing... We knew we would never get away with that. But we went as far as we could, although each time I felt there could be a problem with the MPAA, I shot further away, from another angle, with a different light or whatever, so I had a lot of different possibilities and the MPAA could not force me to cut things out. I always offered them another solution that was less explicit without changing the scene. So if you compare the NC-17 to the R-rated version in terms of running time, they're not very different, but their intensity is different. The impact in the NC-17 version is much harsher, more powerful.

You can really feel the difference in the so-called date-rape scene with Jeanne Tripplehorn. The original version of that sequence was much harsher, it was... WOW! He's really doing something to that girl. In the American version, it's kind of indicated, but then it's over. In the European version, it really hits several times, WOW, WOW, WOW! Ultimately I had to take out about twenty seconds.

LB: In the European version, it's more obvious that she's consenting... I noticed you said "the so-called date-rape scene." Do you not agree? What would you call it?
PV: A date rape would really be that she is raped and that at no moment is there any consent. I think this scene floats between consent and being angry or half angry. There is consent and there are moments when you feel it's going too far, and then she consents anyhow for whatever reason. I would certainly morally question the scene from the point of view of the guy who does it.

Michael is behaving in a way that I would not behave. He is aggressively imposing himself and finds out that she is accepting it. The fact that she accepts is the second phase; he pushes her in to a situation and ultimately I don't know if she enjoys it, but she seems to accept it to a certain degree. But when he does it, there are clearly moments and seconds when you feel that she might not and he is pushing anyhow. So I would say that he is going into an unknown territory where he should be aware of her hesitations. I could never do that to a woman.

There is no doubt that when she invites him in she wants to fuck. Of course she wants to fuck, because she wants him back, you know. The question is that the way he fucks is not exactly the way that she imagined she would be fucked.

She says that later. At several points in the scene, you definitely feel that there is a mutual understanding between the two of them that this isn't big fun. That's what I wanted, and his aggression has to do with the fact that he doesn't want to fuck her, he wants to fuck Sharon Stone. The sex with her would probably be on that level, and he is already imagining or playing out the fantasy of how it would be with that other woman. That's what this scene is about. From a moral point of view, the character played by Michael Douglas is to be accused, and I wanted him that way.

LB: I think that of all the scenes that you had to rearrange for the R-rated version, the opening sequence with the murder of Johnny Boz is the one that lost most of its initial impact.
PV: The murder in the European version is, I think, eight seconds. It's about seven seconds in the US version. So time-wise, it's practically the same scene, but the impact of it is gone. The close-up of the ice pick going through his nose and the full body shot where you see the blood and her stabbing on top of him have all been taken out. The shock of the scene in the European version is . . . you're really blown away. It's what I wanted. It's strange because it's so short! I mean, it's probably shorter than the shower sequence in *Psycho*, but it's so powerful. I wanted it to be that shocking because for a very long time after that scene, nothing really happens. And later, when we have a bed scene again and you see her, you should know that this might happen again and that it's horrible.

LB: What about Gus's murder in the elevator?
It's softer in the American version, but I think losing the impact in the opening scene is more important, because when you see Gus, you know he's going to die. And so it's less unexpected than in the opening love scene. There, it's love and then that complete reversion into death.

LB: What would you call the MPAA?
PV: Warning-system agents or something. If you want to use the term censorship, which I'm hesitant to use, I think you would have to call it more of an economic censorship. They don't censor your movie. They don't say you cannot release your movie. After showing the MPAA the first cut of *Basic Instinct*, they said this is great, it's a wonderful movie, please don't change it, it's an NC-17. They wanted to protect children or warn parents, but also they felt that it was a powerful movie, done with artistic integrity. They wanted to legitimize the NC-17. Then, of course, the studio said we cannot release this film with an NC-17 because in a lot of cases, and that's why I call it an economic censorship, theaters won't show NC-17 movies, especially in malls.

LB: Do you think *Basic Instinct* would have been less successful if it had been released with an NC-17?

PV: Yes. It would have done half the business it did; sixty million dollars would be my guess, if that much. The studio said that with an NC-17 we would only get five hundred theaters at the maximum, probably four hundred. Ultimately, the R-rated version came out into sixteen or seventeen hundred theaters.

Especially when you make a movie for $45, $65 million you cannot say, well, you know, forget the money, I'm an artist. It is a strange thing that this medium has two values, an artistic one and a commercial one. If you want to be in this business, you have to realize that people, companies are investing money and are dependent on the success of a movie in order to survive. I think you kill both the industry and good movies too if you consider film only as art. If there's no industry, there can't be good movies, you kill yourself, you kill your own babies, you kill life. We should be somewhere in the middle. Making ten *Home Alone*'s, I think that's cookie-making, but *Home Alone* one is not cookie-making. *Home Alone 2* is dangerous, and 3 and 4 and 5 will be cookie-making, unless a genius picks it up somewhere. If you only make art movies like in Europe, you're killing what's essential to this medium. As an artist, you have to be aware of the economic environment.

Take the example of Rembrandt in Holland. In his time, art was something that was paid for by the middle class, by the merchants, and they wanted certain things. They wanted certain portraits, and they wanted the faces of the people who had ordered the portraits to be recognized in the paintings. Some of the problems with *The Nightwatch* when it was finished was that Rembrandt put so many people in the shadows that you couldn't recognize them. These were very important people in town who had ordered this canvas because they wanted to prove how great they were. Even da Vinci was paid by people who wanted to see themselves in paintings. So, you can't isolate art completely from its economic environment.

LB: Does the MPAA call you? How does it work?

PV: No, you call them. In this case the producer or sometimes a representative from the studio calls them and asks for their opinion. They have a spokesperson who gives you indications where the problems are. So in the case of *Basic Instinct* they said we have problems with the violence in the first act and in the scene of the stabbing. Then we have a problem in the fifth reel and we have a problem in reel seven, etc. I think they had problems in four or five reels altogether. They didn't say that shot or this shot. In fact, we tried to get them to be more specific, but they said, "We won't tell you; we're not going to cut your movie. You cut your movie; you give us something we can accept. All we can tell you is that it's too long and too strong."

LB: How many people are on the board?
PV: I think about nine or ten. They're probably people who represent what the MPAA feels is the movie-going audience, people who have children, because kids is always the one issue that they bring up. It is supposed to be a system to warn parents about what their kids are going to see—that's the essence of it.

Of course, you do think about your kids. I show my kids all my movies, always, even when they were nine or ten, but never without explaining to them what they are going to see and warning them and never without my wife and me sitting with them. We watch the films on video, and then we stop and explain how it is done. My wife will say, "It's going to be violent but only because Paul is throwing fake blood on the actors," and then we show them. I think you can show kids anything, but you really have to be aware under what circumstances you do that. I don't think preventing kids from seeing movies is a solution.

You should tell them what sexuality is. You should tell what a prick is and a vagina and how it works, and what homosexuality is. I think you should explain that to children when they're three, because a kid can accept everything. If they're exposed to these things without any warning, it could hurt them but that shock and hurt can still lead later in life to being a wonderful artist. It can also lead you to seeing a psychiatrist every three days. For me, being exposed to violence when I was young, especially in the war and later in reading books that I shouldn't have read at that age, was and still is for me a source of inspiration for my work.

Sex, Cinema, and *Showgirls*

Paul Verhoeven / 1995

Excerpted from *Showgirls: Portrait of a Film*, Newmarket Press, 1995. Reprinted with permission by Paul Verhoeven.

Is it all just tits and ass? Looking at the photographs in this book and seeing my film *Showgirls*, some people might say so. Even if this perception were true, that's fine with me: Why shouldn't we enjoy the beauty of the human body? Like it or not, we are biologically destined to enjoy sexual attraction as the means by which we continue the species. However, the experience of making *Showgirls*, and the aesthetic, emotional, and thematic elements expressed in these photographs, mean considerably more to me.

As a young Dutchman, I was entranced by American musical films, and the opportunity to direct one has been the fulfillment of a lifelong dream. Because the project emerged so quickly, and because the actors are primarily young people who have not yet become Hollywood mega-stars, parts of my work on this production reminded me of the exhilarating, hurried time when I began to make movies in Holland in the seventies. Also, because this movie takes place in the unique American atmosphere of Las Vegas, it gave me the opportunity to deal with the American obsessions with sex, violence, power, and success—themes that clearly pervade all my European work.

The genesis of *Showgirls* was a lunch at The Ivy, a Beverly Hills restaurant, with Joe Eszterhas, to see if there was anything left of our friendship after the explosive disagreement we had over the script for *Basic Instinct*. (For those who mercifully have forgotten, some gay and lesbian groups protested the way in which homosexual characters were portrayed in Joe's script. He agreed to make changes; I refused.) Our mutual friend Ben Myron was along as a peacekeeper. Joe was gracious enough to admit that I had been correct to ignore the pressure groups and to make the film the way he wrote it. We had a few drinks, a few laughs, rediscovered our friendship, and began to discuss the possibility of doing another project together. During an hour or so, the three of us talked about dozens of movie ideas. Ben had the original concept, but Joe was the one who proposed, "What about a musical about Las Vegas?"

I was hooked immediately. Joe claims that my eyes began to glisten. I was remembering all those big MGM musicals that I had watched over and over as a kid. I loved what Robert Wise and Jerome Robbins had done with *West Side Story*. I really like ballet and when I was about fifteen or sixteen, I thought about becoming a dancer. Nothing ever came of it, except I filled sketchbooks with drawings of ballets and ideas for choreography. I always wanted to make a movie with a lot of music and dancing, and I liked the idea that this was not going to be a "highbrow" musical.

Right from the beginning, Joe and I saw this as a story about Las Vegas showgirls. For most of my career, I have been interested in subcultures that are not at the top of the ladder. One of my favorite creations is *Spetters,* a movie about a group of blue collar kids with no education, no money, no power—nothing but dreams about motorcycle racing. As it turns out, *Showgirls* has a lot in common with that earlier movie of mine. It isn't just people at the top who are filled with ambitions. Both Nomi and those blue collar kids in *Spetters* reach for goals in the same way. Although Nomi comes from a similar hardscrabble background, she discovers that there are some things she just won't do.

Shortly thereafter, Joe and Ben (who became co-producer) and I went to Las Vegas for some preliminary research. Of course, in the new "family oriented" Vegas, there are still a few shows that feature the real, old fashioned showgirls with their feathered costumes such as Bally's "Jubilee." A couple of others, however, such as "Splash" and "Into the Night," feature topless nudity and sexy dancing, and this was much closer to what we had in mind. We talked to showgirls, dancers, choreographers, casino bosses, bouncers, entertainment directors, public relations people, and anyone else who would give us insights, but we didn't find the story we were looking for.

Then, we explored the world of the strip clubs, such as the Cheetah, the Crazy Horse, and the Palomino. We found more interesting stories there. The women in these clubs certainly are not showgirls or even dancers, for the most part. But we liked the raucous, sleazy atmosphere, and we were surprised at how much raw sexuality there was in the private rooms where "lap dancing"—in which a naked woman basically bumps and grinds over and on top of a seated male customer—is the preferred entertainment.

Most of the strippers don't really dance. They just move sensuously to the music. But we saw several women who really were dancers. This formed the seed for the character of Nomi in the film. In other interviews we heard of some strippers' aspirations to jump over into one of the big Vegas shows. And some of them did.

Some of the women we talked with had very strong personalities—real "fuck you" attitudes. They were difficult to deal with and had sharp tongues, but out of their collective voices we heard a character developing. Realizing that some dancers used sexual relationships to get the top spots in the big Vegas shows, Joe then quickly made the leap to a story about a young unknown who will do anything to steal a job as a lead dancer in a show. We later realized that there were elements from Joe Mankiewicz's brilliant 1950 film, *All About Eve,* in our story. You may remember how Anne Baxter undermines Bette Davis in that movie.

Out of all of this emerged a film about a young woman with a disturbed background that is not revealed until the end of the picture. Her name is Nomi, and she goes to Las Vegas with the dream of becoming a dancer in one of the big shows. She has to begin in one of the strip clubs, in which she claws and manipulates her way up the ladder of success. She uses her strange and complex relationship with Cristal, the lead dancer in the biggest show, to get what she wants. And she discovers that at each rung of the ladder, she has to pay a higher and higher price for what she is getting. Ultimately, she refuses to pay with her soul. Joe Eszterhas calls it the dark side of the American Dream.

At first, I thought of *West Side Story* and *Flashdance* as the musical inspirations for this movie. The choreography in *West Side Story* was innovative in 1961 and it still holds up. *Flashdance* is a story about a strong willed girl who wants to dance, and, of course, that was one of the first projects for which Joe Eszterhas received writing credit. More important, it was the first theatrical film to use music video techniques in both dramatic and dance sequences.

The more I thought about it, however, the more I realized that *Showgirls* would have to be more extravagant, more excessive in the big productions. After all, this is a Las Vegas show. It takes place in a town where everyday sights are a giant pyramid, an erupting volcano, white tigers, and acres of neon so bright it looks like daytime at midnight. People are winning and losing millions of dollars on the turn of a card. It is literally a completely extravagant town. The Hollywood version of a Las Vegas production number has to dazzle moviegoers who have seen the real thing.

For cinematic style, I wanted a very free, fluid look, something that would work with all of the movement and spectacle of the story. I ended up studying Federico Fellini's *8 1/2* and Orson Welles' *Touch of Evil* for inspiration. Fellini moves so fluidly through that movie and does so much with the camera that I learn something new every time I see it. *Touch of Evil* is a *film noir* that is very much choreographed for the camera. When the camera makes the moves, the actors are all choreographed in a way that the camera can go from here to there, passing through the different angles that the director had in mind—all done so beautifully you don't notice unless you are really looking for it. Although they didn't have the technology—in fact, I can't figure out how they did some of the camera moves—the technique is very much what we do with Steadicam today.

Probably seventy percent of *Showgirls* was shot with Steadicam. Larry McConkey was my first camera operator and Steadicam operator. He and Jost Vacano, my director of photography—who had used a similar technique in *Soldier of Orange* and especially in *Das Boot*—helped me get that loose feeling I wanted. On the screen, it appears as though the camera is following the actors, as it might do in a *cinema verité* documentary. In fact, the actors are moved or choreographed by me, so that the camera can move when and where I want it to go. The actors handled some complex moves and some detailed choreography, and Larry gave them a lot of freedom to work within those moves. Basically, you never see the camera moving without being motivated by an actor, but I have choreographed the actor so that the camera can find a new angle. It is a technique that always uses the movement of the actor to camouflage the movement of the camera.

Alfred Hitchcock, who is another director I admire greatly, sometimes used that technique during his middle years. Of course, it was more complicated for him as the Steadicam did not exist and he had to do all those camera moves on a dolly, but the choreography was the same. You can see a lot of Hitchcock's influence in *Basic Instinct*, but not so much in *Showgirls*. There is a scene, however, in which Cristal and Nomi are talking in a restaurant at Caesar's Forum shopping mall which I "steal" from *North by Northwest*. If you recall the scene between Cary Grant and Eva Marie Saint on the train, he shoots first over the shoulders, and then moves closer and closer, in a very simple and elegant way. That's one of my favorite dialogue scenes in all of moviemaking, and I borrowed from it shamelessly.

An aspect of filmmaking that I think you see clearly in *Showgirls* is the potential for expressing emotion through movement. When I was a young man, I wanted to be a painter, because I see painting as such a great expressive medium, a way to put a deeper sense of yourself, of your emotions, on canvas with the use of only a brush and some tubes of paint. Then, when I got a movie camera from my uncle, I moved slowly from painting to filmmaking over a period of five or six years—during which time I saw how I could use the camera like a brush, to use movement to express emotion. If you look at the later films of Sergei Eisenstein, such as *Ivan the Terrible*, you can see how he stylized the movement of the actors to express emotion, using the static framing to provide a measure for that movement.

European filmmakers have explored the possibilities of "painting" with the camera more than Americans because their movies are much more based on psychology, rather than storytelling. The "Hollywood formula" of three acts with a precise dramatic structure is so drummed into young filmmakers in the United States that they find it difficult to think in other terms. Most of the so-called masterpieces of European cinema cannot be understood in those terms at all. Movies by people such as Truffaut and Fellini are essentially nonlinear. There's no second or third act in *La Dolce Vita* because the film doesn't develop that way. It's much more like music, in that it moves from *allegro* to *allegretto* to *adagio* and so on. It follows feelings, emotional lines, rather than plot lines.

(Having said this I have to confess that, in general, I would rather watch American movies than European movies, which are generally too slow paced for me. Also, by now I've learned to like more dramatic structure than European films allow for.)

The first time I read Joe's script for *Showgirls*, I knew that I could not make this film in a way to satisfy myself, ethically and artistically, and at the same time satisfy the normal studio requirement that a director must meet the MPAA Rating Board minimum standards for an "R" rating. We knew rather early in the development of this movie that sexuality and sexual power would be one of the core dramatic issues, but we didn't think in terms of ratings. The emerging prospect of trying to direct an adult movie that deals with naked dancers within the arbitrary "R" strictures of the Rating Board made me very unhappy.

With *Basic Instinct*, I had been forced to submit and resubmit the film nine times before receiving their R-rated blessing. All that was removed was twenty-two seconds of "objectionable" material, and another twenty seconds were changed into closer or wider shots of the same take. Every second of the original can now be seen on videotape. Joe and I agreed that we would only discuss offers from production organizations willing to accept an "NC-17" rating for a film that would cost $30-40 million. Five studios made offers—which I thought was quite amazing—and Chargeurs/Carolco, which will distribute through MGM/UA, made the best one. Ironically, with *Showgirls*, I got to direct an MGM musical!

I have been accused of being deliberately provocative in insisting upon making an NC-17 film, and I suppose that my insistence is a provocation in a way. But I think of myself as provocative in a different sense: as a director who explores the difference between reality and the way in which we usually see reality portrayed. I feel that there is a huge discrepancy between what life really is and what we are supposed to see in the movies. There are many aspects of life that are not publicly acknowledged and that many people don't want to see as reality. For example, if you had tried a year ago to make a movie about the dangers of paramilitary militia groups in the United States, you would have been a revolutionary. Today, you would be a TV news producer who is too late with the story. There are a large number of other social and political facts in this country that are quietly ignored, and perhaps the most obvious one is sexual behavior.

Despite the fact that everybody fucks and that sexuality is simply a mammalian characteristic, American movies do not portray sex particularly realistically, if at all. There is both official censorship and economic censorship of sexual material at all levels in this country. Strangely enough, even hate speech and the stockpiling of military weaponry is better protected than sexual information, in a nation that prides itself on openness and the freedoms guaranteed in the Bill of Rights. I think that the First Amendment is one of the cornerstones of democracy, a true sign of strength. It tells us that in American society you can say or show whatever you want to say or show—even if it is irritating, disgusting, unpleasant, shocking, or offensive to everyone else.

Censorship is a sign of a society's weakness. It demonstrates that the censors are afraid of ideas that are different from their own. It suggests that some people are too weak to deal with words or images with which they disagree. The First Amendment, however, supposes that the American people are strong enough to deal even with ideas and words that they abhor. The First Amendment is a statement of belief in the strength of the American citizen.

The best scientific studies on the influence of sex and violence in the media are all rather clear, too. No causal relationship has been found between being a frequent *Playboy* reader and becoming a rapist. There is no causal relationship between someone watching *RoboCop* and holding up a gas station. There is often correlation, which is a different matter. Sex offenders may like to see pornography; people prone to violence may like violent movies. But that doesn't mean that one causes the other. In my films, I hold the mirror up to life. What you see is the sex and the violence that already exists in modern societies. But, of course, I sometimes push beyond the framework of reality, because that's my pleasure.

Politicians attack Hollywood because they—and perhaps the American public—don't want to look at the real problems. The big problems are in the American social structure: crime, drugs, the urban environment, poverty, lack of education, and the availability of guns. The politicians don't deal too much with those problems; it is much easier to blame Hollywood for causing decadence in American society—which seems heartless and cynical.

I don't think that the religious moralists or right-wing feminists are heartless or cynical, but I think that they are similarly misguided in their attacks on sex in movies. Fundamentally, they both argue that a woman showing her tits is being degraded, is being exploited, is being humiliated, and that the act of showing her tits contributes to the downfall of civilization.

I don't think that's true. What that woman is doing is demonstrating our strong instinct for procreation. Most heterosexual and bisexual men like to see tits and ass because those sights stimulate our sexual drives, our natural desire to fuck and create babies. Most women like to show off their bodies in skirts that reveal their legs or blouses that emphasize their breasts because they like to use their sexual power—they know that dressing this way will attract men who will ultimately give them babies. (Of course, this is not a conscious process.) That's the simple biology lesson of it all. We need to accept that we are just mammals who are running around doing one thing rather effectively, which is to procreate.

Sexuality and the uses of sexual power are central to *Showgirls*. However, all of the sex scenes in this film have a purpose in addition to simply stimulating sexual enjoyment. For example, one of the key scenes takes place early in the movie when Cristal visits the Cheetah strip club, and insists upon buying Nomi to perform a lap dance for Cristal's boyfriend, Zack. Nomi refuses until the club manager hears Cristal offer five hundred dollars. He forces Nomi to go with them. Essentially, what we see next is Nomi fucking a fully clothed Zack, without really fucking him, while Cristal watches.

The levels of meaning within this scene and the interplay among the three primary characters here is rather complex. Ostensibly, Cristal is humiliating Nomi and demonstrating her power over Nomi by "renting" her against her will—literally imposing a form of slavery on her. However, Nomi had created an opportunity to meet Cristal earlier by manipulation and was aware of Cristal's interest in her. Nomi also knows that Zack, the entertainment director of a hotel, watched her pole dance.

When she begins the lap dance over Zack, Nomi reverses the power game. She uses her body to exert her power over Cristal's boyfriend who is, not coincidentally, Nomi's potential employer. Although Cristal bought the lap dance for Zack, it is obvious that he is really just a substitute for Cristal herself. Cristal is seduced and riveted by Nomi's sexuality. You could argue that Cristal is trying to seduce Nomi in a very complex way, and that the danger of losing her lover to this woman is part of the excitement for her. You might also say that Nomi is deliberately playing the "victim game" to draw Cristal into her trap. Although it seems as though she is being exploited, she is well aware that five hundred dollars is a lot of money for a lap dance and that her relationship with Al, the club manager, would have allowed her to refuse the dance. But the resistance that she displays makes the encounter even more exciting for both Zack and Cristal. And, in the end, she might be the seductress and controller of both of them. (For more details of my thinking about this scene, see the excerpt from my shooting script in the storyboard drawings that follow.)

When Cristal sends someone over to the club the next day to offer Nomi an audition for the chorus of "Goddess," is she successfully continuing her seduction and bringing her closer? Who's leading whom? Who's really in charge here?

There's a lot of ambiguity in the lap dance scene—the same sort of ambiguity that exists in the script for *Basic Instinct*. Some people are still not sure who the murderer is.

Contrary to what you read in movie magazines, the shooting of erotic scenes is rarely erotic on the set. It's acting; it's not real sex. In my films, the actors have seen detailed storyboards of the sex scene and are often receiving precise instructions from me while they are doing it. I have heard that some directors simply tell the actors to "Go for it, baby," and then mush the scene together with a series of dissolves. Those sex scenes simply suggest two people copulating.

But I prefer to use sex scenes for something else. The sex scene between Michael Douglas and Sharon Stone in *Basic Instinct* is a good example. I storyboarded precisely every move and every angle in the scene and gave the boards to Sharon and Michael weeks ahead of time. It was a fairly long and complicated sex scene. Sharon would ask me what the camera was picking up. And I would explain to her what I wanted the camera to capture and why.

On the day of the shooting, there was no discussion necessary. Michael and Sharon knew what I wanted them to do. They took off their clothes and did it. I directed them very exactly, with no euphemisms: "Now you go down to her mouth, turn to this side, kiss her and move slowly down to her nipple so we can see your face. Now, lick her nipple . . ." and so forth. I try to be very neutral in the tone of my instructions because actors are often insecure about these scenes.

I know that when all those moves and angles that I storyboarded for Sharon and Michael were edited together, people thought that was a "hot" scene. And it probably is. But I like that scene not because it is about sex, but because it is a thriller scene expressed through sex. It is a scene in which the audience knows that this woman could be the same woman they saw committing the murder with the ice pick at the beginning of the movie. There are shots repeated from the first scene, and the music is the same as the first scene, so that the audience is constantly being reminded that Michael may be in danger. We see the same shots of the mirror on the ceiling, the brass bed, the tying up, the position, and the woman getting on top of him. And the audience is thinking: There's a blond woman, he gets an orgasm, and she will kill him. So I take them through the same psychological trajectory and maintain the tension while they look for clues. Otherwise, what would be the point of simply showing three minutes of fucking?

In a later scene in *Showgirls*, after Nomi has learned that Zack will be holding auditions for Cristal's understudy in "Goddess," she goes home with him and fucks him in his swimming pool. I shot it with a kind of romantic feeling, but again, I'm using the knowledge that the audience has about her ulterior motive. I don't do it as straight fucking. I have her fuck him the way she did in the lap dance, so that this scene echoes the earlier one and the audience can see that Nomi is doing essentially the same thing in a different way. It is camouflaged as a romantic sex scene, but the audience emotionally absorbs that it is about something else, and they gain another insight into her character.

Nomi plays at being innocent, but proves to be quite calculating and manipulative. She also appears to be willing to pay any price for success, but eventually she finds the tab too high. Cristal has it all and likes to play with fire. Does she realize how much she endangers her life when she toys with Nomi? Zack helps both of them and fucks both of them—and is used by both of them. As the three of them swirl around in this intricate dance, their motives become more and more ambiguous. Like most of us, I believe that these three characters are not entirely sure of their own motivations. I am fascinated by that lack of clarity. The human mind is not a "normal" computer, and people are often unaware of their own motives, in some ways, that is the essence of life for me: We want things desperately, but we don't know exactly why we want them. I think that we are propelled by ideas and motivations that are often beyond our consciousness. We cannot pin these hidden drives down. You cannot say exactly what it is. It is as if there is no "real" reality. There are many realities.

One explanation of my interests as a filmmaker is that I was trained as a mathematician at the University of Leiden in Holland. I studied mathematical physics and completed my doctorate in mathematics, with a special concentration on the general theory of relativity. From a physicist's point of view, there is no single reality. There are many realities coexisting at one time. This is part of my philosophy of life and I suppose it is also a continuing theme in my films. Even in an action movie such as *Total Recall*, I enjoyed developing the idea that Arnold Schwarzenegger and the audience were experiencing two realities simultaneously, and both are consistent throughout the movie. Is Arnold in a dream or is it real? Did he save Mars or is he still sitting in the machine dreaming? It is my own feeling that both versions of reality are true. There are similar levels of reality in *RoboCop* and *Basic Instinct*—and certainly in *Showgirls*.

Nomi is an interesting character to me because she appears to be an ordinary pretty girl and yet has many sides; she seems willing to do anything to achieve her goals but makes a moral choice in the end. She is a particularly rich character because she is a shadowy one. When Cristal tells her, "We're all whores, darlin'" she doesn't realize that she is pressing a hot button for Nomi. We discover that Nomi had been a prostitute after her parents were killed, so that words such as "whore" or "mother" cause her to react. She's linked traumatically to that word "whore," because that is the past she is trying to escape. The movie is partly about just how far she will go.

When Nomi's friend Molly is raped at a party and no one in that tight Las Vegas show business world is willing to defend her or even speak up on her behalf Nomi reaches the breaking point. My interpretation of her character would be that she has accepted the exploitation of herself and played by their amoral rules because she feels strong enough to turn the tables, to defend herself. It is only when she sees the cruelty of those Vegas rules applied to a defenseless person such as Molly that her ethical sense is awakened. Molly may be the only truly decent person in the whole movie. She is certainly the ethical center of the story. All of the men are sleazy and dominating; most of the other women have their own hungry agendas. Molly is the only person who is sincerely concerned about Nomi, who sees her talent, supports her, and then sees her going down the road of corruption. She warns Nomi not to let herself be "sucked into it." When Nomi pushes Cristal from the staircase, she crosses a line. Molly turns her back on Nomi. Even then, Nomi pursues her goals. It is only when Nomi sees her friend hurt and deserted by the rest of the Vegas pack that she realizes that if she accepts this completely corrupt society, she would accept anything. It is the last step toward sacrificing her soul.

There are many parallels between *Showgirls* and *Keetje Tippel*, a film I made in Holland in 1975. Keetje, or Katie, comes with her family to Amsterdam to find fortune. In this rather Dickensian story, set in the 19th century, Katie starts as a prostitute, then becomes a nude model, and finally marries a charming opportunist (played by Rutger Hauer). Eventually, she loses him. Not defeated, she finds another guy who is richer and aristocratic, and marries him.

Katie is a country girl who comes to the big city and becomes corrupted by the world of capitalism ushered in with the Industrial Revolution. The difference between Katie and Nomi is that although both make immoral decisions in the pursuit of success or money, Katie never looks back. She just gets richer and richer, without having ethical qualms. In the last scene in the movie, in which Katie is licking the blood from the wound on this rich guy's head, she is literally sucking him dry—like a vampire. It is a harsh, but honest, view of life.

Because Nomi finally rejects the corrupt world that is offering her success for her soul, she is saved, redeemed. It is sort of a Christian morality tale. As she picks up her bags and is hitchhiking out of Las Vegas, the guy who gives her a ride asks her what she won. She answers, "Me."

Despite all of the manipulative and immoral things she did, she emerges with her dignity and is off to another life with a clean slate. As I think about it, this is a very American vision, a tale of redemption. In reality, most people who are willing to compromise everything and finally have the prize in their hands don't throw it away as Nomi does. They behave much more like Katie Tippel, or like the girl at the end of *Spetters*, who starts to build her fortune on the ruins of the young man who has just committed suicide. They take the money and don't look back.

This theme of redemption is part of American mythology. American movies are filled with these fairy tales in which everything comes out right and everybody goes to the seashore. It is an illusion that is supported by the whole culture, and is probably part of the larger unwillingness to look at unpleasant realities.

Of course, my American movies reflect that mythology of redemption, too. I have been living and working in the United States for almost a decade and I can see changes in my attitudes, my life, and my films. It is inevitable that I am becoming Americanized. If you look at the difference between the films Alfred Hitchcock made in England and the ones he made in the United States, you can see the same sort of change. I am sure that it was not something he tried to do. It's something that just happens. When your surroundings change you, your perceptions also change, as do your interests and your rhythms. I have a much different rhythm when I work here than when I worked in Holland. In my country, things are much greyer. In the United States there is more contrast, more social and political tension. More drama. More fun!

I suppose that if my films reflect that tension, and even if they provoke strong responses, I fulfill some function as an artist. Perhaps, now, as an American artist.

Showgirls: Shooting the Script

Paul Verhoeven / 1995

Excerpted from *Showgirls: Portrait of a Film*, Newmarket Press, 1995. Reprinted with permission by Paul Verhoeven.

Normally, when I direct a movie, I make detailed drawings of each scene of the script in sequence, indicating the type of shots, the angles, and the way in which I envision the shots being edited together. This process, called storyboarding, produces a sort of lengthy cartoon strip of the whole movie. I conceptualize visually, and the process of making these drawings helps me to think through every step in the making of a film. When I directed *The Fourth Man*, all of the storyboards were completed before we started shooting, and I have had the luxury of elaborate storyboards on all my American movies.

However, with *Showgirls*, we were rushed into production and there was no time to prepare storyboards in advance. I ended up making the drawings right in my script before the next day's shooting on a day-to-day basis. What you see in these four sample pages is a sort of sketchbook, a visual diary of my thoughts about how this film should come together.

Actually, I am just as happy that I did not make my usual detailed preparations in this case. I think it might have been unnecessary and perhaps even hampering to be too precise and too clear from the beginning. I was working with a cast with many young actors I had not worked with before, and I was not sure how far I could push them in certain directions. So I tried to use my knowledge of the people who I was working with as I created the storyboards each day.

Day by day I felt better, because I could see how the actors worked together and how they looked through the lens, and I used that in the drawings. It was a kind of direct feedback that I never tried before. I could integrate my feelings about who they were and how they behaved into the drawings. Each night, before or after dinner, I sat down with my script and spent an hour or so creating the storyboards for the next day's shooting. I truly came to enjoy the spontaneity that it allowed me to have.

Another advantage this daily exercise gave me was that I knew the locations of the sets I would be working on, so I had in my mind very clear images of where I would be shooting the actors. I knew what was possible and not possible. For example, I watched the carpenters building the sets for the Cheetah strip club because they were working in the studio next to me. I saw how they did it and I knew exactly where I needed my camera setups. I would know the lights already, more or less, and I would know where the poles for the pole dance were. The construction of the whole thing would be clear to me, so I could storyboard it carefully.

Sometimes, you prepare all your shots in advance and then discover that you can't shoot what you had imagined because the situation is against you. The corner you wanted is not on the left; it's on the right. You want to move the camera this way, but find out it has to go that way. If you start your storyboards three or four months before your shooting, there are plenty of things that will have to change on the set. But that was rarely the case with this movie. Each night, I would just eat something and sketch the scenes for the next day and enjoy myself.

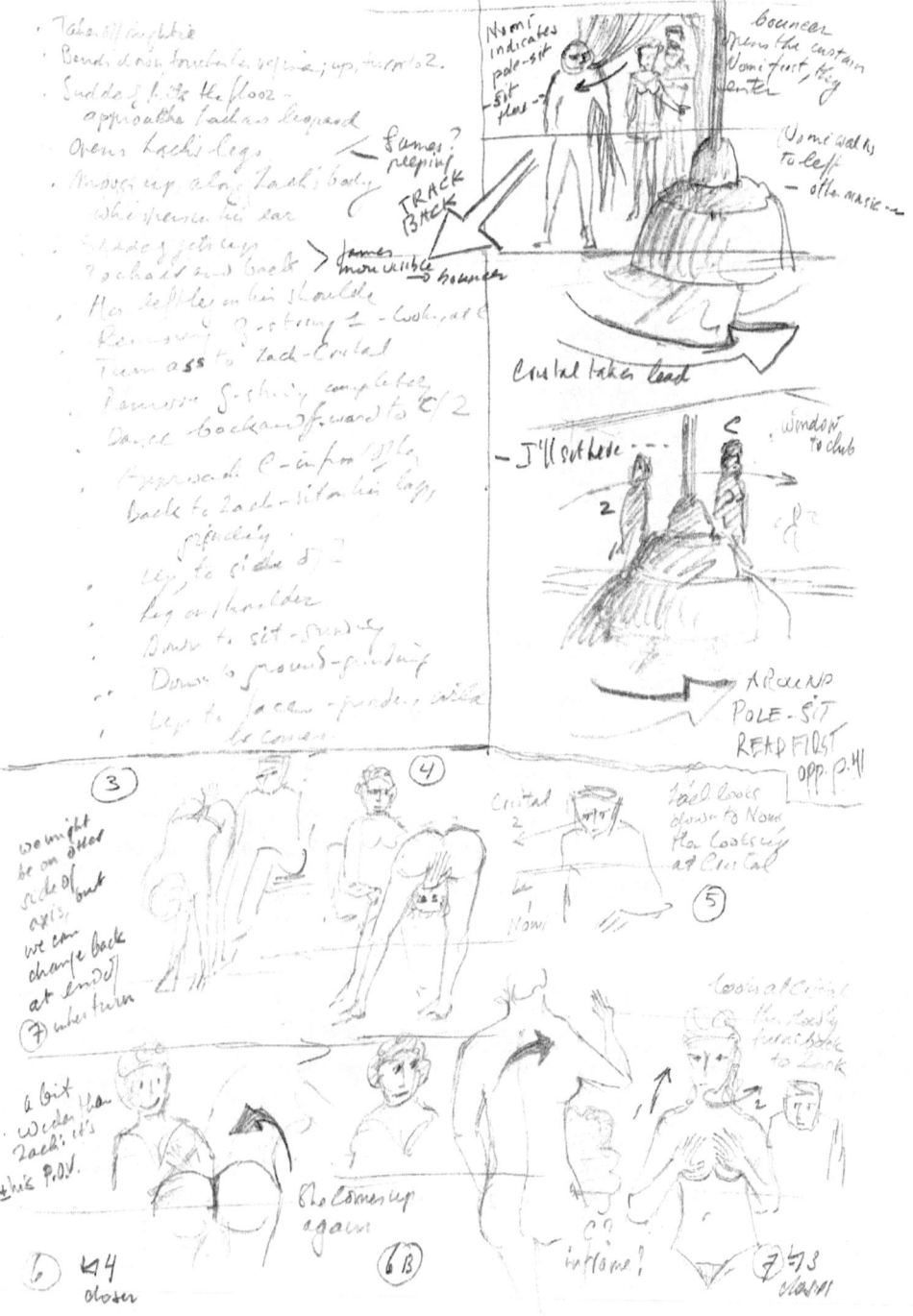

Verhoeven carefully storyboarded the action and camera angles for the climactic *Showgirls* striptease scene.

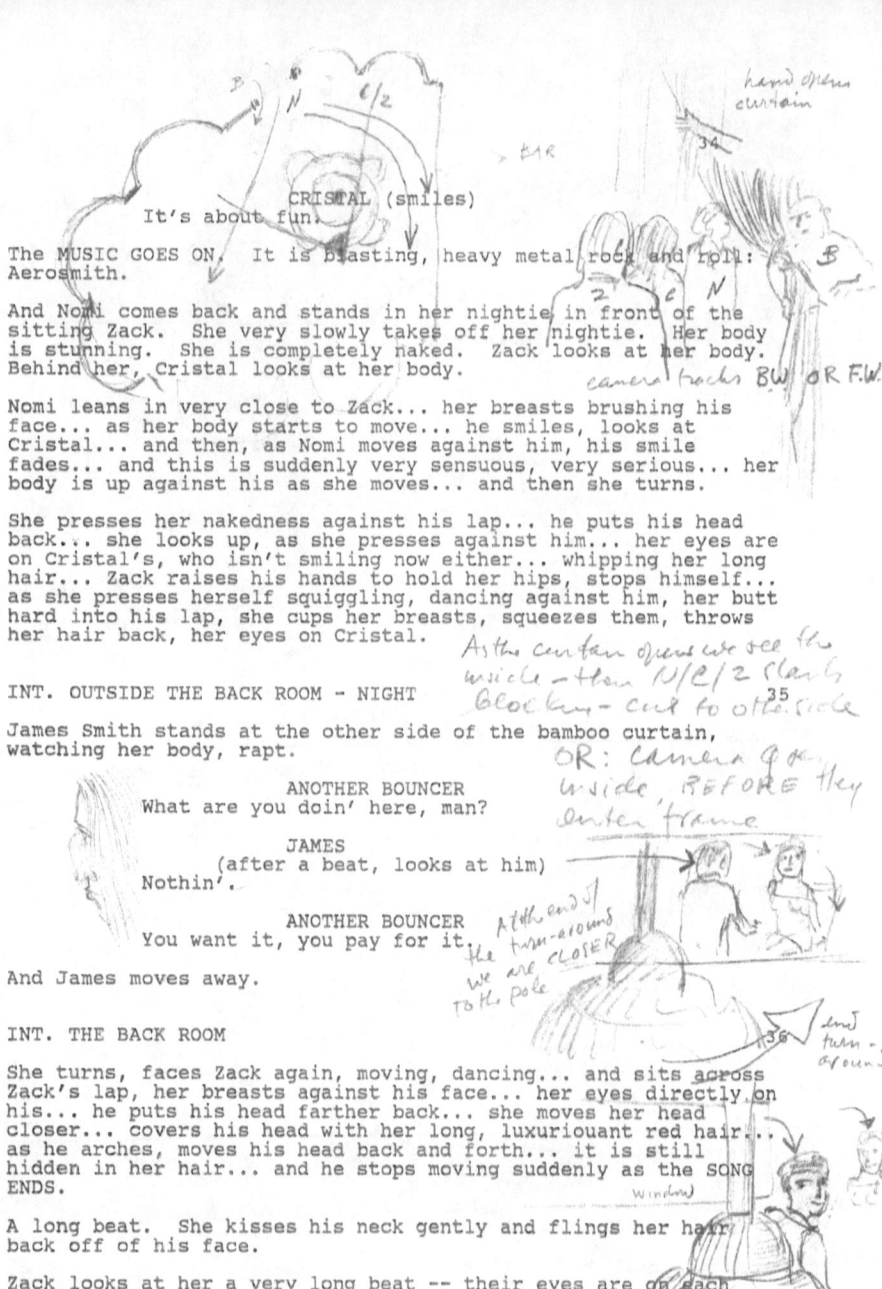

CRISTAL (smiles)
It's about fun.

The MUSIC GOES ON. It is blasting, heavy metal rock and roll: Aerosmith.

And Nomi comes back and stands in her nightie in front of the sitting Zack. She very slowly takes off her nightie. Her body is stunning. She is completely naked. Zack looks at her body. Behind her, Cristal looks at her body.

Nomi leans in very close to Zack... her breasts brushing his face... as her body starts to move... he smiles, looks at Cristal... and then, as Nomi moves against him, his smile fades... and this is suddenly very sensuous, very serious... her body is up against his as she moves... and then she turns.

She presses her nakedness against his lap... he puts his head back... she looks up, as she presses against him... her eyes are on Cristal's, who isn't smiling now either... whipping her long hair... Zack raises his hands to hold her hips, stops himself... as she presses herself squiggling, dancing against him, her butt hard into his lap, she cups her breasts, squeezes them, throws her hair back, her eyes on Cristal.

35   INT. OUTSIDE THE BACK ROOM - NIGHT

James Smith stands at the other side of the bamboo curtain, watching her body, rapt.

ANOTHER BOUNCER
What are you doin' here, man?

JAMES
(after a beat, looks at him)
Nothin'.

ANOTHER BOUNCER
You want it, you pay for it.

And James moves away.

36   INT. THE BACK ROOM

She turns, faces Zack again, moving, dancing... and sits across Zack's lap, her breasts against his face... her eyes directly on his... he puts his head farther back... she moves her head closer... covers his head with her long, luxuriouant red hair... as he arches, moves his head back and forth... it is still hidden in her hair... and he stops moving suddenly as the SONG ENDS.

A long beat. She kisses his neck gently and flings her hair back off of his face.

Zack looks at her a very long beat -- their eyes are on each other.

Verhoeven's last-minute storyboards for the climactic *Showgirls* striptease scene demonstrating the scripted love+power triangle between Nomi, Cristal, and Zack.

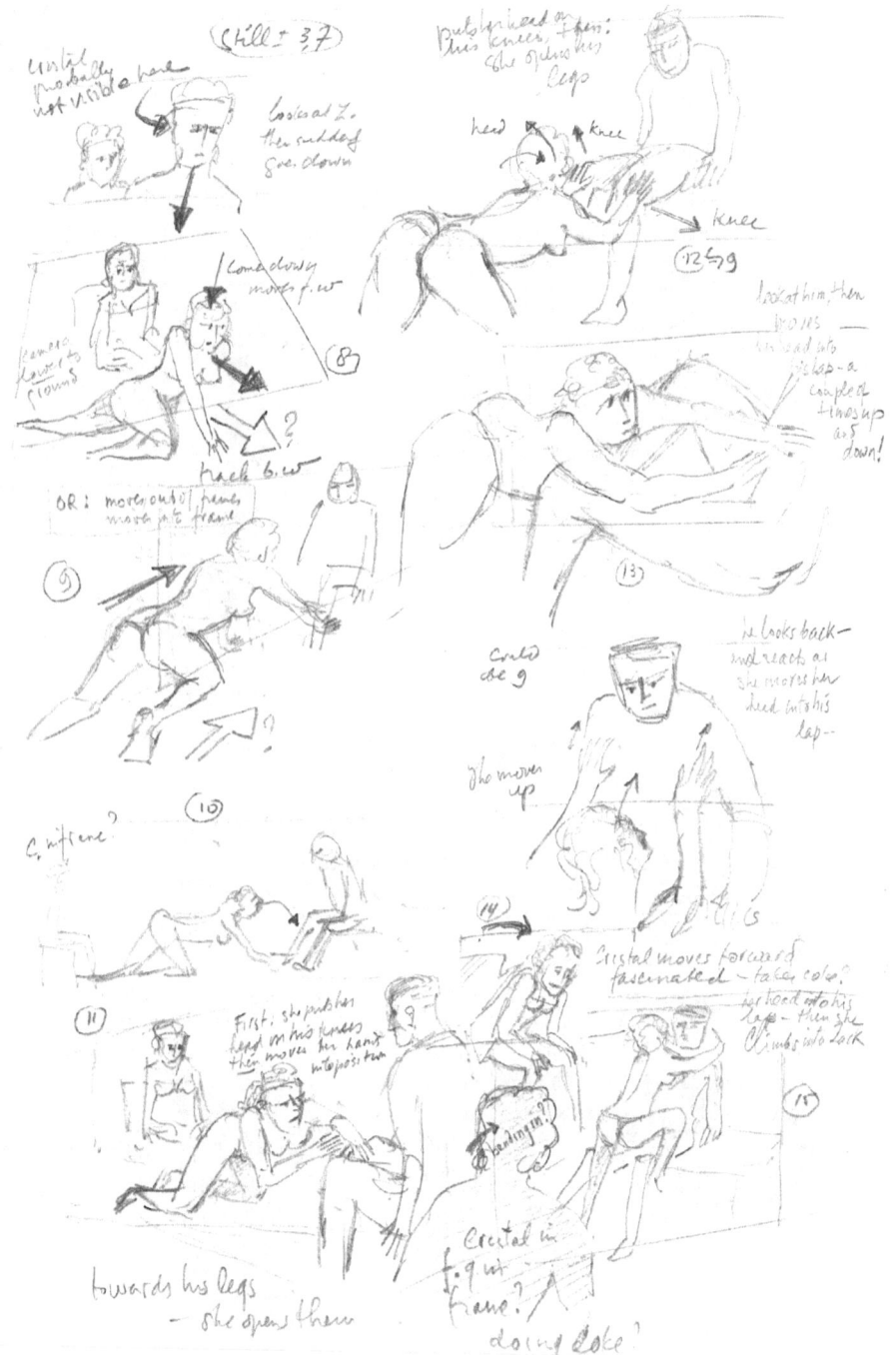

Cristal watches Nomi take command of the performance.

                    CRISTAL (behind them)
          Thank you.

And Nomi gets up and turns to her. Her face is expressionless
as she looks at Cristal, but there is a triumph in her eyes.
She's still completely naked.

Cristal opens her bag, counts out five one hundred dollar bills
and holds her hand out with the money. A beat as they look at
each other, and Nomi takes the money, reaches for her nightie,
and walks out the bamboo curtain.

Cristal and Zack look at each other a beat.

                    CRISTAL (smiles)
          It was fun, wasn't it?

                    ZACK (straight)
          You're such a bitch.

                    CRISTAL (smiles)
          But you love me. Can you walk?

He looks at her. And starts to get up, slowly.

37 INT. THE DRESSING ROOM - NIGHT   37

All the girls are getting dressed. Al comes in, puts his hand
out. Nomi peels two hundred dollars off, hands it to him. Her
face is expressionless.

                    AL (grins, to Nomi)
          Hey, you oughta go out and celebrate.

She doesn't even look at him.

                    DEE
          We can go over to my place and smoke
          some dope.

                    CARMI
          You still got that Thai stuff?

                    NADIA (Russian accent)
          Russia, end of day, salami and vodka.
          Here, marijuana. God bless America.

                    DEE
          Nomi. You wanna come?

                    NOMI
          Not me.

She looks very disturbed. She starts to head out.

Cristal spitefully pays Nomi when the striptease is over.

Christine strikes a boyish figure in *The Fourth Man* in low light, then steps over Gerard in her high heels.

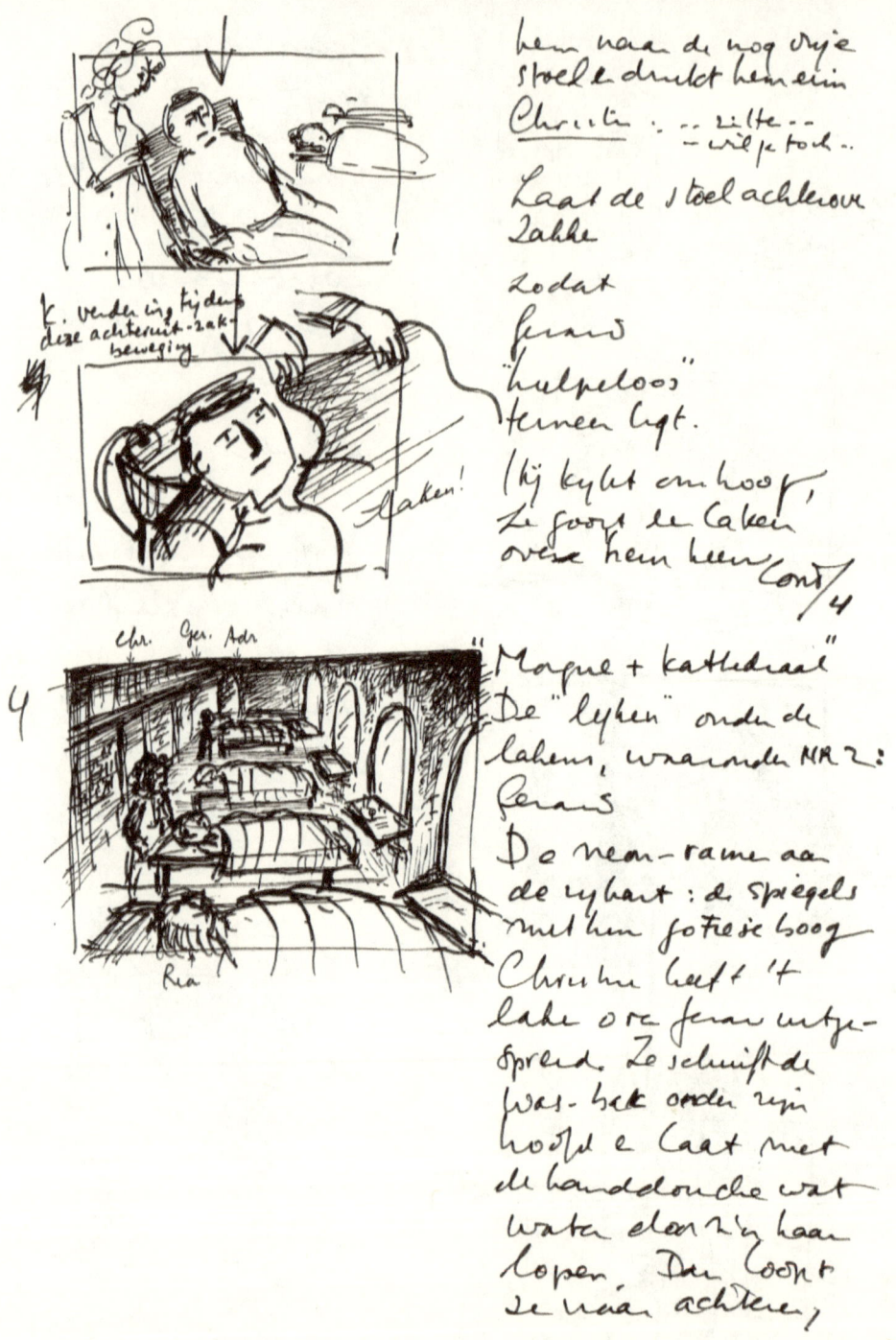

Customers lay out in Christine's salon in *The Fourth Man* as if in a "morgue" or "cathedral".

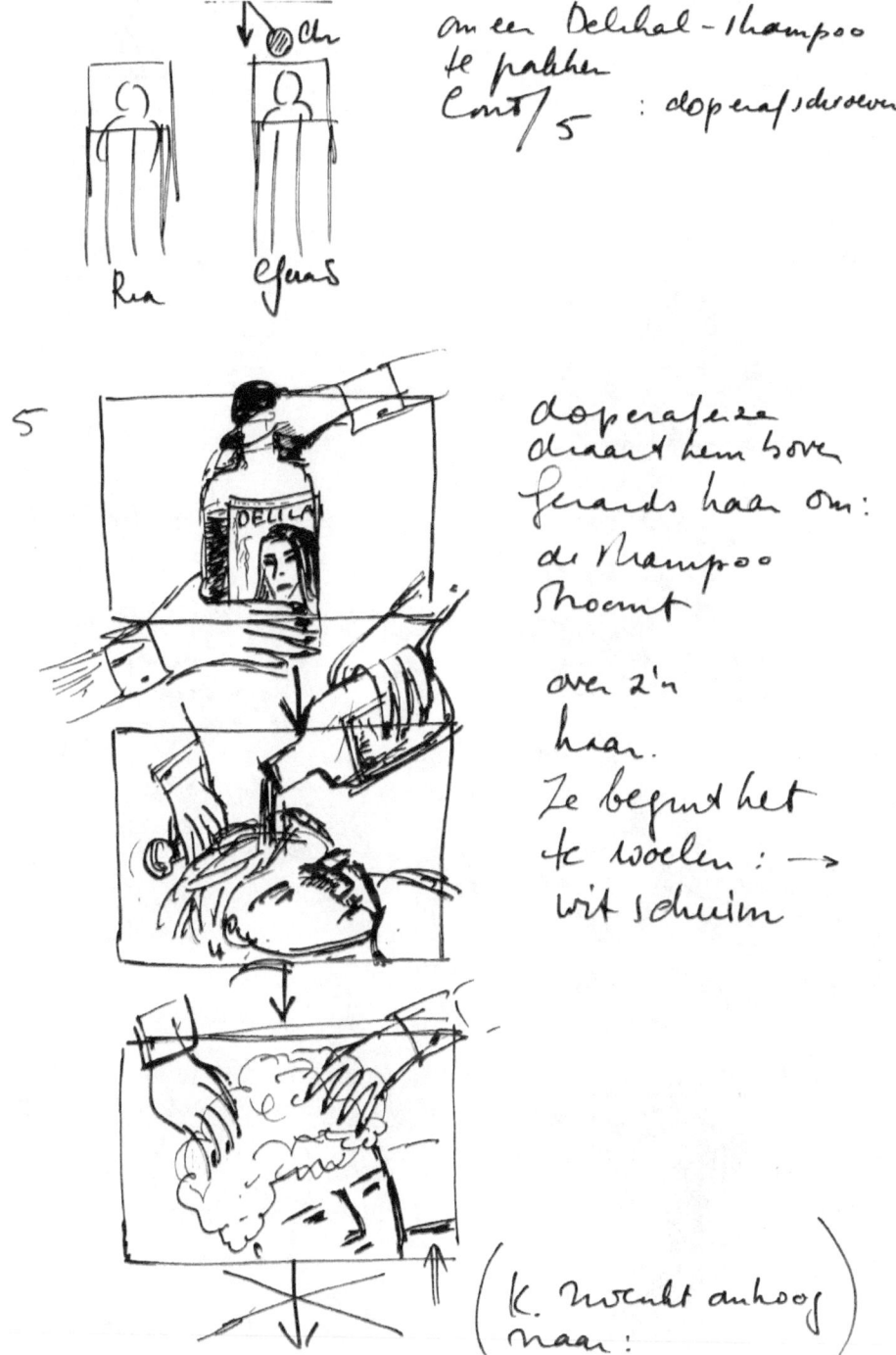

Christine washes Gerard's hair with her trademark "Delilah" shampoo.

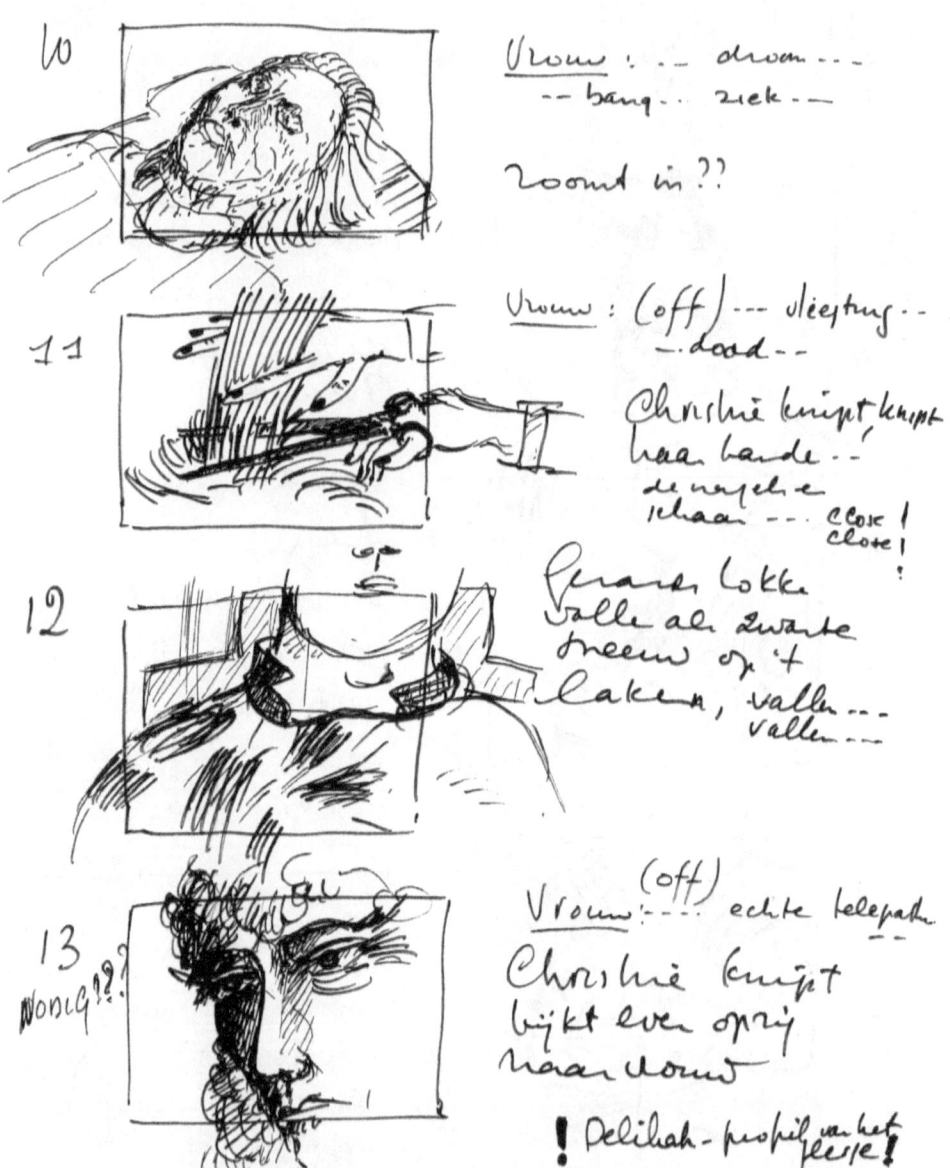

Christine cuts Gerard's hair while a mysterious woman in a clay mask (representing the Virgin Mary) relays a deadly premonition.

en 'kijkt' met haar watten- ogen
richting Gerard + Christie = föhn
(Houdt op met praten)

17

Ongeveer haar
"blik"-richting

18

18 = 16 - lim : de Vrouw neemt de watjes
van haar ogen

19 = 17 Christine schuift vóór Gerard
(knipt met vinger)

Christine: — Dochje Abie!
Op de achtergrond komt
Adrienne in beweging
Doorspelen Zie op de volgde bladzijde

20. Van de andere kant:
Christine manipuleert
zichzelf en haar mooie
kietje tussen Gerard + Vrouw
in...
Ze glimlacht lief/geil

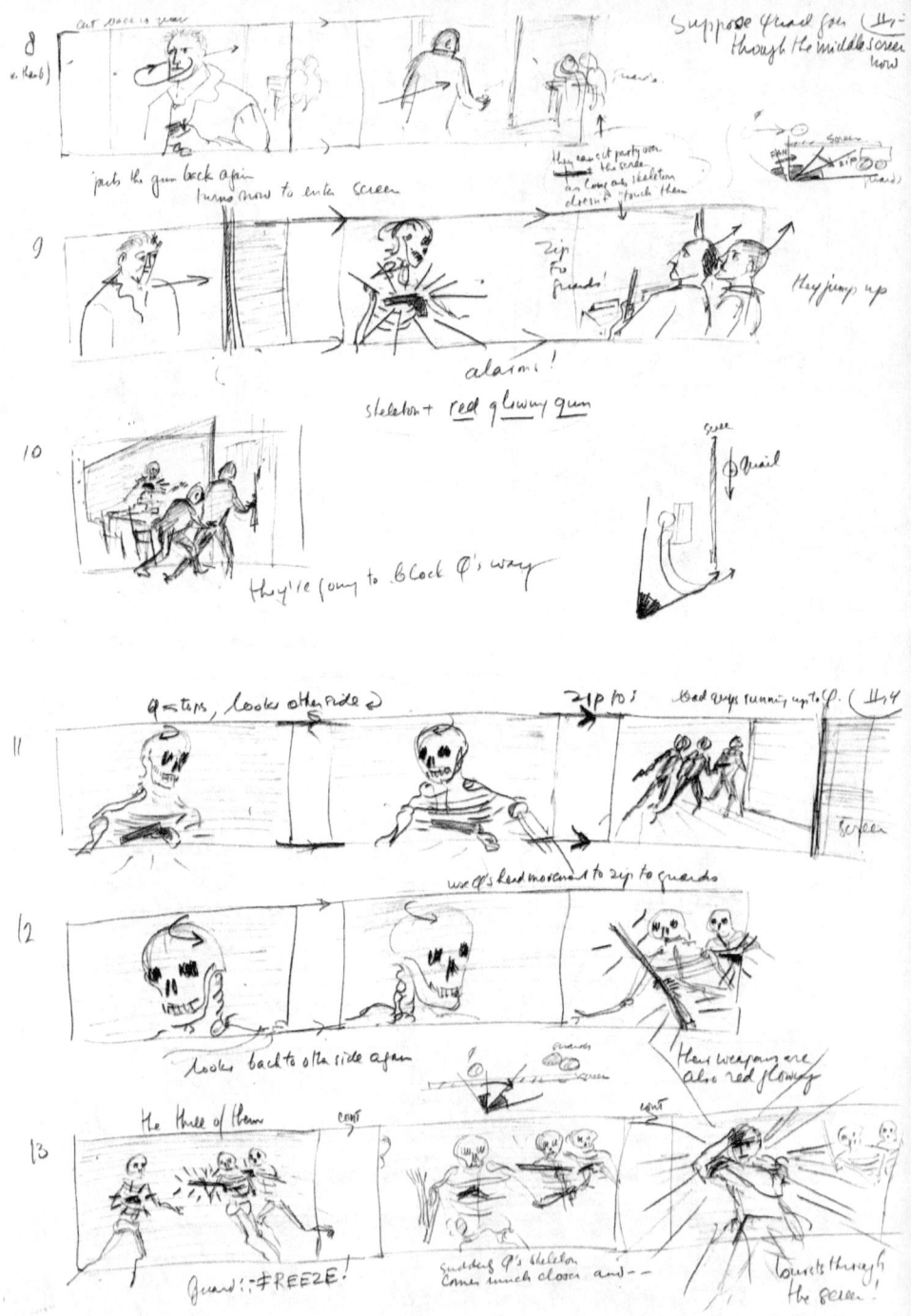

In *Total Recall*, Douglas Quaid runs through a security scanner that reveals him as a skeleton holding a "red glowing gun" (top). Quaid sets off the alarm, and when the guards chase after him, he bursts through the screen toward the audience (bottom).

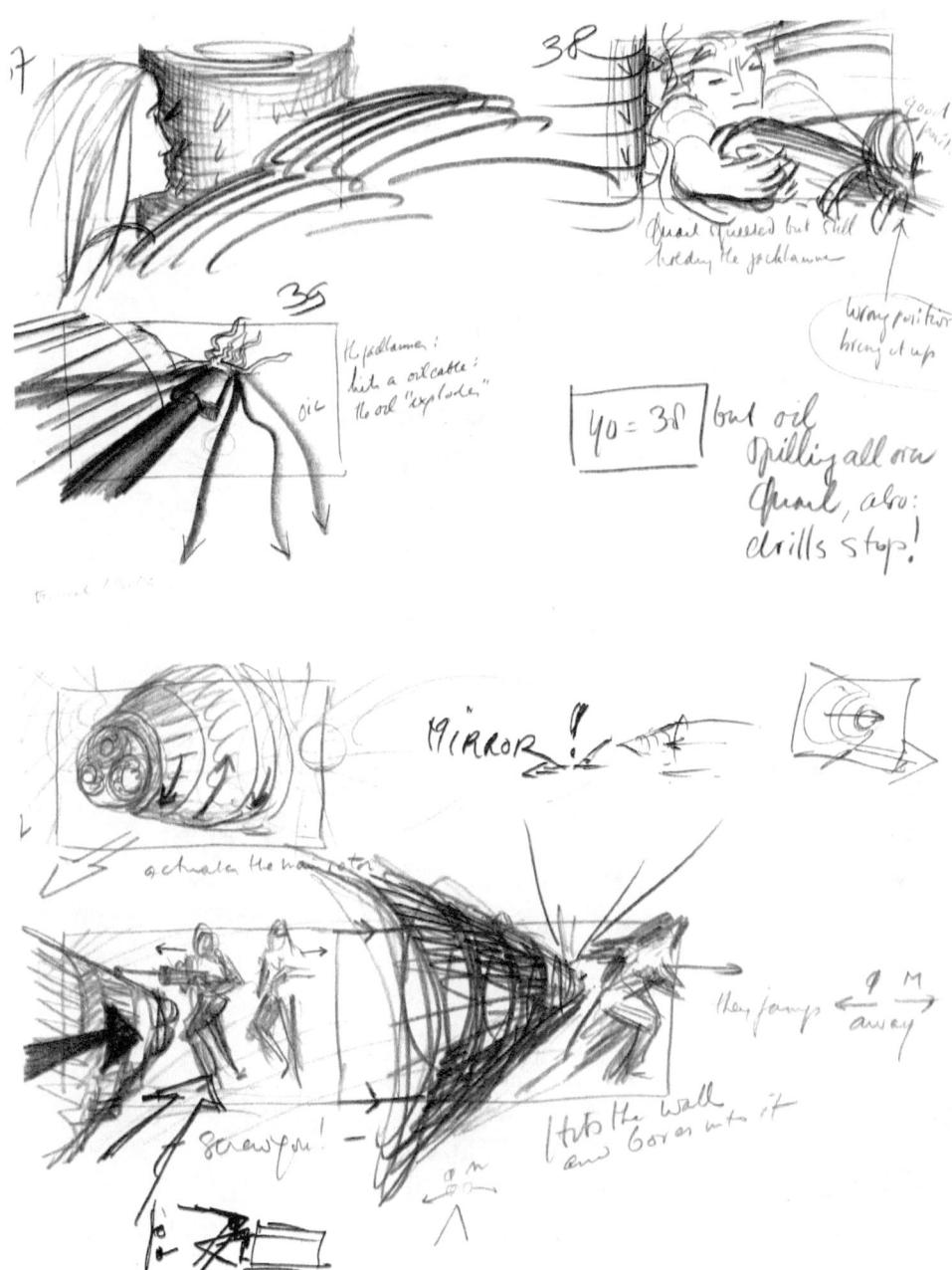

Trapped with Melina at a dead end in *Total Recall*, Quaid uses a power drill to break an "oil cable" and delay Benny's approaching tank (top). The giant drill on the tank reactivates but Quaid strikes out just in time, screaming at Benny, "Screw you!" (bottom).

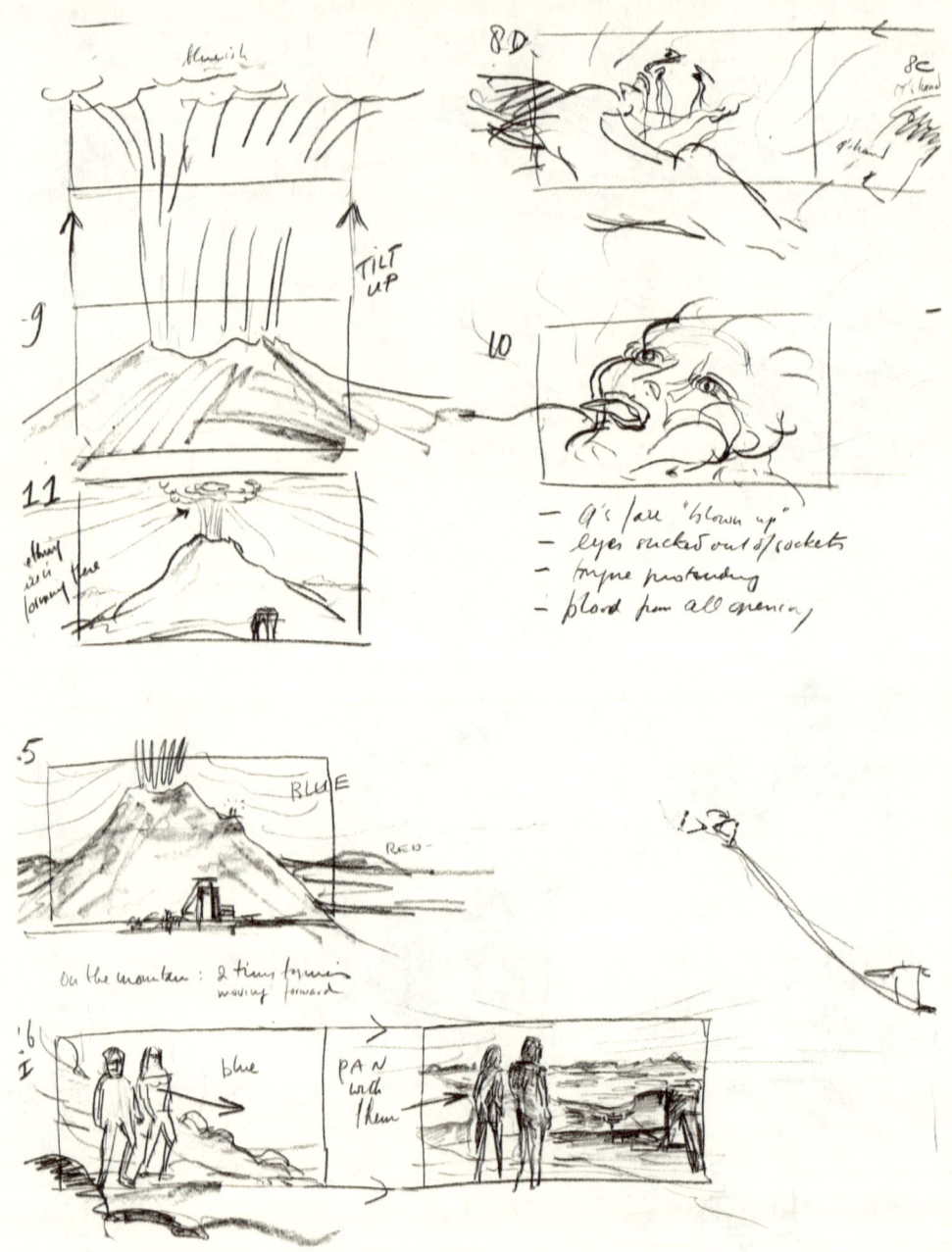

Quaid and Melina begin to suffer from asphyxiation on Mars without space suits (top). Air is finally released into the atmosphere and the couple admires the Martian landscape as it shifts from red to blue (bottom).

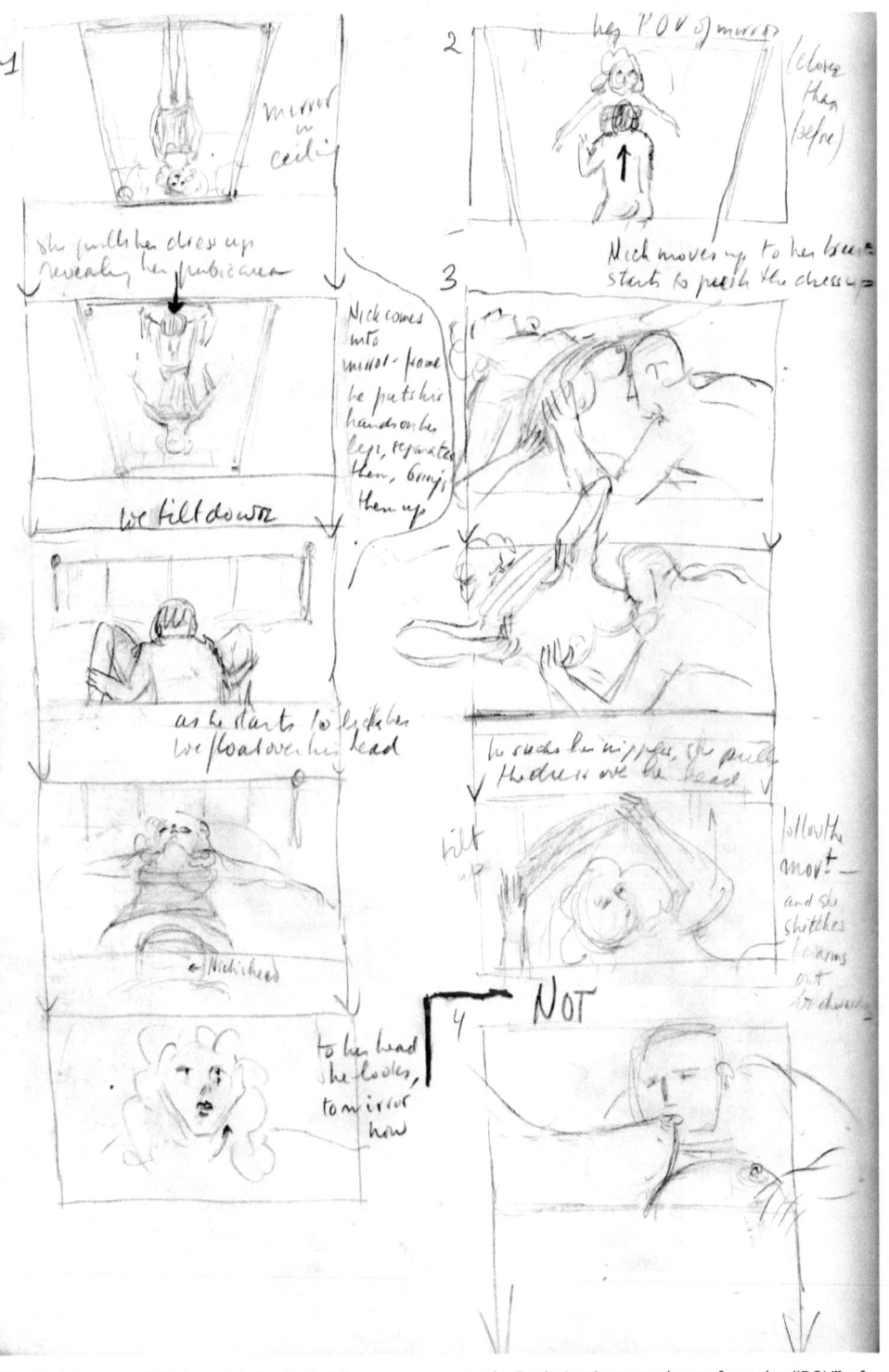

The first images of Nick and Catherine's infamous sex scene in *Basic Instinct* are shown from the "POV" of an overhead mirror...

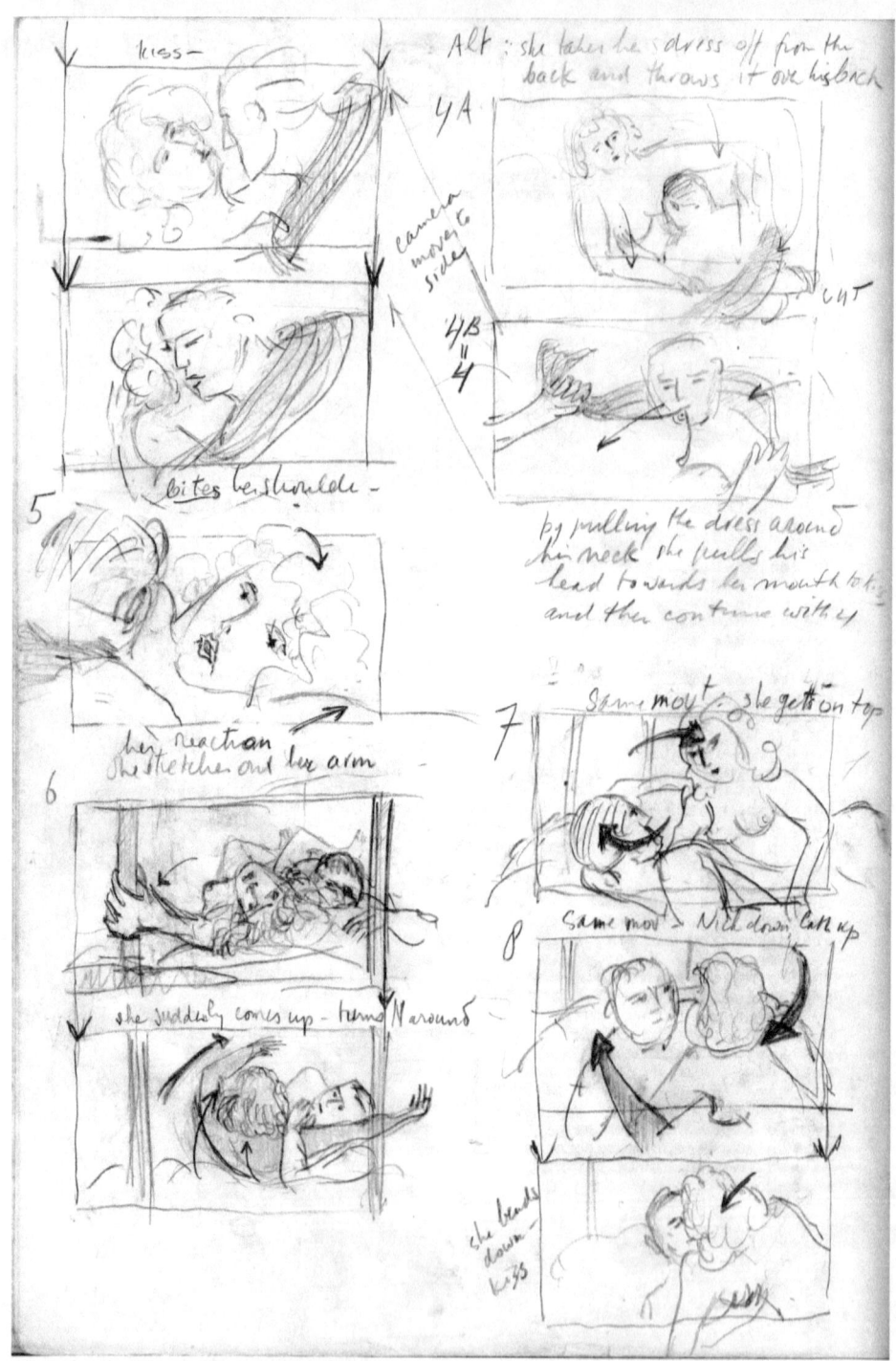

and depict certain acts that the MPAA deemed too explicit for an R-rating.

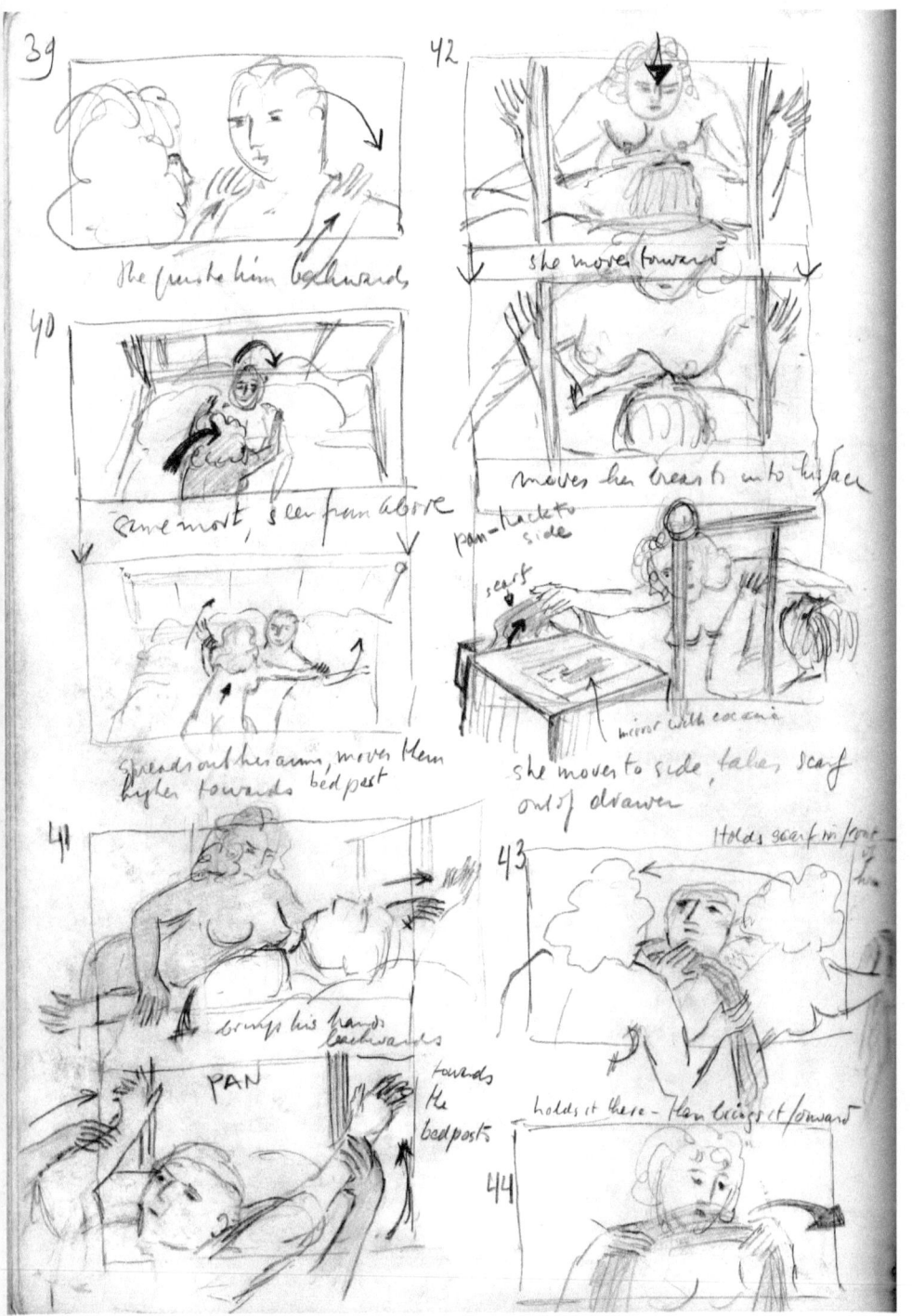

With a mound of cocaine on the side table, Catherine ties Nick to the bedpost . . .

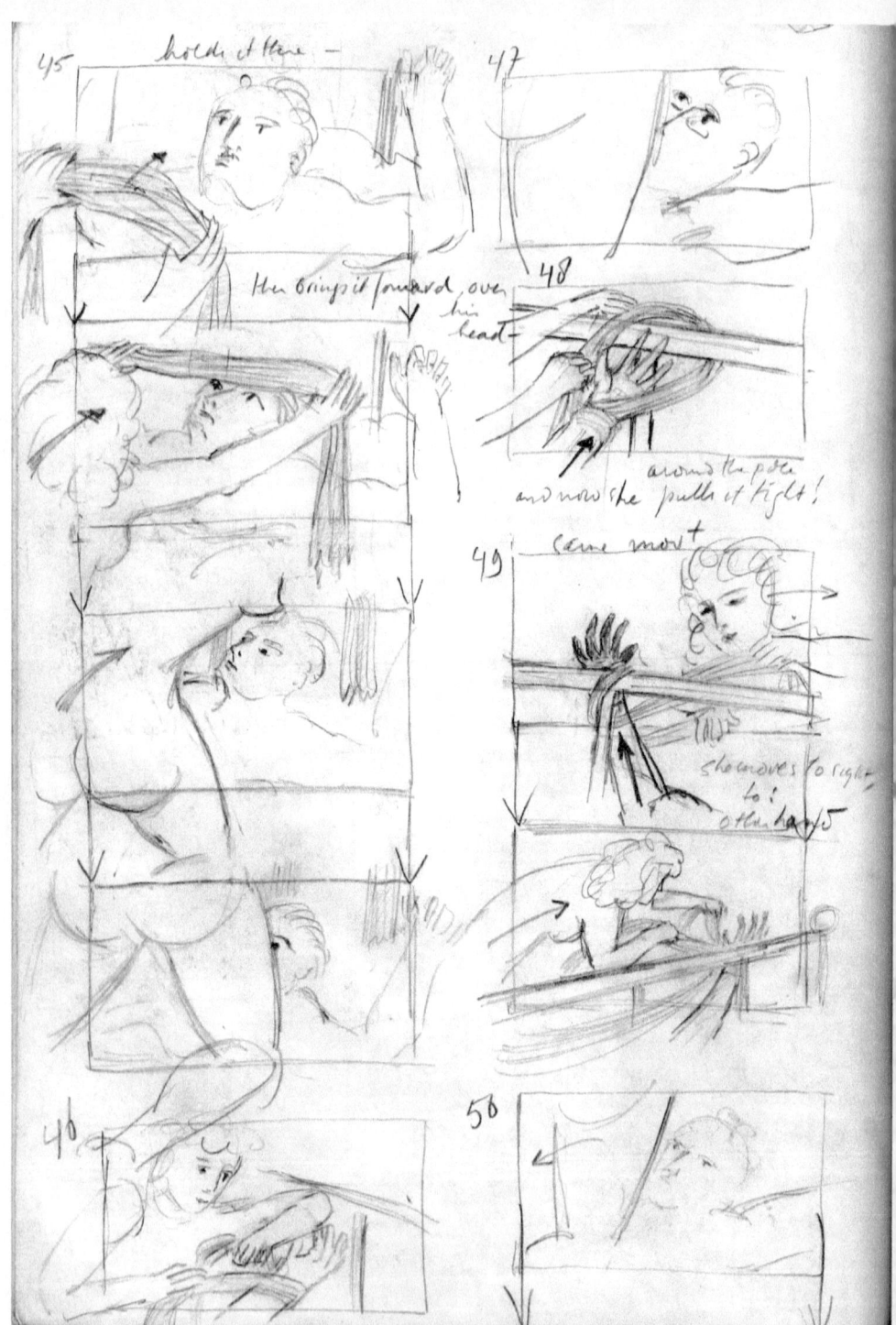

in an exact replica of the murder scene that opened the film.

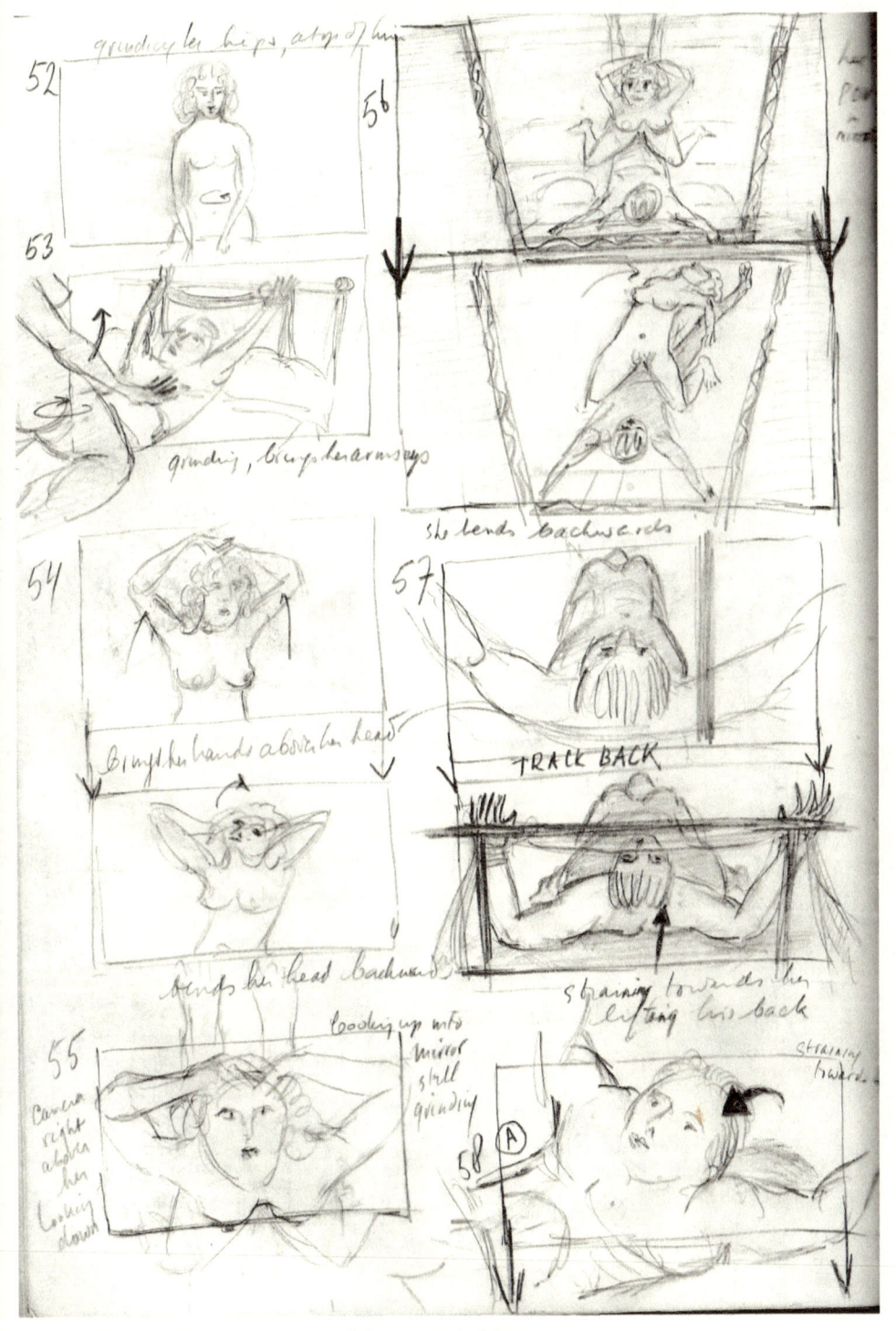

Verhoeven toys with the audience up until the very end of the scene, . . .

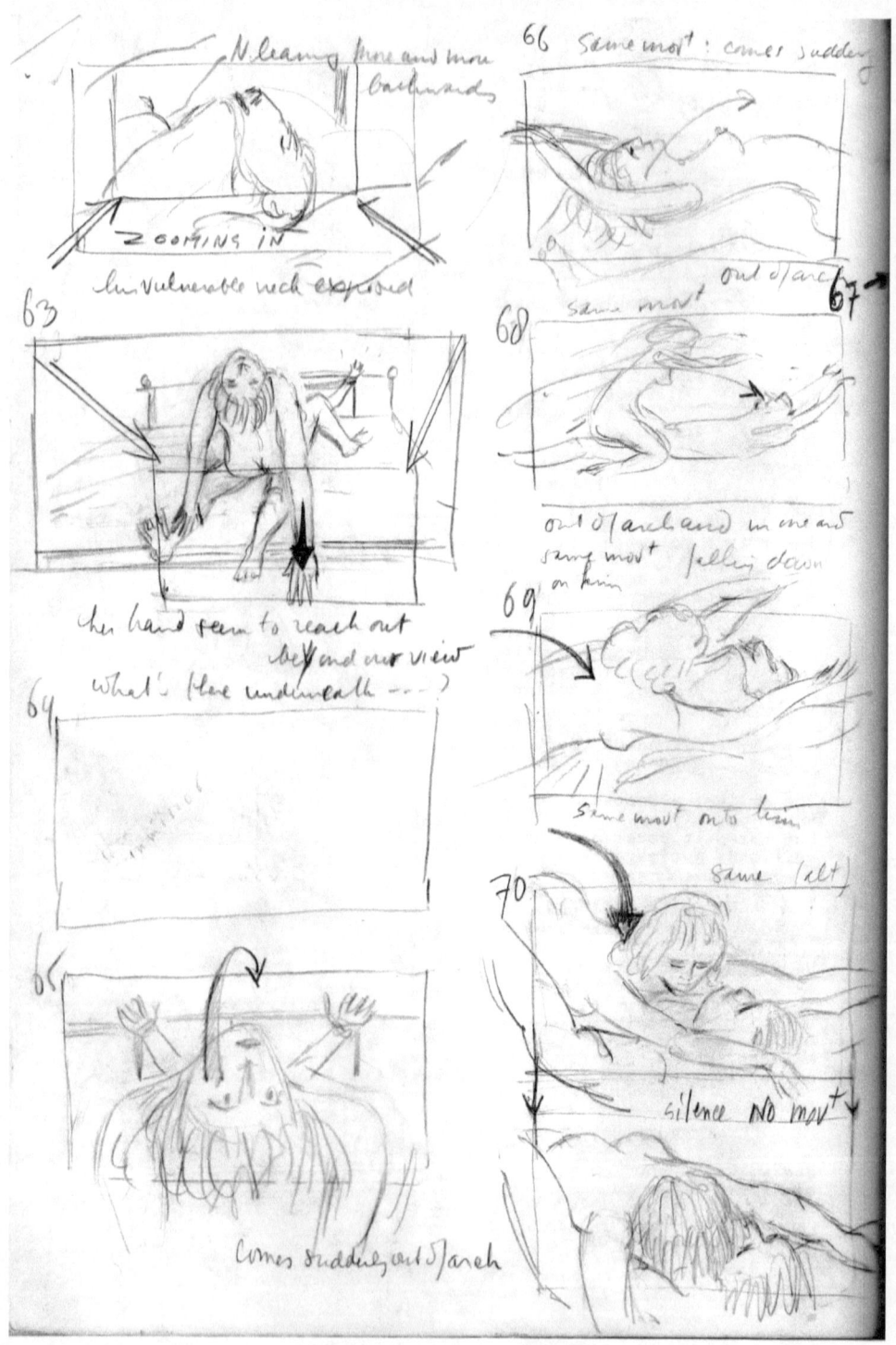

when Catherine appears to "reach out beyond our view" like the murderess, presumably for an ice pick, but comes up empty-handed.

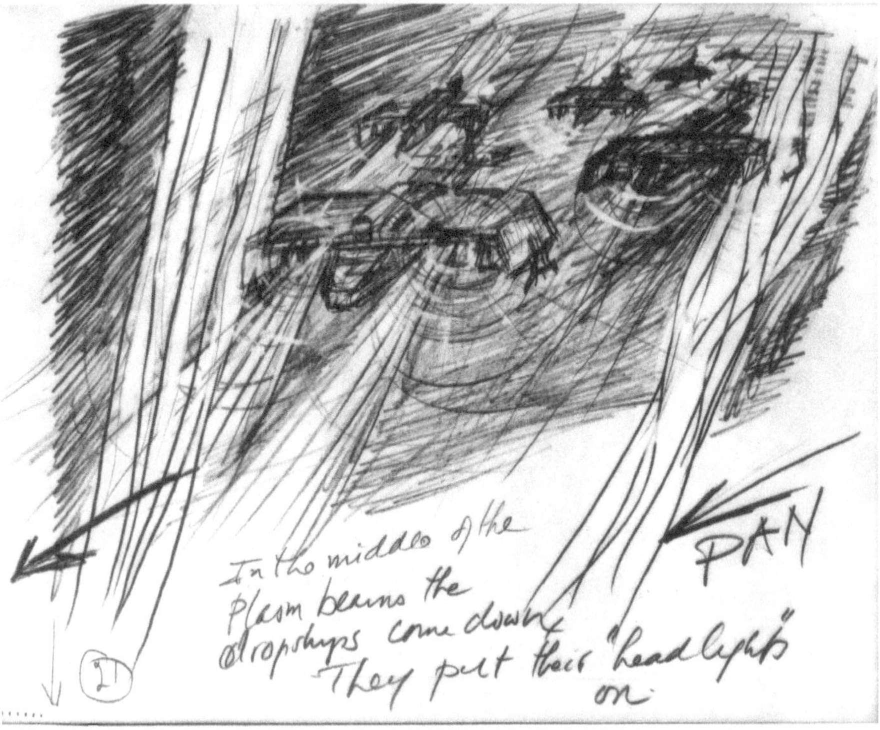

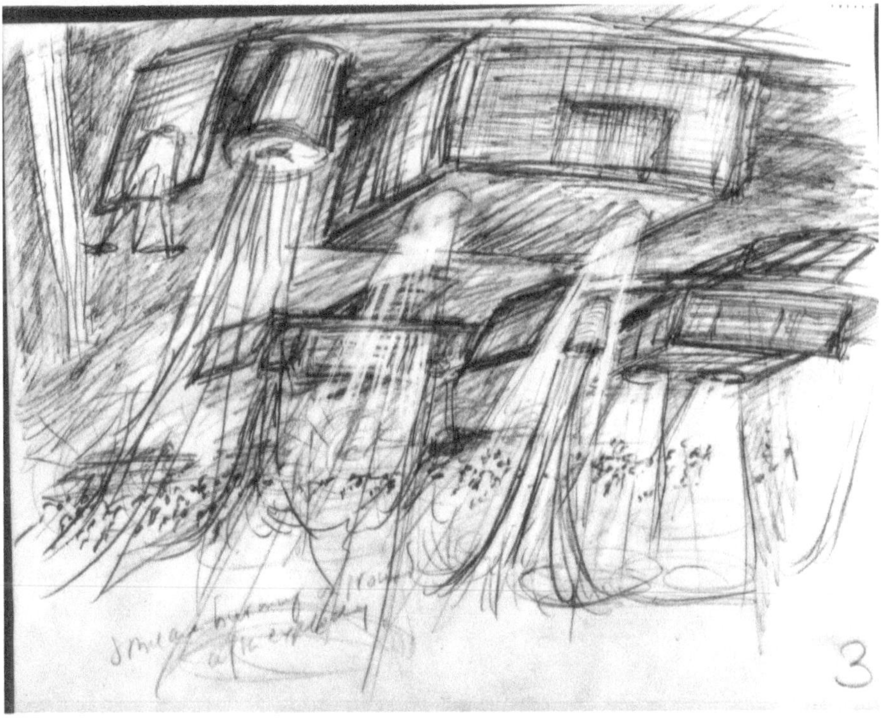

In the middle of the plasm beams the dropships come down. They put their "headlights" on.

Verhoeven's sketches of spacecraft in action for *Starship Troopers*.

The troopers round up on Klendathu in *Starship Troopers*.

Behind glaring spotlights, German soldiers in *Black Book* shoot at an ususpecting group of Jewish Dutch passengers, killing nearly everyone onboard the boat.

Rachel can be seen in the background diving into the water (bottom).

Multiple cameras cover Verhoeven's precise staging of the scene, in which our heroine's family and beau are ruthlessly killed.

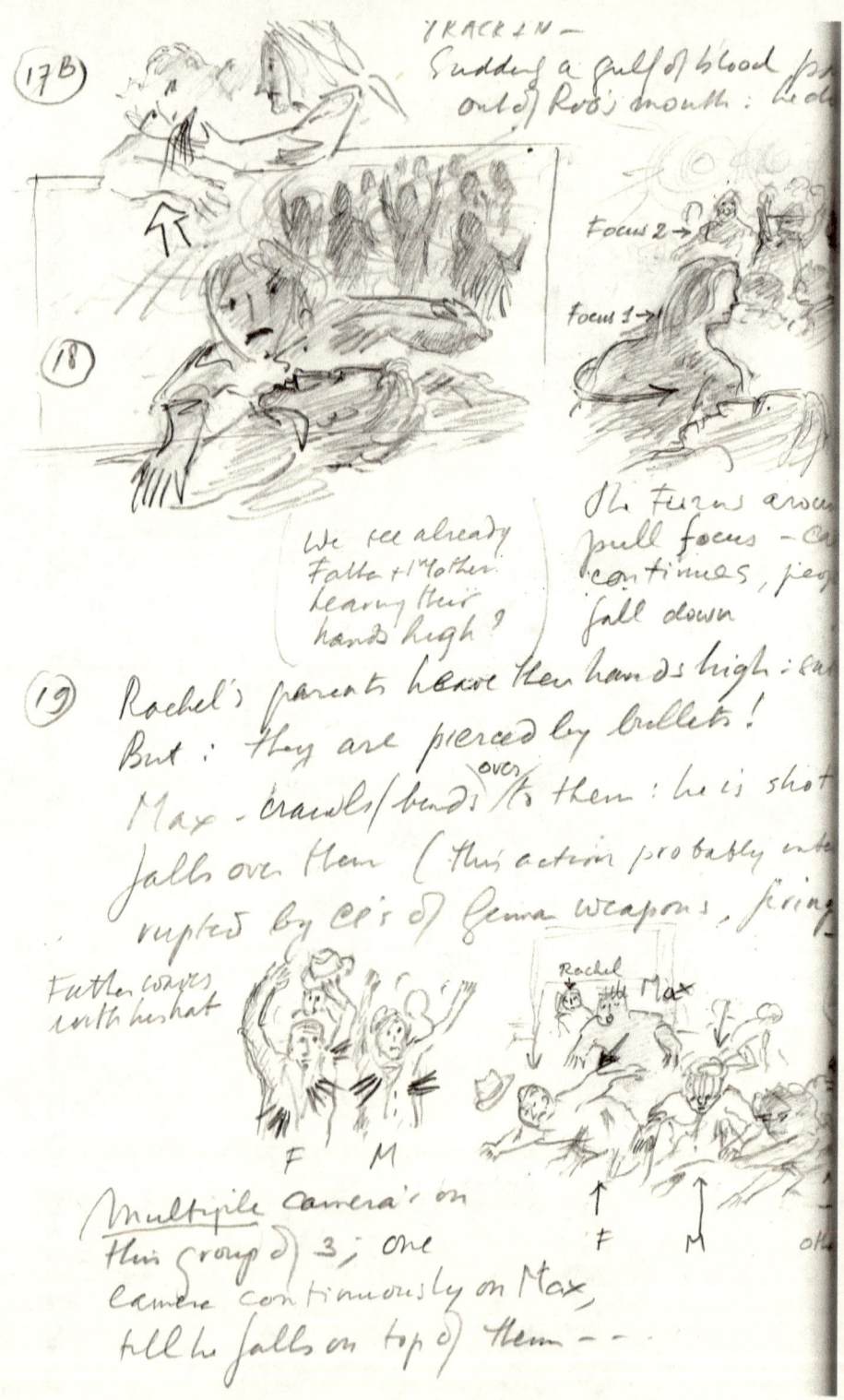

Arrows pointing to "F" and "M" in the bottom image indicate the movement of Rachel's parents.

The scene closes on alternating views of "our" boat and the German's (top); the former illuminated by moonlight after the spotlights shut off (bottom).

Working undercover for the Dutch resistance, Rachel/Ellis sings the song "Die fesche Lola" as Marlene Dietrich did in Joseph von Sternberg's *The Blue Angel*.

Ellis and her friend Ronnie use the opportunity to playfully kick out at the German officers.

The Showgirl Must Go On

Dennis Hensley / 1995

From *Detour*, Fall 1995. Reprinted with permission by Dennis Hensley.

I've just seen the appropriately named teaser reel for Paul Verhoeven's *Showgirls* and I'm recovering from the experience in a Sunset Boulevard cafe near the screening room. Though I'll eventually see the whole film—and believe me, I'm counting the minutes—for my first encounter with the film's star, Elizabeth Berkley, I'll have to make do with just the thirteen minutes of source material provided. But what a magnificent thirteen minutes they are. Based on these few stellar minutes, the twenty-two-year old also looks to be acting and dancing her ass off in the film. This, of course, I mean figuratively, for who wants to see a movie about a stripper with no ass?

Based on what I know about Hollywood and what I've just witnessed on screen, I'm half expecting Berkley to sulk in to see me in baggy sweats and no makeup, claim she didn't know what she was getting into, and get pissed off when I ask about the nude scenes.

What a refreshing surprise it is, then, when Berkley makes her entrance. Dressed to kill in a backless lace top, and shiny drawstring pants that reflect the light in all the right places, the 5'10" stunner appears to have left the straight-laced character she played on *Saved By the Bell* back in high school.

"I was just at the gym," she says breathlessly, "and the *Showgirls* publicist calls and says, 'Elizabeth, you're on Sunset Boulevard.' Did you see that over there? It's the billboard for *Showgirls*. So I said to my trainer, 'I'll be back, I just need to go take a drive,' so I drove up here and just stood there. I mean, it's like a dream come true."

"I can't see it through the tree," I complain.

"OK," she says. "Let's go on a field trip."

ELIZABETH BERKLEY: Now we're back in the restaurant, folks, and there's a giant-sized pole right by our table.

DENNIS HENSLEY: It's too big to do a pole dance with, isn't it?
EB: Yeah, it is. You can't grip it.

DH: What's the operative width?
EB: About half this. Something that your hand can almost go around. (*Laughs*) So, I'm a connoisseur now.

DH: Have you seen the finished film yet?
EB: Oh my God, I just saw it like a week ago. You have to understand, I've been working at this since I was like five years old so it was pretty overwhelming. I sat in the screening room by myself. The lights went down and I started to cry because it was just overwhelming at first. I'm such a perfectionist, but at a certain point, I was able to get lost in the story, which was a good sign to me. I really thought that I was watching another girl.

DH: So what's the story of *Showgirls*?
EB: It's about this young girl whose been dealt a really bad set of cards in life and she comes to Vegas to become a showgirl. Ultimately it's about moral choices, really, like how far would you go to get what you want, what would you give up for love. It's a very dark drama, but it's also entertaining because of the production numbers. I don't think there's ever been anything quite like it.

DH: What's your character's name?
EB: Nomi. It's spelled N-o-m-i but the way I've always thought of her is Know Me. She's not going to obey other people's rules. She'll stop at nothing to get what she wants. What drives her is her dancing. It's the one time that she feels the most alive.

DH: How much dance training did you have before this movie?
EB: Dancing has always been one of my biggest loves. I've always taken classes and people have always said to me, "Well, if you're an actress, why do you take dance class every day?" and now I'm saying to them, "Honey, this is what it was for, this movie right here."

DH: What did you think when you first read the script?
EB: I thought, "I have to do this." I mean, this role, I would kill for. It's very rare you read a script where the whole focus of the film is on a woman. Also, I'm so passionate about what I go after and I really felt a lot of connection with the character right away. I just knew I had to get in the room with Paul and show him what I can

do so that he could see because I really felt this strong connection. Plus it's a little scary, you know. I didn't become an actress to do things that are safe.

DH: Did you read any scenes and think, "I can't do that, there's no way they can get me to do that?"
EB: No, I didn't. I thought, "Oh, when can I do that?"

DH: It never crossed over the line for you?
EB: No. In the beginning, I was a little nervous about the nudity but after the first day that I did it, it was fine. Paul made me feel really safe. I knew I had to feel that trust with him otherwise half the things I had to do, I could not have done.

DH: Did you go to craft services naked?
EB: Yeah, everyone did. People would be sitting there, talking, eating bananas, smoking, whatever. The thing is, the way it was shot is so beautiful. Even though there are twenty one pretty much naked bodies on the stage it's not like you go, "Oh, breasts, breasts, breasts."

DH: There must have been a zillion horny extras wanting to appear in the club scenes.
EB: Uh-huh, just as there are guys that go to these strip clubs. Everyone goes in for a different reason. Like some go because it's a power trip. They can reject any girl they want and take any girl they want if they pay the money. The girls all work there for one reason, the cash.

DH: If you weren't an actress, would being a Vegas showgirl appeal to you as a dancer?
EB: My mind can't even go to thinking about my life without acting, to tell you the truth.

DH: Were you aware that the project existed before you auditioned for it?
EB: Yes. The year before I met Paul I saw an article in the trades that talked about Eszterhas selling the script and what it was about and I thought, "Oh my God, I have to get ahold of this script." Then they put it on hold for a year and in that time I was so curious about these strip clubs and lap dancing clubs that when I was in New York or Vegas I went to see what it was all about. I watched and talked to the girls but I never got up there. I think for a lot of them it's very hard to disconnect from what's happening and to not have anger towards men. Sometimes when I would leave there I would be sad.

DH: How many auditions did you have to go through before you got the role?
EB: Four. Plus I just had to get past my agents and people telling me, "They're definitely going to give this to a big name star."

DH: Wouldn't it be hard to find a name that can dance and that would be willing to do what the role required?
EB: Believe me, a lot of people wanted to kill for this. Everyone and their mother went in for this.

DH: I know. My mom didn't even get a callback.
EB: The fact is, they would have used a dance double, so the bottom line was the acting because she carries the movie.

DH: At what point did they ask to see you dance?
EB: The third audition was a dance audition and after that I went to Idaho to do this TV movie for Disney called *Cry of the White Wolf*.

DH: Is there any lap dancing in that movie?
EB: No, but I was practicing pole dancing in the woods in case I had to go back for another interview.

DH: Did Paul have to go to the studio and fight for you?
EB: No. He just said, "This is who I want." They really trust him. Look, this is the first director who in his contract, knowing that it's going to be NC-17, was able to release it as a wide release movie in like 1,000 or 1,500 theaters.

DH: Where are you from originally?
EB: Farmington Hills, Michigan. Everyone knows everyone. I went from kindergarten through high school with the same people. I finished up high school out here actually. I live with my parents out here.

DH: What do your parents think of *Showgirls*?
EB: They're excited. Matter of fact, I called my dad at work today and he's going to drive by to see the billboard. They're very supportive. They knew what it was before I did it.

DH: Did they come to the set?
EB: No. They're not stage parents. My mom saw the eight-minute trailer and loved it. She actually had a similar reaction to me. She saw someone else up there. I

mean, it's not gratuitous. The nudity is necessary and essential to the story. To portray her any other way would be a lie, you know. She's a stripper. You wear a G-string and five inch heels.

DH: Do you have brothers and sisters?
EB: I have a brother named Jason.

DH: Isn't it weird to imagine him watching you doing a lap dance?
EB: Oh my God. Well, he'll get turned on by the other girls in the movie. He'll be grossed out by me. His friends, who have seen me grow up, used to tease me about being flat-chested because I didn't develop until later in life—I was like seventeen—so they haven't seen me since then so they're going to be in for a surprise. And his friend said, "Okay, I don't have a lot of cash right now so I'm going to put $7.50 for a movie ticket in an envelope and save it for September 22nd."

DH: Did you get to keep any of the clothes?
EB: I'm going to get some of it, like these suede hip-hugger pants that lace up the front and of course, the S&M outfit with the thigh-high boots. Where I'll wear that, I have no idea.

DH: Did you ever get turned on while you were shooting?
EB: Oh yeah. Definitely. I can't tell you which scenes because it was pretty constant. I mean, I'm dancing to amazing music, Prince and Dave Stewart from the Eurhythmics, that's enough right there. The dancing scenes were a real turn on. The music in this movie really got me. I could hear it twenty-million times and it still gets me. It's all new and original in the movie. There's one song by Prince called, "Rip, Pop Go Da Zippa."

DH: Did you get to meet him?
EB: I met him by chance right there in Tower Records. I was walking down an aisle and he saw me and he went, "Nomi?" because they had sent him a tape of me. And I turned around and it was him.

DH: What did you say?
EB: I didn't know what to say, because I didn't know what to call him. So I told him how much I've loved dancing to his music.

A few weeks later, I see *Showgirls* in all its naked glory and I howl with laughter at a hundred or so things I don't think I'm meant to, I still find myself getting into the characters, appreciating the performances (particularly Berkley's and Gina

Gershon's) and want to know what's going to happen next. But then, I had a good time at Exit to Eden, so what does that tell you?

If I said I was upset or offended in any enduring way, I'd be lying. Color me screwy, but I'd rather see a movie that treats lap dancers like lap dancers than one that treats hookers like ingénues. Besides, I've always been a sucker for the unmitigated tackiness of Vegas. What's not to love about a film that appears to have been treated head-to-foot by a Ronco Be-Dazzler?

I talk to *Showgirls* director Paul Verhoeven a few days after I see his film, and despite the backlash I can feel brewing in the media, my thumb's still turned up. Fittingly, he calls just as I'm about to welcome guests to my annual Miss America party. Though I forget to ask, I have a hunch Verhoeven is in favor of keeping the bathing suit competition.

DH: Do you remember the first time you laid eyes on Elizabeth?
PAUL VERHOEVEN: Of course. She came into my office on the second day of the auditions and said, "Well you can stop looking because I am Nomi." Of course I was testing everybody in the Central United States that I could get to; actors that can dance or dancers that can act or strippers that can do both but after a certain amount of weeks, it was more and more clear that the surest choice would be Elizabeth.

DH: After seeing the film, it seems to me that you not only needed a girl who was pretty and talented, but one that was completely devoid of inhibitions.
PV: Yes. When I felt that she was confident in both acting and dancing, I started discussing what was necessary for the movie which was that she should not be inhibited by any of the scenes that were in the script, especially, the pole dance, lap dance and some of the more sexual scenes. But it turned out that she was extremely easy with all of that. She seemed to have no problem and I believed her and I was right.

DH: Were there ever times on the set that she balked?
PV: No. That never happened. Long before we started shooting I described the scenes and tried to prepare her for the fact that she had to face two or three hundred people being completely naked. Ultimately when it happened, she seemed to be prepared because she never was afraid of doing anything that was written in the script.

DH: Did her lack of inhibitions surprise you?
PV: Yes. Especially for an American woman. You would expect this attitude more from a European actress than an American one. Yeah, I was highly surprised, but

of course, it was great that she felt that way about her own sexuality or about her own body. I think she's very confident about how she looks and she seems to not be inhibited in any way. I've never seen her inhibited in any way throughout the process of shooting.

DH: Did you ask to see her body during casting?
PV: No. You could just tell it was hot? The way she was dressed, yes. I mean, she had a very flimsy dress on and I don't think she had any bra on so basically, you didn't need much imagination to check out if she would look good naked or not. And I asked her precisely if she had any scars or things that would be difficult, and nothing was there of that kind.

DH: It seemed that the film paralleled her own life in that the character does morally questionable things to be come a "star" and Elizabeth does what some people would consider morally questionable things in a film that could make her a star.
PV: Yes, it does. Basically, you could even argue at the end of the movie showing her on the road to Los Angeles is exactly what might happen when the movie comes out, isn't it? The character Nomi is driven by ambition, to a large degree, and Elizabeth is also well aware of the ambition in her life to get to some place.

DH: The ending seems ripe for a sequel. If the film hits, would you like to do one?
PV: I've never done one. I'm easily bored when I've done a certain kind of movie to do it again. The ending was more winking to the audience what the next step might be. I'm not sure really that any of us is really interested in continuing that story although I know that Joe Eszterhas in some interviews has said that the sequel will be called *Bimbos*. If I would do a sequel, I guess it would be about a girl making her way in Hollywood or it could be a movie about Marilyn Monroe. If you study the life of Monroe, then it's clear that the movie about her life in Los Angeles would probably be expressed the same as we are expressing in this movie about Vegas.

DH: Did you do anything wild or unconventional to coax a certain performance out her?
PV: Not really, no. I'm not that kind of director. I'm not very manipulative in trying to obtain goals. I'm much more into telling them exactly what I want and trying to describe it as precisely as possible. I'm not a director that gives them information that is A but means B. If I want B, I'll propose B. I'll try to clarify what B means and how it could be done. The only thing with Elizabeth is that sometimes she's so thrown into the part that she overachieves so I have to relax her more than anything else. Sometimes she would hang on to the original design

and choreography and needed some psychological guidance to loosen her up to say, "Forget what you learned, it's in your body now. Just give yourself over to the music and it will come." That is the only thing really where I would say that I did something psychological, but it was in all openness.

DH: What do you see for her future?

PV: The possibility to do other movies, I would say, and I think she's dying to do so. It depends a little bit how the movie is doing. If the movie does very well, then basically she will be a star but she will also have to carry the burden of being a star, which to a certain degree, is something that is enjoyable, but on the other hand, especially because it's put in such a sexual context, the movie might propel her into a direction that can be a burden as we all know about Marilyn Monroe. Of course, Monroe was a much more unbalanced personality than Elizabeth is, who has much more better support systems with her family and friends, so I think she is certainly much better prepared to deal with the fact that the attention would go to her for some time in a certain direction.

DH: What was it like meeting her parents?

PV: Very nice. Her mother seemed to be as open to the whole thing as Elizabeth herself. Her father, I saw only once on the set for a moment. It was in the disco so it was pretty much a normal scene. I think her mother might have been a little bit thrown off when she saw the first shots of Elizabeth on the tapes but never expressed that to me and always seemed to be extremely supportive and really, I think, had an attitude like, "Go for it. Let's just do it. This is something that is important. This is something that you can do. This is something that you have been dreaming of doing and now you should just do it." It's a little bit weird probably for parents to see their child in her full natural glory, but hers seem to be liberated enough to not worry too much about that really. I never got a feeling from her mother, who I met really several times, that there were any inhibitions from her side. It was like the inhibitions were left behind when she was growing up. I think she probably got an education that made this vision possible.

DH: In what ways was working with Elizabeth similar or different than working with Sharon Stone on *Basic Instinct*?

PV: With Elizabeth, in the beginning, it was more finding out who her character was and how she would react on direction and what you should say and what you shouldn't say and what would propel her in a good direction. With Sharon Stone, I knew much better of course when I did *Basic Instinct* how to approach her because I had worked with her in *Total Recall* and had my fights with Sharon already there as I had my fights with Sharon when I was doing *Basic Instinct*. It's a different situation because the relationship between me and Sharon was often more antagonistic that it ever was with Elizabeth.

DH: Did you ever fight with Elizabeth?
PV: Yeah. Sometimes I'm a little bit crude, you know. If she'd say, "Can I have thirty seconds of intro to the music?" I would say something like, "Okay, give her ten minutes." Which is kind of irritating to her. And then I'd feel bad and apologize. But I think we never got to any clash on any serious level, ever. While with Sharon doing *Basic Instinct*, there was an antagonism that certainly, in the second part of the movie, made the set a really tense place.

DH: What did you learn from your ratings battles on *Basic Instinct* that affected the making of *Showgirls*?
PV: Basically, that I felt very unhappy at the end of *Basic Instinct* when I thought that the movie was kind of perfect, at least in my eyes, and then I had to cut it down and tone it down to get an R rating which the studio required. It was like cutting your own flesh a little bit and I decided that if I would ever feel that another movie would require a real NC-17, that I would only do it on that condition that it could be given an NC-17. So when this project came along, it was clear to me that in that environment it would never be possible to tell that story as an R and I said to Joe then, "If you want me to direct that movie, you have to auction it as an NC-17" and so he did. And Carolco and later Chargeurs bought it and MGM-UA had the audacity to go for that kind of rating.

DH: Looks like there's no need to release a Director's Cut on video?
PV: No, there is not. There is no other version. There are no other scenes of any relevance. This is it. This will be the movie that goes to Europe and to whatever country. They might cut it themselves, but not me.

DH: Who do you think is the audience for this movie?
PV: I would say everybody over seventeen but I think young people would probably, I think, have a good time. I think that people that are older could really enjoy the dancing and perhaps even the sexual freedom of the movie. Because of the policy that MGM/UA set up, which is a little bit different than the way Joe Eszterhas has expressed it lately, we are of course, in a position where we have to enforce the NC-17. I mean, I think to a large degree it's possible to argue that a young woman of sixteen years old would have enough understanding of the world to see this, but we are now living in a situation where the rules are as such and I think that should be the rule for the moment.

DH: Seeing your movie, I felt, was like a way of rebelling against Bob Dole's idea of what we should watch. Did you intend it to serve as counter-programming in that way?
PV: Well, we didn't know that this thing would happen. The situation with Dole started to happen six or seven months ago when the movie was almost shot. But I think you could argue that Joe Eszterhas made this movie because he intuitively felt this kind of climate and felt that it would be interesting to put an alternative there. And I think it is an alternative, in so far as it says, if you are an adult, you should be able to see this and you might appreciate it. Instead of saying, like Bob Dole, that sexuality is a wrong thing and that basically seeing sexuality—let's forget about violence for a moment because that's such a different issue—that seeing sexuality would lead to depravity or moral decline which I strongly disagree with. I think that people seeing this movie will simply not go into moral decline because of seeing it.

DH: I enjoyed seeing a movie that didn't seem compromised. It seemed like one clear vision as opposed to something that had been tinkered and test screened and sanitized to death.
PV: It's not a top heavy movie at all. It's not trying to make a sexual statement. It just has a certain lightness and freedom in expressing itself in sexual or nudity terms which I feel is refreshing if you see how American filmmakers in general are forced to treat sexuality in their movies because they cannot show anything.

DH: How do you think this film will play in Europe?
PV: I'm sure that it will be much less provocative and much more based on the dancing and the music and the story and the characters than that they would be so much intrigued by the nudity which, I'm not saying is completely common in Europe, but it's a lot more acceptable.

DH: Was it a conscious decision to not have male nudity? I mean, would it have killed you to give a little dick?
PV: To be honest, I could not find a really good actor that wanted to do it. I wanted to show it at that moment that they go to the swimming pool because I felt that it would be natural. I'm sure I could have found somebody that wanted to do the nudity, but I could not find somebody that could do the acting and the nudity. Of course, Kyle is nude throughout the whole scene on the set and I thought that was already pretty audacious for an American actor to spend all night nude in front of a fifty or sixty-man crew. You could argue that male nudity in a sexual situation like that would lead to an erection anyhow and that's very difficult to show. I mean,

you could, but basically, it's a bit too much to ask from an actor to perform that right in front of the camera. I think it's not that much of an acting thing and as nobody wanted to do the nudity anyhow, it seemed to be a farfetched situation.

DH: Is it true that Gina Gershon bought you a lap dance?
PV: Yeah. She and Elizabeth sat on both sides of me while the woman was doing it so they both could see exactly what it was all about.

DH: Did you learn anything from it?
PV: I probably learned to be humble because you feel pretty silly if two women are looking at you while another woman tries to make you come. It was much more for them than for me. I didn't do it for myself because I had been lap danced before in the same club when we started to do our research. The natural reaction would be for me to say, "I'm not going to do that," but I felt that it would be unfair to not stand in for two or three minutes when they were supposed to start doing this for days.

DH: If the man doesn't climax, when does the lap dance end?
PV: When the song's done. You don't get a second chance unless you pay another thirty or forty dollars. I think it might be rare that you would really come so easily, you know. (*Laughs*) You might have to spend a little bit more money to get to that point.

DH: What do you make of these rumors that you and Elizabeth are having an affair?
PV: That started from the beginning because of the way that I behave on the set. Normally, I'm a director that when somebody is upset about something, especially if it would be a female, I would just put my arms around them and just try to console them in a very nice and warm way. Of course, if you do that on the set with a naked woman it looks pretty strange and I think that the rumor probably started in Tahoe when there were probably five hundred people in the audience sitting there. My behavior might have been a little bit strange to them and I think that probably evoked the idea that there was something going on. I mean, it has been said before in the case of Sharon Stone and other actresses and basically as a rule I feel that if you have a sexual relationship with your actress, I feel that you cannot get to what you want in the movie. I think that's inhibiting. I think that what you feel in an artistic sexual way for your actress if you would consume that in bed then I think that you cannot portray it very well on the screen anymore. Because that interest seems to be consumed. I felt exactly the same with Sharon where I had the same kind of feeling of sexual attraction to as with Elizabeth,

but that if you give in and say, "Okay, let's do that in reality," then I think that there's no way that you get it on the screen. So in both cases, I felt that it should be something that is not consumed although it's clearly something you feel. Sure, I felt a strong attraction to both women. It certainly was there. But for me, it feels like if you go in that direction that you will never be able to transcend it and that's what you should do because it should not be in my personal life, it should be on the screen.

DH: When you meet actresses that you haven't worked with socially, how do they react to you?

PV: I think they see me probably as God and the devil, you know. That I'm the person that could do something special with them, but on the other hand ask them to do things that they might not be immediately willing to do. They have to be confident that everything you do with them is something that ultimately they won't regret. In the case of Sharon, I think she regretted that she had put her trust so much in me and herself at the moment where she opens her legs and she has no panties on. When it happened I think the relationship was such that she felt that it was okay to do so. I think five months later when she saw that scene in the presence of her friends, her manager and agents, she felt that the situation was so different that she could not accept her openness at the moment that it happened. I think it was feared that people would be abhorred by seeing that and that it would hurt her career. So she tried to make it undone and basically because I felt that it was very important and it had been discussed and she had seen it on the video and had accepted it that it would be too late now to go back. I felt that was not fair. I felt that it should not be taken out and I refused. Ultimately of course, you know that Sharon, after protesting and accusing me of having betrayed her, ultimately the last stand on that story of hers, in the last half year, is that she invented that scene. So now she tells everybody that it was her idea. After two years of accusing me that I betrayed her, she changes her tune and now it's suddenly her idea. I think she accepts it in her heart because she knows it's such a strong scene. I think that the strength of the scene is probably proven by the fact that so many people remember that shot of her, and any shot of her sitting in the white dress in the chair is symbolic for sexual power, isn't it?

DH: It was the defining moment of the movie.

PV: Yes, it was. It turned out to be. It was not when we shot it. I was never aware of that until the movie came out.

DH: When you meet men socially do they ever say like, "Hey, thanks dude. Keep it up."

PV: Some men do, but there are also men that are telling me that from a feminine point of view people could be really offended by this movie. I don't know if they think that for themselves or if they take that position for the sake of argument. I haven't gotten the feeling that there was a very strong difference between the opinion of men and women. But I hope it stays that way.

DH: One thing I enjoyed about talking to Elizabeth is that she's not at all coy or ashamed about her work in the movie.
PV: No, because I think that her convictions are real. When she told me that she would be able to handle it, it was based on something that's internally hers. That was not something that she faked to get the part. It was something that turned out to be the reality of her inner being and I think that's why she can talk about it and can defend it and strongly stand behind it. I think it's an essential thing to her. It's an inner truth of hers; that these things can be shown and that you can behave that way and that it is fine.

DH: Would you work with Elizabeth again?
PV: Yes. For sure. I think she's great. I had great time. I admire her. I like her. She has a great personality. She's very audacious. It's difficult to upset her. She's a very strong independent woman and it's fun to be with her in an artistic situation where you can really direct her as a director wants to direct actors so that the best things come out for both.

DH: Would you have cast Elizabeth if she wasn't a strong dancer and used a double for the dance scenes?
PV: No. The dancing was so much a part of the story that you could never have done that with a double like in *Flashdance* because you couldn't be close enough. Here you had to express a relationship on stage, where the psychology should be visible in the faces and in the dancing and that would never allow you to do stand-in work.

The next day, Elizabeth Berkley calls from a limo on her way to JFK airport. She's been in New York City to do more promotion for *Showgirls*, and if her lap dancing love-in with David Letterman is any indication, her enthusiasm for plugging the film show no signs of waning. Berkley gave good Letterman.

Not only did she take the uptight Midwesterner to "Lap Land," but she spoke out about herself and *Showgirls* with the kind of no-apologies bravado that I've decided, as Verhoeven said, can't be faked. And though David is famous for making pretty young things blush, this time it was he who was seeing red.

DH: What question are you the most tired of hearing?
EB: "Weren't you nervous about the nudity?" But I can understand why people ask that though, especially in America. When I was at the Cannes Film Festival that was never really a question that was asked because it's such a natural thing there. They kind of embrace that in movies.

DH: Did you know that in the press kit there's a picture of you actually licking the pole. Can't wait to see that turn up in *USA Today*.
EB: It's classic, isn't it. It's funny because that came literally out of the moment. I mean, how could you choreograph a tongue lick?

DH: If you weren't in this movie and went to see it, what would you think about the way young women are portrayed in it?
EB: One of the things I like is that the women in the film are definitely in their power. They're in control of their destiny and making their own choices. I think that that's really important to show, especially, within Nomi's character, this woman who's on this discovery of her self worth and knowing that she's enough and kind of tested with the questions of "How far would you go to get what you want? What part of your soul would you sacrifice to get what you want?" I think these are important issues and I think it's exciting that it's explored in a very sexually charged place.

DH: Do you wonder if *Showgirls* is going to do for you what *Basic Instinct* did for Sharon Stone?
EB: People have asked me that. The thing that I would love from it is this is my beginning as a feature actress and I hope that people really love my work in it. Hopefully, it will open a lot of opportunities. It already has. Since I completed the film, I've had a few meetings and some offers that were really lucrative but I want to make smart choices about my next thing. I'm not saying, "Oh I won't play sexy" because sexuality can be explored different ways. It just depends on the script, the directors, the character, the other actors. I'm also going to college. I'm a sophomore English Literature major at a major university. I'm going to have to take this so it's going to take me a long time to graduate but that's okay.

DH: Have you suspected that some male producers and directors called in so they could "check out the chick from *Showgirls*"?
EB: If someone wants to meet me because they're curious about *Showgirls* or whatever, that's fine. I don't let people take advantage of me. I can see through that when that's happening. Some men are curious just because it's a young pretty girl,

maybe more so with this type of movie, but that's okay. I mean, if they're curious, that's good. Let people be curious.

DH: Joe Eszterhas has come out and said that young women should do what they have to do to see this movie because it speaks to them. What do you think this movie says to young women?
EB: I think it's like an everybody kind of a movie, but for some women I think that the message would be that it's great to have goals and you should go after them and not sacrifice yourself along the way.

DH: Are you prepared for the backlash if, when this comes out, people argue that it's exploiting women?
EB: Well, here's the thing. First of all, I'm a very strong woman. I go after what I want, you know. Paul, in his films, portrays women only in their power. I mean, they're not victims. Look at Sharon Stone in *Basic Instinct*. No one can say she's a victim. Nomi Malone, my character, is not a victim. The film itself explores the exploitation that goes on in Vegas which is a reality there, believe me. I talked to showgirls and the things that happen in the film are things that happen to them throughout their careers. Because it is provocative, this kind of movie will evoke a strong reaction.

DH: And you're prepared for that?
EB: Yeah. I mean, I don't do things just to get a reaction but I know that it definitely will get a strong reaction, especially with what's going on right now in the political world, but the reality is these strip clubs are popping up all over the world now. These lap dance clubs are part of the sexual culture of the 90's.

DH: What was Joe Eszterhas like?
EB: He's very intense, really wonderful. First of all, I went up to him and said, "I just want to thank you for creating this woman."

DH: Was the invasion of the *Showgirls* cast and crew big news in Vegas?
EB: Well, we were there and so was *Casino* at the same time.

DH: Did you meet Sharon Stone?
EB: Not while we were filming, but I've met her before. We had the same acting teacher, Roy London, who passed away two years ago. He was unbelievable. He was one of the biggest nurturing forces in my life.

DH: You still live with your parents, right?
EB: Yeah. I do my own thing. There's a lot of mutual respect in my family and it's like I have complete freedom. If I didn't, I wouldn't be there. It's great because I can go upstairs and have a lot of love around me.

DH: Was it tricky introducing them to Paul Verhoeven?
EB: No, it wasn't at all. Are you kidding? Here, I've been working at this my whole life and here's someone who believes in me and gave me a big shot. My parents think he's wonderful.

DH: How do you feel about the rumors that you and Paul are having an affair?
EB: First of all, it's not true. I mean, I love him. We have a wonderful artistic and professional relationship and the thing of it is, it's the nature of the movie. The nature of the movie causes people's fantasies to go kind of wild. They want to think that things went beyond the work.

DH: Did it hurt having the rhinestones removed from your nipples?
EB: Gina put rhinestones on her nipples. I didn't.

DH: Were the women in the film curious about each other's nipples? It seemed to me like every size, shape and color was represented.
EB: Definitely. That's the beauty of it. You look on the stage, everyone's bodies are so different. It's not like they all went for a certain type. It was kind of celebrating the human body in an artistic way. I remember running toward one of my partners and doing a high kick where I put it on his shoulder and do like a back bend and I came up and he's like, "Wow, that looks great!" Everyone was just complimenting each other.

DH: Have people been telling you, "Your life is going to change—are you ready?"
EB: I try not to have any expectation of what will be. One thing I am prepared to do is continue working. That's what makes me happy.

DH: What's your fantasy scenario for *Showgirls 2*?
EB: Maybe Nomi's hitchhiking into L.A. and Paul Verhoeven picks her up and wants to put her a starring role in his next movie.

Dreams of War

Bill Warren / 1997

From *Starlog*, December, 1997. Reprinted by permission of the publisher.

"I read science fiction when I was younger," says *Starship Troopers* director Paul Verhoeven. "Mostly comic books, at least what was available in Holland—*Flash Gordon* at that time. And I saw a lot of American science fiction movies. I saw movies about Tarzan, then I realized there were books about Tarzan, and I started to read those. Then, I realized the same writer [Edgar Rice Burroughs] had also done science fiction, so I read *A Princess of Mars*. But that was when I was very young, twelve or something. I *really* started to read science fiction when I was in my early twenties."

Those SF-reading years would have been when Verhoeven, born in 1938, was studying math and physics at the University of Leiden. He served for a time in the Royal Netherlands Navy, advancing to the rank of lieutenant. In the Navy, he began making films, documentaries on the service. After returning to civilian life, he immersed himself in filmmaking, shot more documentaries, and finally made fictional films for television. He also directed episodes of the Dutch series *Floris*, about a medieval knight, which starred Rutger Hauer.

"I didn't look at science fiction any more for a while, because I was really caught up in European culture, and also in the European kind of filmmaking, like Italian Neo-Realism and the French New Wave. That seemed to be a more appropriate way of doing movies—much closer to reality. It was only after coming to the United States that I felt this possibility that I had never really considered seriously: to do movies that were not close to reality. Most of my movies in Holland were taken from biographies or autobiographies, so they always had a kind of realistic content. It's only in the United States that I realized I could dream again."

And dream he has. When producer Jon Davison announced that Verhoeven had been chosen to direct the very American *RoboCop*, film fans were puzzled. Verhoeven? The man who had directed the realistic *Turkish Delight*, *Spetters*, and *Soldier of Orange*? And yet he turned out to be the right man for the job; *RoboCop* wasn't just a SF-action picture—though it's certainly that—but also a wry, cynical, yet affectionate comment on American society. Verhoeven followed that with *Total Recall* and *Basic Instinct*.

Verhoeven's decision to make his first US-made movie a science fiction film was not made just because he liked the material. "In the beginning, I felt [making a SF movie] would protect me better against my lack of knowledge about American society. I didn't go for films that would really be embedded in American culture, because I didn't know American culture very well. Making science fiction, where things are not so rigid and where your knowledge of society is replaced by your fantasy of society, was a good thing for me. *RoboCop* and *Total Recall* were both done because I thought that with science fiction, my lack of knowledge wouldn't show so much.

"I don't think I went to *Starship Troopers* because of that, though," Verhoeven admits. "This third movie is more a coincidence. It came from me being intrigued, talking about the script, and working together with Phil Tippett on creating another society and another race on a foreign planet. Those are basically what brought me to the project. Also, there are many of my childhood dreams in it. Science fiction is, to a degree, escapism: to go to places that you will never be able to go in your lifetime."

OFF TO WAR

Now the *RoboCop* team of Verhoeven, producer Davison, effects maestro Tippett, and writer Ed Neumeier have been reunited for *Starship Troopers*. "I was not even involved in the beginning," Verhoeven notes. But he had stayed friendly with Neumeier, who asked him to read his outline for a movie based on Robert A. Heinlein's SF classic. "Jon optioned that book because he felt it was close to something that he and Ed wanted to do anyhow," the director explains. "Then, using the book as a vertebrae for the movie, he started to develop an outline of about thirty pages. That was the first thing I read, and I got very intrigued about the possibilities. I thought it would be interesting to do a war movie like the ones made in the forties and the fifties, based on World War II. To do that kind of movie, to deal with the behavior of young soldiers, what they go through and how they get there, and to do that in a science fiction form with the enemy not being Japanese or Germans, but giant insects, was intriguing, and it would be politically completely correct to kill the enemy.

"I thought it would be combining many of my interests in life. I'm really interested in diaries of war, mostly the Second World War, of course, because I grew up in that period, and was living close by [the fighting] when I was a child in Holland. But it also had the SF elements, it would be about high school, it would be about boot camp. It would bring back memories of my childhood, my high school time or when I was drafted. It had many of these things that were happening to me when I was in my early twenties, and I thought a science fiction movie was a nice way to project the emotions of that time."

While there have been movies about space combat, and a few that include scenes of the military battling aliens, monsters and so forth, there are really very few full-scale SF war movies, particularly set in the future. So, *Starship Troopers* is breaking new ground. It also revives the idea of the "giant bug" movies of the 1950s, but puts the critters into an altogether new context—organized mass warfare. The movie actually has more scenes of battle than can be found in Heinlein's novel, which is more about the interior journey of Johnny Rico from a callow young man to a seasoned, expert warrior.

One of Verhoeven's most notable films from when he was still in Holland was *Soldier of Orange*, a powerful look at Dutch soldiers in WWII, starring Rutger Hauer. The director says that in some ways, *Starship Troopers* is similar to that 1979 film, "Only it's an American *Soldier of Orange*, where the enemy is not Germans, but giant insects. It has that idea; it's about young people, you meet a lot of them, and some of them survive while many of them die. That feeling of innocence, of being a young kid and thinking the world is wonderful and everything will go well, that feeling that is then destroyed by the cruelty of war was the idea that attracted me.

"But the real reason to do it, from an emotional and creative point-of-view, was the fact that I could re-establish my relationship with Phil Tippett, whom I had not worked with or seen very much after *RoboCop*. He's an extremely interesting artist. I always felt that we should find a project together, and this was the one."

Ever since they met in 1977 (and were married the same year), Tippett and his wife Jules Roman have been working closely together on all his projects, from *Piranha* through *Starship Troopers*; Verhoeven is also impressed by Roman. "She is doing a lot of the scheduling and logistical operations. They are like one body; one arm does this, the other does that. They both supervise this enormous group of people, more than a hundred when we were doing the movie. Some of them had never worked in this field at all, and didn't know much about computers. Phil and Jules did an excellent job of getting everything done in time and on the level we wanted it. I was very confident from the beginning that they could do that, although few could have done it so well in such a short time. The results are really good."

KNOW THE ENEMY

The Bugs represented the hardest aspect of the movie for Verhoeven. After all, he had to prepare and shoot a movie about warfare in which the enemy forces simply could not be on the set. In *Soldier of Orange*, for example, he says, "The enemy was real; they had personality; they were actors, and you could ask them to play the part. That is not the case here. These people are continuously fighting elements that are, in the story, right in front of them, but they never see on the set. They are all filled in later by the computer.

"It was pretty tough to get consistency in the [actors'] performances, to give them motivation—to be angry, sad, pleased or afraid based on a virtual enemy that they had to imagine. I was trying to help them by performing sometimes as a Bug; Phil did the same. He was running around with an assistant with two high poles in their hands, so the actors could get a feeling for the size and speed of these animals."

Verhoeven sighs. "What applied to the actors applied even more to *me*. I had to do my storyboarding based on the continuity of these insects which would be made later. We storyboarded all this very precisely, more than I've ever done for any movie in my life. We were sticking to the storyboards, because that was the only, shall we say, bible we had that would hopefully be so good that later when they would fill in the insects, there would be a consistency in the actors' performances and their positioning, in the display of action or whatever."

The director points out that there are important differences between an SF/war movie like *Starship Troopers* and an SF/horror movie. "It's not really a movie where the enemy is invisible in the story, or just slightly visible, or just around the corner, or just there for a moment, like *Alien*, is it? In *Alien*, the enemy has a very short visibility in the cuts, and is always spooky and not a substantial enemy you have in front of you very long. All that is different here, because the enemy has to be right in front of you, and not presented in quick cuts. There are horror elements in the movie, but the general tone is that of a war movie."

FOLLOW THE LEADER

Verhoeven is a warm and passionate man, and genuinely modest, so what he cites as the most pleasing aspect of making *Starship Troopers* is not a major surprise. "It was the cooperation between the different talents, the cooperation with the, let's say, co-directors of the movie. The cooperation with Phil Tippett, the cooperation with Scott Anderson here at Sony ImageWorks for the starships, the cooperation with my assistant director Gregg Goldstone, the cooperation with Vic Armstrong, my second unit director—all these people were so extremely important and creative together.

"There is a leader, whoever it is, but the other people are so extremely important that it was very fruitful to be in a dialogue with four or five people every moment of the day, really, and to try to find a common solution. That was something unique. Normally when you direct a movie, it's only your word that seems to be felt. But in this case, that was not possible. Every time, we had to find a solution together, and that was nice. We had problems, but they were technical, logistical; we had no emotional, psychological problems among us. There were three, four, five people that you could really in some ways call the co-directors."

Initially, Sony Pictures intended to release *Starship Troopers* in the middle of the summer, but it became so crowded with other big-scale movies that it was decided to delay the release. The change of date, Verhoeven admits, "certainly made the film better, because we had more time. It took some time to get the film into position here at Sony ImageWorks, who are doing most of the starship FX. We certainly lost a lot of time there until I got Scott Anderson, now my supervisor, to take over that position in October [1996]. From then on, it became a very smooth ride, but before that, it was not. The fact that the movie was moved to November helped us to get everything under control again, and also made it possible for Scott to do as good a job as Phil was doing."

But this also gave time for Internet rumors about *Starship Troopers* to spread even further. Heinlein is one of those writers who inspires, in some readers, a kind of worship. These Heinlein True Believers became outraged when they learned that the power suits, one of the "coolest" aspects of the novel *Starship Troopers*, were not going to be used in the film, for several good reasons.

Another complaint suggested that while in the novel, the soldiers were all volunteers, in the movie the troopers would include draftees. This simply isn't true, but Verhoeven does point out an interesting fact. "In a way, they are *not* volunteers. In the Heinlein book, there is the Federal Service, and there is a differentiation between a citizen and a civilian. Yes, you don't have to go into the military, but if you want to be a respected citizen, if you want to vote or hold office, you *must* go into Federal Service. And that's still a premise of the movie: If you don't go into Federal Service, you stay a civilian. If you go two years in the Federal Service, not necessarily as a a soldier, then you become a citizen. So you can't say it's completely voluntary, because it's really the pressure of the society that makes it for many people not possible to skip the Federal Service. If you want to be a politician, you have to go through Federal Service; if you want to have babies, you have to go through Federal Service. It's a little Orwellian in a way, although it's not portrayed as a malevolent society."

DEFEND YOUR SOCIETY

Hardcore Heinlein fans also claim that none of his philosophy from the book is in the movie. They ignore the fact that the novel was written in a period in which Heinlein was deliberately attacking the mores of American society by offering alternative cultures. Heinlein presented the society in *Starship Troopers*, and showed how it worked, and why. But he was neither attacking nor endorsing the society. He merely presented it.

"The philosophy of Heinlein," Verhoeven asserts, "is certainly in the movie. Whether I adhere to that society myself is something else, but it *is* the philosophy of the world he described, and we took that from his book. We are stating it continuously throughout the movie, but we don't offer an opinion about it. Of course, we have the news moments in it; our movie is interrupted sometimes with the news breaking through on the Federal Net. These items can be read in an ironic way, so there is some commentary on this society by the writer and director of the movie, but the characters in it all accept the society completely."

And yes, there are no power suits, though they were originally intended to be part of the film—Davison's office wall is covered with designs for the suits. "Yes," Verhoeven concedes, "people might regret that there are no power suits, but there are many other things. Heinlein didn't spend much time on the bugs; the book is not really about that, is it? The book is about boot camp, becoming an officer, how to be a soldier and how the society works. The battles with the Bugs were not essential to the book at all; there are only a few pages about the war itself, in the beginning a little bit, and at the end. But our movie is really about a war. First, it shows the characters and the society, and then in the second part, they go to war and they die. There is much more in the film about the alien insects and about their society, so the viewers might not get power suits, but they get really good Bugs.

"To be honest," concludes Paul Verhoeven, "I do not think the fans will be disappointed. There will be many people who will go to this movie, even if they are prejudiced before, and will come out not as prejudiced. Yes, there are no power suits, but the philosophy is there. There are some you cannot make happy, but I think anybody who has an open mind will feel they have not been betrayed.

Interview with Paul Verhoeven

Olivier Guéret / 1997

From www.cinopsis.be, December 1997. Reprinted by permission of the author. Translated from the French by Alexandra Valentine Proulx.

Amsterdam, December 6, 1997—We were warned that Mr. Verhoeven was very unhappy about the fascist interpretation of his film that certain members of the press had chosen to promote. "Gentlemen of the press," we were instructed, "please avoid the topic." Far from discouraged, *Cinopsis* took the necessary steps to find out everything there is to know about *Starship Troopers*.

OLIVIER GUÉRET: In all of your science fiction films, such as *Total Recall* and *RoboCop*, the protagonist is going through an identity crisis. Was this aspect important for you to develop in your latest film?

PAUL VERHOEVEN: In *Starship Troopers*, the identity crisis was actually more along the lines of human development—a growth. The crises in *RoboCop* and *Total Recall* were much more complex because of the existence of two realities. However, I don't think that's the essence of the film. In this case, the protagonist is very young and naïve. He doesn't have an understanding of these two realities. His relationship to life evolves significantly after his confrontation with death. He jumps from childhood to what some might consider manhood, by becoming an officer in the Terra Mobile Infantry.

It isn't an identity crisis. He grows in phases that coincide with what the government expects of him. He would probably have been very different if it weren't for the war. He is a direct consequence of the world he lives in. The main difference between this film and other American films is that here the audience has a difficult time identifying the hero's cause for which he is fighting for. He doesn't see the big picture. When we think of the film as a whole, it might lead us to questions about the government's motivations. Usually, in American films, we identify with the hero. He fights for the right cause and wins: Everything is good. Here, the situation is much more ambiguous.

OG: To what extent do you think this film mirrors American society?
PV: The film is a mirror of American society, although that wasn't the initial premise. It was originally devoid of any political ideas whatsoever. It was simply a film about a space war between humans and giant insects. Heinlein's novel was added on at the film's preliminary stage. The book contains certain political ideas that we interpreted as a denouncement of America. It's a commentary on power politics and civil policies such as gun control and the way the judicial system works—things that reflect the American establishment. It was over four or five years of preparation that these additional political elements slowly made their way into the film. Many of the film's scenes depict in an ironic fashion how Americans see themselves as the masters of the universe; it's a little like the Roman Empire.

OG: Why did you choose to mix a high-tech universe with the one of the Second World War?
PV: We were looking for a representative model, above all else. The most important recent conflicts were in Kuwait and Vietnam. The Kuwait war was a little strange because of US supremacy. It wasn't really a battle; it was more of an invasion. As for the situation in Vietnam, it wasn't a convenient model. That war was full of hidden things, ambushes and fringe groups fighting in their separate corners. There was no battlefield. The Second World War's look and imagery was closer to Heinlein's book which in fact was written right after it. It was also interesting to me because I lived through that period. It was the obvious choice given the time the book was written.

OG: Did you encounter any problems because of that choice?
PV: What do you mean? Political problems? I had problems with the American press (*The Washington Post*), problems that were picked up by the European press (*Libération*), comments about the so-called fascist aspects of my film, if that's what you're getting at . . . It warps the story's potential. The film isn't a comment on fascism; it's a comment on imperialism in the broadest sense. Making that choice was obviously going to attract controversy, and it did, much more than I had expected. At first there were no issues. It was the *Washington Post*'s reaction that generated the polemic. It's true that fascism isn't dead and that it remains present in several countries around the world—but that isn't what the film is about. When you see the topics that I raise using the Federation's newsreels, I'm pointing out dysfunctions within the current American regime—for example, how easy it is to purchase a weapon despite gun control being in effect, or the judiciary system, which has only accelerated the process of sending people to death row and the electric chair. In the newsreels, the question "Would you like to know more?" begs the question "Do you want this type of society? Do you want to dive even further into this

system that already exists in America?" Regardless of all this, I maintain that the main subject of this film is giant insects! (*Laughs*)

OG: And the use of violence? I find your film quite violent. Do you believe that is the best way to denounce violence?
PV: I have no idea. I don't know if it's the best way. I'm not sure I'm even fighting against violence. I'm simply describing it. Violence is something that I hate, yet it is an integral part of life. I never moralize in any of my work. Look at this century—you'll see that wars have killed over 200 million people. Some died because of fascism and others because of communism. Wouldn't you call that violent? I don't understand how to avoid the topic when the world has become a slaughterhouse. Violence is omnipresent. My cinematographic violence is a symbol of protest, and if I exaggerate the concept it becomes a philosophical argument against ambivalent violence. You can't deny that violence is an integral part of humanity.

OG: Why did you choose to cast unknown actors?
PV: Because the famous actors of that generation weren't available. That's the only reason. Also, there aren't that many. I thought of Chris O'Donnell, but he was already working on *Batman & Robin*. We should have skipped half a generation to get better known actors like Christian Slater, but since the film opens in a high school it would have looked stupid. It wouldn't have been credible. Using older actors would have made the characters' lose their naiveté, which meant a lot to me. I wanted to give the audience the impression that my heroes were leaving the age of innocence and entering the slaughterhouse. They needed to look innocent and vulnerable. If there were twenty-three-year-old celebrities available, I would have worked with them and spent less on special effects. Is that a good or bad decision? Commercially, maybe I should have taken a different strategy. We'll be able to judge that decision after we see how much it grosses internationally.

OG: What was the biggest challenge in the making of this film?
PV: To direct a scene like the ambush on the outpost, with all of the insects barreling down hills and climbing up walls. Directing the actors, going left to right and then backward, simulating special effects to make the actors react. That sequence is based on the film *The Charge of the Light Brigade*. The challenge was to make the film without there being any insects on set. Almost every shot involves special effects. It was hard to visualize and to make the actors visualize the fifty percent of the action that was completely digital. We had to motivate people to react to things that did not exist in the material world. In order to direct those scenes, I literally put myself in the place of the insects . . . shouting, running around, attacking and jumping. I was always right next to the camera yelling: "Watch out!

They're coming! Look right, look left, behind you . . ." We tried all kinds of things to indicate the insects' positions—with lighting, etcetera—but it was always my voice that worked the best . . .

Dutchman's Breaches

Brian D'Amato and David Rimanelli / 2000

© Artforum, Summer 2000, "Dutchman's Breaches: Brian D'Amato and David Rimanelli talk with Paul Verhoeven."

One day in college I went to the local art house to see Paul Verhoeven's *The Fourth Man* (1983). The director was unknown to me, but the promise of gaudy violence and AC/DC sex scenes no doubt lured me in. Verhoeven, as I later learned, was at that time probably the Netherlands' most renowned filmmaker, having directed such critically acclaimed features as *Turkish Delight* (1973), which received an Oscar nomination for Best Foreign Language Film, *Soldier of Orange* (1977), and *Spetters* (1980). I had no idea that *The Fourth Man*, a less than completely successful film, would prove the "bridge" between Verhoeven's European art-house past and the string of controversial Hollywood blockbusters that lay in his future, beginning with *RoboCop* in 1987. There's something weirdly disjunctive about the elegant if gory killings in Verhoeven's last Dutch film and the out-of-control body counts amassed in subsequent Hollywood productions, especially the assassination-a-go-go of *Total Recall* (1990) and the giddy celebration of sex-hungry lesbian serial killers that is *Basic Instinct* (1992). People complained about the unrelenting violence and about the socially unredeeming (albeit extremely glamorous) portrayals of ice pick-wielding dykes. The movies were smash hits.

Subsequent Verhoeven films such as *Showgirls* (1995) and *Starship Troopers* (1997) fared less well at the box office and were typically savaged in the popular press. Being misunderstood is the common fate of strange and original art, but the stubborn obtuseness of most mainstream critics in response to Verhoeven has been risible. No point is served by arguing with the popular press over its presupposed dumbness, but Brian D'Amato and I did fervently believe that our enthusiasm for Verhoeven's movies was a legitimate art—and Hollywood—passion. He's our favorite mass-market auteur, a real genius. Naming *Starship Troopers* one of the top ten artistic achievements in *Artforum*'s 1998 year-end roundup, I asseverated that Verhoeven had created a new kind of cinema. The extravagance of my claim has been more than borne out in one important taste demographic: art schools, where I frequently screen Verhoeven films with the same earnest seriousness I would accord Straub-Huillet. Was not the ideological import of *Cahiers du Cinema* to rehabilitate trash Hollywood noir as the highest art? Maybe our excitement over Verhoeven is the compliment that vice pays to virtue. Part of the thrill of Verhoeven's American films derives from the narrative ambiguities and off-register tone common to all his work—a link, however unexpected, to the European art cinema of the seventies and to his youth. His upcoming feature, *Hollow Man* (English majors will recall the similarly titled T. S. Eliot poem), which opens nationally on August 4, stars Kevin Bacon and Elisabeth Shue in a horror drama about the highs and lows of discovering a formula for human invisibility. Maybe the ultimate in voyeuristic stalking fantasies isn't the dream we imagine. It is our hope that *Hollow Man* may yet portend a general reappraisal of the Verhoeven oeuvre. For perverse fun alone, he deserves a retrospective at Anthology Film Archives.

BRIAN D'AMATO: We wanted to ask you about some problems in your films—
PAUL VERHOEVEN: Problems?

BD: Well, issues—
DAVID RIMANELLI: Problems for some people.
BD: We've been rereading the reviews of *Starship Troopers* [1997], and it doesn't seem as if many of the critics realized there was any irony in the film.
PV: I don't think they got that, no. The movie has a lot of irony or whatever you want to call it. It's saying, "This is wonderful! You have to fight! And don't forget—you're going to die, too!"

BD: We also read an interview with the film's leading lady—Denise Richards—and she didn't seem to get it either.
PV: No.

DR: Maybe that worked for the benefit of the concept.
PV: Well, that is a pretty good summation of the characters, isn't it? (*Laughs*) Because they don't seem to understand very well what they're doing. You know that line where Michael Ironside [Lieutenant Rasczak] says, "Want to live forever?" I think that's from Frederick the Great. That was one of his most famous lines: "Come on, guys! You want to live forever? Let's fight!" And of course throughout the film there are these nearly verbatim visual quotes from *Triumph of the Will*. I don't know if you ever read the article that was in the *Washington Post*, two weeks after the release, accusing me of being a neo-Nazi—

BD: The inventor of modern warfare. (*fumbling in notebook*) Yeah, here it is. It's by Stephen Hunter: (*reading*) "It's spiritually Nazi, psychologically Nazi. It comes directly out of the Nazi imagination, and is set in the Nazi universe . . . Unlike films from a civilized society that see war as a debilitating, tragic necessity . . . this movie sees it as a profoundly moving experience."

PV: That article was picked up by all the European newspapers: They were all saying, "Beware! This movie's coming to your country!" (*Laughs*) And the more fascist the nation had been, the less they were willing to see it as a description of their country. I had terrible interviews where they just said, "You're a Nazi." And I'd say, "No, no, I'm talking about some fascist mentality in the film." And then they'd say, "Well, isn't that something you admire?" They were set in their belief that the film was promoting fascism. Now, of course it plays with that, because it shows how these kids accept that and glory in it, in all these clichés—which have been used by propagandists not just in Germany but in the United States as well. But the movie isn't saying, "Okay, now, our message is that the US is a fascist, imperialist country." I try and avoid being someone with a big message. I always feel that comes at the cost of the movie. I think a movie is its own thing.

DR: I watched *Starship Troopers* over and over, and if it were simply an allegory of fascism I don't think I would have gotten so interested in it.

PV: No, it touches on these things without becoming them. It's more just about me than anything else, I think. All these things are living inside me—my interest or fascination with authoritarian systems, but also my knowledge that if I had lived in Germany in the thirties, I would never have been able to stand in the crowd and raise my hand in that salute. But I'm certainly able to understand how crowd emotions feel.

DR: The excitement of the bestial, insectoid masses?

PV: Well, in *Starship Troopers* the animals aren't organized much differently from the people who fight them, are they? But I don't think you can say it's this or that. Ultimately a movie is expression, or at least this one became expression because I was involved with it for so long—much longer than any of the other movies I've done in the US. Most of the others came my way with a nearly final script. Although I think I did add layers to *RoboCop* [1987] and the others, but somehow they were vaguely there anyhow. We developed *Starship Troopers* practically from scratch, over three or four years. In that sense it became more like *Soldier of Orange* [1977], although that certainly was not an ironic film. It's more of a humanitarian movie; more about acceptance and about how everybody's a hero—or nobody's a hero. You know how at the end of that film two people stand next to each other and toast the future, and one is the hero and the other is the guy who didn't do anything during the war? He just sat over his books and studied the whole time. But they are equalized in the last shot, meaning, "I'm not going to pass final judgment on them. The hero is here, and the antihero is there, and, basically, that's life." *Starship Troopers* is about something else altogether: my unrest when it comes to the United States in general, my wondering, "What is this society about?"

DR: Does that explain the much-commented-on fact that so many of the stars of *Starship Troopers* were picked from *Beverly Hills, 90210* and *Melrose Place*?
PV: Well, I won't say that's pure coincidence. But I didn't set out to pick people from television shows just to say, "How superficial everything is here!" I was looking for a certain physical type that happens to abound in television shows—superficial characters, people who have a certain one-dimensional quality, nearly comic-book characters. You know, there's now this animated TV series based on *Starship Troopers*, and the faces are all drawn in that chiseled way. But they already look like that in the movie, don't they? They are really kind of . . . well, I was looking for chins and noses to match Leni Riefenstahl's vision of the ideal soldier.

DR: Or Arno Breker's.
PV: Right, right. That was on purpose. I was looking for something to give the audience that feeling, that these are the kind of people who would do this. Anybody else would say, "What the fuck are you doing? I'm not gonna join the army." And of course I also thought it was interesting to show all this beauty being destroyed.

BD: Nazi propaganda films had all these really sweet-seeming people—
PV: Definitely. You know the shot at the beginning of *Starship Troopers* where they all turn to the camera and say, "I'm doing my part!"? That's straight out of Leni's film, where the one guy turns and says, "I'm from Silesia!" And then another one says, "I'm from Bavaria!" So, yes, I tried to give it that kind of feeling. And I don't really know why.

BD: People have a problem with ambiguity. They think everything's deadly serious unless Adam Sandler walks on honking a bicycle horn.
PV: Even the advertising people had a hard time with it. They had no idea how to market that movie. There was only one campaign that was absolutely marvelous, the one in England with these giant teaser posters all over town with the different catch phrases in huge letters, like "THE ONLY GOOD BUG IS A DEAD BUG!" They understood that sort of irony. But even if you look at the more normal movies—*Total Recall* [1990] and *Basic Instinct* [1992]—there's also a gigantic layer of ambiguity in those. Although it's more in the story, isn't it?

DR: It's a narrative ambiguity.

PV: Right. *Starship Troopers* was more some sort of "politicized pop." But again, I have to say it's not a political movie. It's not done to say "fascism is bad" or "fascism is good" or "you should become a soldier" or "you shouldn't become a soldier." It's more just my own observations, expressed in film language. Observations of any, let's say, imperialist country. It could be in the future or it could be the Roman Empire—which has lots of similarities, of course, with the United States.

BD: A few weeks after *Starship Troopers* came out, I saw an ad on TV for the US Army Reserves, with this GI Jane–type woman working in an office, and she says, "No problem, this weekend I just refueled sixteen Apache helicopters!" That's almost exactly the same line Denise Richards has in the movie: "Imagine piloting half a million tons of starship!"

PV: It's ridiculous, of course. And with those insects—but at the same time the insects are truly devastating. And then there's also some beauty in all the destruction, isn't there? You know the scene in Patton where he looks out at all those tanks that have been destroyed and says, "God forgive me, but I love this!"? (*Laughs*) Somehow, that's also part of me. I love to see movies on war and destruction. And I could say, "God forgive me for liking them." Perhaps it's because I grew up during the bombardments in The Hague. And a lot of houses in our quarter—not our street, but the whole area around it—were destroyed. So sometimes I think, "Oh, maybe it's my youth, you know?" That's why that sort of thing fascinates me. Anyway, it's why I feel that movie is about me, really. It's about how contradictory I am, myself, and how ambivalent I am about all those things. I mean, of course, the Allies freed us from the Germans, for God's sake. Which was good. But, on the other hand, I still can jump into the German thinking and live there in my imagination, as an artist, if you like, not as a person. As a human being, I'd just say, "You fucking idiot!" You know that scene in *Starship Troopers* with the little kids stomping on the tiny insects? And then their mother starts applauding them, screaming ecstatically. (*Laughs*) I mean, that's an expression of the idiotic ideas that go with liking to fight, right? And loving destruction. But it's something of a commentary on myself, too. Saying how crazy it is to think that way. It's the same way I'm fascinated with religion. As you may know, I'm working on a movie about Jesus. And basically it asks: How can millions and millions of people, for two thousand years—year in, year out—how can they all believe this and have this, say, this "light psychosis"? It's taken me fifty years of studying even to figure out what I can say that's really different enough to be said. Not to antagonize people—it'll do that anyway—but to say something I believe is true. I mean, it's difficult to find the truth in this story. And, of course, to the postmodern mind truth isn't much of an existing particle anymore anyway. For me the question remains, what do I think really happened there, two thousand years ago? And that's the issue of the movie.

BD: But it's not going to be in ancient Aramaic?
PV: No, that would be too truthful. (*Laughs*) Then nobody would want to see it.

BD: So when is the record going to be set straight about *Starship Troopers*?
PV: I don't know. In retrospect, you could argue that we should have cared about the audience much more—from a commercial point of view. But I didn't, unfortunately.

DR: But from an artistic point of view, who cares?
PV: Yes. But from a commercial point of view—well, we spent a lot of money on that movie.

BD: It's doing well on DVD.
PV: Yes, but it'll probably take the studio twenty years to get their money back.

DR: So it was too much of an art film?
PV: Right. That's just what [creature effects supervisor] Phil Tippett said to me. He said, "Paul, this is once in a lifetime. Never again will you be able to spend $100 million on an art film."

DR: *Showgirls* [1995] was something of an art film—
PV: Yeah, but it didn't cost $100 million. (*Laughs*) It was much cheaper. But yes, *Showgirls* was just so negative and so cynical about American society, reducing everything to opportunism. Almost everyone in it was bad, and it was expressed in the most vulgar—or let's say, the most realistic—way. I mean, the ironic thing is that *Showgirls* is the most realistic movie I've ever made in the United States. It's all based on months and months of interviews with chorus girls, choreographers, producers, and theater owners—and that's really the way they are. Even the singer who rapes the girl at the end—that was also based on things that had really happened and were covered up by the police because it's Vegas.

The same thing happened with *Spetters* [1980]. That film was also based on interviews and articles. We gathered material for a couple of years to get those characters exactly right. And then everybody in Holland was completely upset when *Spetters* came out. They said, "This doesn't happen in our society, this male-rape stuff." But it was all from news stories that we'd just gathered and put together.

BD: But isn't there an implication in *Showgirls* that it's all just the main character's fantasy? You know, the way she gets into the same car at the end, and it swerves in just the same way, and the way she never gets hurt or even hit all through the picture, like that might wake her up—

PV: No, I don't think it's all her fantasy. Although perhaps that would have made the movie a little more interesting. Maybe. But it is clearly a fairy tale, if you want to use that word. It's purposely a cyclical story. The idea for the ending was to predict that what she'd just done as a showgirl in Vegas, she was now going to do as an actress in LA. Did you see that big sign at the end that shows they're going to LA? It wasn't in the script, but I added it to give the idea that now the story would spread out to the whole world, because LA reaches the whole world. That mentality is the norm in LA, as much as it is in Vegas. So for me, *Showgirls* was just Part One. Actually for some time [screenwriter] Joe Eszterhas and I discussed a sequel. It was going to be set in LA and called *Bimbos*.

BD: That's a good idea.
PV: No, I don't think so anymore, I've already had too many problems because of *Showgirls*. I underestimated how genuinely shocked people can be. The public—and also the critics—were really pissed off. Because it got them personally. They couldn't just sit back and just say, "This is bad." In fact, I even warned Elizabeth Berkley before we made that movie that people would end up hating her for it, that long before the movie was released they'd be writing that she can't act, can't dance . . .

DR: She was great.
PV: I think she was great. And extremely audacious. But the critics went for the kill. I think they couldn't stand that anyone had been able to push them right in the nose. They hadn't expected it.

DR: But from the aficionado you had acceptance—an instant camp classic.
PV: Yeah, right. (*Laughter*)

DR: And in that context, camp is reality.
PV: I understand, that's all true—and that was also kind of nice. That's why I went to the Raspberry Awards. You know, *Showgirls* won Worst Movie, Worst Director, Worst Actress, even Worst Music.

BD: Weren't you the first to accept the award in person?
PV: Yeah. I went there because I thought, mmm, well, somehow, I wanted this "trash." So I should get that award, you know? (*Laughs*) But of course it also cleaned the slate for me, a bit, neutralizing the complete negativity. I mean, you

read the reviews and try to say, "I'm above that. I've trained my whole life to get bad reviews." Especially in Holland—*Spetters* was an even worse experience in that regard than *Showgirls*. Because *Spetters* was the first time, and I didn't expect it; I was completely overwhelmed by so much personal negativity—by them really attacking you, in your most personal being, like you're a brainless fucking idiot. And now I look back at *Showgirls* and say, for God's sake, how did we dare to do that? I mean, I'm amazed at my own naiveté, to think that this was fine. (*Laughs*)

DR: There's a question of camp and intentionality with that film. Isn't camp one thing that still depends on authorial intention?
PV: Of course it's intentionally campy, but on the other hand it wasn't a deliberate attempt to make camp. Because I never try, really, to do that. I'd say that comes into the movie. I didn't start out saying, "Okay, *Starship Troopers* is going to be ironic." It became that way while I was working on it.

DR: So irony and camp are byproducts.
PV: For me they are. I think you set out to do something you think is outrageous or that goes beyond current thinking, something nobody has dared to do in a Hollywood movie. We wanted *Showgirls* to have a layer of brutal realism on the one hand and a layer of fairytale fantasy on the other. A girl comes in from nowhere, and she's picked up because she dances so well. And then she takes somebody out and grabs the best spot.

BD: It's inexorable.
PV: Yes. And it would have been all right if we'd done that story in an inoffensive way—like *All About Eve*, which is basically the same tale, isn't it? But to apply it to the "dirtiest" level of society—although I don't think it's dirty, but that's how people look at Vegas—and then to present that as glamorous, in a way. (*Laughs*)

DR: It had the pleasure of self-revulsion.
PV: Right. I think it played with that, me shooting one of the scenes in the first club—the one with the two girls dancing together on the pole? That scene is no different from what you see in Vegas. If you go to the less high-level clubs, that is. And there are things worse than that. I even took a few shots out that were just too far beyond.

DR: While we're talking about camp, there's something about the tone of your early Dutch movies like *Spetters* and *Turkish Delight* [1973] that makes me wonder whether you'd seen any Warhol movies at that time.
PV: Yeah, Morrissey, Paul Morrissey.

DR: *Trash? Flesh?*

PV: And *Heat*. Yeah. I'm a big admirer of those early Morrissey movies. And of course I know Warhol's work. But I'm not so sure that I used that. I think it was more just the feeling of freedom, and the way Joe Dallesandro—isn't it?—how he behaved in nudity.

DR: His animality.

PV: Yeah, and his directness. It was like, "Okay, do you want to have a man or woman, do you want to be fucked, or sucked, or whatever? Fine, it doesn't matter—man, woman—oh, yeah, another woman, okay, no big deal, whatever." Isn't there this scene in *Flesh* or *Trash* where he's in bed with these two women and he thinks there's going to be a great threesome? And then the two women are much more attracted to each other. So in the end he goes to sleep off to the side. I mean, that whole kind of nonchalance, not insisting too much—especially in *Heat*. That's the one set in the little motel, isn't it? Joe Dallesandro is in this motel, and he has all these sexual encounters, and out at the swimming pool there's this boy who always has a sheet over him, and he's masturbating through the whole movie. I loved that.

DR: That's the audience, I guess.

PV: Yeah—that's what I thought. When that came out it became a strong influence. I'm sure some of that reflects in my early movies.

DR: People said *Turkish Delight* was the Dutch *Last Tango in Paris*. Except *Last Tango* was so dirgey.

PV: Yeah. No, *Turkish Delight* took pleasure in it. Especially if you can see the original version in Dutch, it's not cut, like that dubbed version you saw on tape. It's not so masturbated—or how do you say it?

BD: Emasculated.

PV: Right. There is the same kind of nonchalance in the sexual encounters. In most Hollywood movies today, you know, if they fuck it's only done to show that they're fucking, isn't it? They put themselves on top of each other, and all the movement starts, and a lot of dissolves—dissolve to the knees, dissolve to this, dissolve to that—and then that's it. Ahhhh! (*Gasps*) And they fall down, and that's the scene. A sex scene needs something more than that. Otherwise, why show it? It's like walking: You don't show people walking if they aren't going somewhere. When we did *Basic* I wanted to do a scene where the characters would be watching each other while they're going at it. I wanted to do that scene in a Hitchcockian style, or let's say, what Hitchcock might have done if he'd been able to do a scene like that in those days. And it's a murder scene at the same time. It's the big scene between Michael Douglas and Sharon Stone, and it has two aspects. There's the sex, but also the question, "Is she going to kill him or not?" Which saves it, of course, from being only a straight love scene, right?

DR: Murder was a pretext.
PV: Murder as a pretext to keep the audience there. And to not make them completely uncomfortable because of all the sex. I mean, you even see Michael Douglas licking Sharon Stone's genitals—especially in the European version. We had to make cuts in the American version because of the MPAA [Motion Picture Association of America], and it became more choppy. But in the "director's cut," everything flows. It's an absolutely beautiful love scene, I think. But it could only be extended that long because there is something else going on, that keeps you on the alert. Otherwise, if you show sex for longer than a minute or two, you start to think you're watching a peep show. So I felt that *Basic* gave me this magnificent opportunity to do a really long sex scene—it's three or four minutes or so—without losing the audience, without everyone starting to look around at each other like, "Uh-oh, my girlfriend's watching this. Should I look over at her? I mean, does she think I'm going to do that myself tonight?" That kind of thing. Of course that's always there anyway. You sit there, and you think, "Hmm, that was interesting. Maybe I've failed in life. I've never done anything that interesting." There's always a little bit of that.

DR: But at that point in the film the audience isn't yet sure that the Sharon Stone character is the killer.
PV: No, I know. But because of the repetition of that shot of the ceiling mirror, and the angles, the hands, the same as when she kills in the very first scene in the film—I wanted that threat to always be present. And he even suspects she's going to do it, but then it's nothing. So it's all playing with that murder possibility, but using it for other reasons.

BD: There's an implication in that film that the Sharon Stone character is just making it up, the way you see her writing novelizations of the movie's upcoming scenes.
PV: Yeah. Well, it's an ambiguous movie. In my opinion, of course, Sharon did it. But all the characters in the movie think it's Jeanne [Tripplehorn], right? It's only we, at the end, who might think: Hmmm . . .

DR: I thought they were in cahoots.
PV: No, no. I think it's nearly as ambiguous as *Total Recall*. You know how in that

film you wonder, "Is the whole movie just the dream he bought at Rekall, Inc.? Or did he buy the dream and then wake up from it, and have the full adventure and become a real hero?" It has this continuous ambiguity of the two levels of reality. I think that's what *Basic* has, too: Is it her? Is it her? Her, her? Or this one? (*Laughter*) That, I think, is the movie.

BD: What about your new film, *Hollow Man*?
PV: Well, it's a more straightforward project. A bit like *RoboCop*. It's a science-fiction film, too. But the narrative is more like *Basic Instinct*, which is about murder. A strange murder. A woman kills men during orgasm to find out if she can get away with it. If you can accept that premise as a reality, then fine. And in *Hollow Man* the premise is, "You can make somebody invisible." And one scientist does it to himself and starts to deteriorate and become evil. Which is the classic story, isn't it?

I just showed this film to my wife. I'm never so sure what I do with movies while I'm working on them, what the levels are. It's only afterward, when I look at the whole movie and start to reflect on it, that I see what I did. Anyway she felt that it was "a study in evil." That it was really about the descent into the abyss of evil. But, of course, if you look at it from a realistic point of view, it's not even campy, it's silly. (*Laughs*) If you want to use that word. Nobody can become invisible in the first place.

BD: And you do have a doctorate in physics—
PV: Yes. I know precisely that it can't be done. (*Laughs*)

The Master of Science Fiction Longs for a Break from Special Effects

Douglas Eby / 2000

From *Cinefantastique,* August 2000. Reprinted by permission of the author.

Regarding his choice of Kevin Bacon for the lead in *Hollow Man,* director Paul Verhoeven noted, "I was always a big admirer of Kevin Bacon, though I'd never worked with him. There were other proposals on the table, but with all the considerations of money and availability and other things, he worked the best."

Agreeing that Bacon can play hero or villain, he said, "And he can go in between. I think it's an excellent choice. I met him in December [1998], in New York, and I thought, 'This is the guy.' I'd always looked at his work with a lot of pleasure, and I thought he could do it. He's very talented. What you need also is a guy who's very down to earth, and wouldn't mind getting painted all the time, blue or green or whatever, or put a suit on. And he's suffering a lot. To get painted is one thing; to get it off is another. And he had full contact lenses on all the time, over the whole eyeball. Very annoying. And on top of that, the latex mask he uses in part of the movie is glued to his skin, and it starts to pull off after three or four hours. So you need a person who knows how to suffer."

Production of the film was delayed about halfway through from a tendon injury that kept Elisabeth Shue out of commission. Shue plays Linda Foster, a fellow scientist who was a former lover of Caine, Bacon's character. "She was working out here on the Sony lot, and mis-stepped getting off a trampoline," Verhoeven explained. "It was a freak accident. Nobody's guilty." Verhoeven admitted having this kind of interruption, and anticipating the need to get the energy of the production up to speed again, was not easy to deal with. "I'm looking at it with fear and dread," he said during the hiatus while Shue healed. "I mean that, more than you think. Shooting a movie is always quite an ordeal, the time and energy you have to put into it to keep it all moving, and keep it aggressive and interesting and edgy." Looking toward getting back into production after the break, he noted, brought up questions like "Will I be motivated enough? Will I be tired? Will I be able to keep doing good work?" But he also recalled an earlier film of his, shot in Holland, that required shooting in different seasons. "So we stopped even longer than here, and in fact, it didn't matter at all. In one or two days we were back in the groove."

There was even some consideration to replace Shue, but Verhoeven noted, "I was very against that. I think she's doing a great job, and gives the movie a lot of warmth, and becomes a warrior at the end, because she has to kill him, or he'll kill her. She doesn't normally play that kind of character. What she adds to the movie immediately, from the beginning, is a lot of warmth and charm. In the beginning, you identify with Sebastian [Bacon] to a certain degree, but when he follows these paths of darkness, the question is how long will the audience follow him? When he gets more evil, their focus will be Elisabeth. At the start, he was the leader of the project, and forces the other scientists to go that way. But then she becomes the hero."

When another scientist in the group, Matt Kensington (Josh Brolin), becomes Linda Foster's new love interest, she still has feelings for Caine, Verhoeven noted: "They were living together, and broke up for some reason, but there's still residual stuff that always plays. Especially with Elisabeth that plays very well, because she has a real talent in communicating sympathy, love or sexuality to people." The script went through a number of drafts in order to make the Kensington and Foster characters "more and more realistic" he said."So they would not be talking clichés, that they would not say all the time, 'Come on, let's go!' or 'We have to go.'"

Asked if he particularly likes making science fiction films, Verhoeven emphatically answered, "No. I like science fiction movies. I've always liked that. But making them is quite an ordeal. It's much more pleasant to do, say, *Showgirls*, than *Hollow Man*. It's tedious, it's time consuming, it's very precise. The movements of the camera are always more restrained than you want, because you realize you have to replace the background, and if the actor is walking, then you have three independent moves that have to be repeated. So you have to use a motion control track all the time, which is very time consuming. These kinds of shots, even if they're six or seven seconds, take three or four hours because the computer has to move the camera over the rails in exactly the same way, and you can't have any variation, or then you'd lose part of the background."

Referring to intensive visual effects work for this film, Verhoeven noted, "Sony is one of the few companies in town that still has their own special effects house. Most have given up, because the profits are so low, and you need crazy people to do it, like Phil Tippett, who works seventeen hours a day, seven days a week, and gets people around him who are willing to do the same for the sake of the art or beauty of effects." One of the challenges of using effects shots is to keep them integrated into the flow of the story.

"So you always feel that a special effect is part of the scene," Verhoeven explained, "and you don't get the feeling, as you often have in special effects movies, that the effect is isolated and cut in." He added that he has tried to keep effects part of other shots as much as possible, "so you feel the time and space are the same" and not disrupted when you make a cut from an effect to an actor reacting. Also, he pointed out, that once the character of Caine is invisible, "There is only a voice, and if you make too many cuts, you have no idea where the person is anymore, because you don't see him in the first place. Of course, in the latter part of the movie, where he's going to be mean, you don't want to know exactly where he is."

Speaking again of his opportunities to do films outside the science fiction genre, Verhoeven said, "I'm very proud of *RoboCop*, I think that's a really interesting movie. And also *Starship Troopers*, but I'm too close to that to judge. So I like that I've done them, but I would appreciate having a little more balance." He pointed out that he's done four science fiction movies: the above titles, plus *Total Recall* and now this project, but only two other films in the US. "And *Showgirls* was kind of a strange experiment," he said, "because you had all these nudity issues. So I've done only one movie that was kind of normal, which was *Basic Instinct*. Of course, I'm coming from a background in Europe, in Holland, where all the movies I've done are normal, all about people; some action, but not too much. They're much more about how people behave in real life. And I'm missing that. Doing one special effect movie out of three is great; three out of three is tough."

The story demands in *Hollow Man* for a photo-realistic depiction of what it would actually look like for an organism to slowly become invisible has pushed Sony to develop some very advanced CGI, Verhoeven said. People at Imageworks spent days in anatomical labs, looking at the complexities of tissue and muscle structure, and body movement. The resulting CG images of Sebastian Caine's body becoming invisible in layers provide a "staggering" amount of detail, the director enthused. The Imageworks team, headed by Scott Anderson (also responsible for *Starship Troopers*) has assured him they can handle the three hundred and fifty or four hundred shots, and these are "not just wire-removal, although there is that, too, but these are much more complex shots than normal," Verhoeven noted. "The heart, everything, is completely expressed digitally. I don't think anyone has gone in that direction. I told Sony they should sell it to universities and medical schools."

The Many Dreams of Paul Verhoeven

Neil Young / 2002

From www.jigsawlounge.co.uk, April 18, 2002. Reprinted by permission of the author.

I met Verhoeven during his visit to Amsterdam's Fantastic Film Festival, where he was to receive the event's Lifetime Achievement award that evening. Though known as Hollywood's favorite "Mad Dutchman," Verhoeven seems eminently sensible in person: engagingly energetic and eager to talk, a hep professor in matching beige cardigan, shirt, pants and trendy slip-on trainers. Though at sixty-four his hair is rather more salt than pepper, his teeth are strikingly Hollywoodish in their size and gleaming brightness—it seems appropriate that "shark" is a word English stole from Dutch, though Verhoeven bares his fangs mainly to smile, at least away from the set.

Rob van Scheers' entertaining authorized biography (published in English by Faber as *Paul Verhoeven*) paints a picture of the director as something of a stern figure when dealing with actors, on movies ranging from Dutch productions like *Turkish Delight, Soldier of Orange, Spetters* and *The Fourth Man*, to his rollercoaster Hollywood career of *RoboCop, Total Recall, Basic Instinct, Showgirls* and *Starship Troopers*.

Though *Hollow Man* seemed to disappoint nearly everybody, my main aim was to cut through the fog of speculation and find out exactly what his follow-up project was going to be—depending on who you listen to, he's been linked with sequels to *RoboCop* and *Basic Instinct*; biopics of Rasputin, Hitler, Christ and the American 19th century spiritualist Victoria Woodhull; the long-gestating *Crusade*, a former 'hot' Arnold Schwarzenegger epic; films based on short stories by French writers Guy de Maupassant and M.F. Aureole; and, most concrete of all, *Official Assassins*, dramatizing how the Americans and the Russians fought over top Nazi scientists after the end of World War II. One internet commentator waggishly suggested Verhoeven might as well combine some of these ideas, and have Rasputin and RoboCop duking it out for Werner Von Braun in the rubble of Berlin.

NEIL YOUNG: So, what *is* your next project? Is it a European-based idea?
PAUL VERHOEVEN: I hope so. I'm working on this project that I *really* want to do which is the first of the series of books by Boris Akunin. He's a Russian detective writer and at the moment, he's *very* famous in Russia. It's set in 1876.

NY: Like a Russian Sherlock Holmes?
PV: Yes, with maybe a little bit of an Indiana Jones touch. It's against a background of Russian terrorism. The first book is called *Azazel*, which is 'scapegoat' in Hebrew. Fandorin is the name of the detective.

NY: What about all these possible projects we keep hearing about—scripts about Von Braun, Rasputin, Woodhull?
PV: *Rasputin* is *out*. The Woodhull project is written, but I have not been able to find financing for that.

NY: Is Nicole Kidman still interested?
PV: I'm waiting to hear from Nicole, I just sent it over to her. *Official Assassins* has been *frozen*, because it's very critical of the US government in 1945.

NY: Did you have to stop because of September 11?
PV: No, the script was written. I had to stop casting because nobody wanted to do it. I was in Moscow, looking at the tanks, when September 11 happened.

NY: Is this where you heard about the Fandorin books?
PV: I found this through my daughter Claudia, who lived in Russia at that time, studying there. She called me about it and said it was wonderful, but of course it was in Russian. Two months later when I was in Paris I saw that it had just been translated into French. Random House USA just bought the English language rights to the first of the nine novels. They're not all set in Russia—the first one is set in St. Petersburg and London.

NY: What about the project involving the ship during the 1600s, the Golden Age of Holland?
PV: That's another project, which was a book written by Mike Dash that just came out. It's called *Batavia's Graveyard*. Film Four bought that book for me. The story is that there's a shipwreck on a coral reef, and a couple of hundred are saved on these islands. But one group goes to the main island, and that becomes a fascist state, and the horror starts.

NY: Would you emphasize the horror aspects or the more political angle?
PV: It would be political, because it's about the creation of a fascist state. But there is a hero—he's a common soldier, who basically became the head of the resistance, and he's there, he's part of the history, it's not some invention of ours. It's a fantastic story, because it gives an ultra-villain—let's say, a proto-Hitler.

NY: Like a Kurtz figure from *Heart of Darkness*?
PV: Something like that.

NY: It sounds like *Lord of the Flies*.
PV: It's an adult *Lord of the Flies*, exactly.

NY: So which do you plan to do first?
PV: *Azazel* first, because the script is written. I wrote it in Dutch and I'm now translating it into English. The other one still has to be written—we just bought the book, and made the deal with a writer.

NY: And you'll do these in Europe, or as a Hollywood production?
PV: Well, I don't think any of these things should be done without an American distribution deal, because otherwise you're sitting with a piece of material. You have to be sure also, through the cast, that an American studio is saying OK, we'll release it in the United States, if you have these and these actors, which is always a problem.

NY: Do you have an actor in mind for Fandorin?
PV: No, not yet. I didn't think too much about that, but it could be somebody like Elijah Wood, or Heath Ledger, or Colin Farrell.

NY: Jared Leto is also very good, he's in *Panic Room*.
PV: Yes, I've seen him. Fandorin starts off in his early twenties, all wide-eyed, and at the end he's [*mimes firing guns*]. But there are great roles for people like Meryl Streep, or Catherine Zeta Jones—there are great parts. The characters are very clearly written.

NY: And is this a definite 'go' project?
PV: This would be my wish—to change gears. As we all know, there are many dreams and many plans with movies, and you can work as hard as you want, as we did with *The Crusades* with Arnold, and the project still might fail, and disappear forever.

NY: Is Hollywood not now desperate to do *Crusades* because it ties into the current situation?

PV: The story of the Crusades is the murderous attack of the Christians on the Arabs and the Jews. Do you think that's a politically interesting situation?

NY: With the right handling, it could be the ultimate time to do this movie.

PV: Yes, if I could do it my way and be historically correct—the reality that the Pope instigates this complete slaughterhouse, which is the reality, that started with pogroms against Jews, and which ultimately had only one goal: to destroy as many Arabs as possible. In the movie the Arabs are the good people and the Christians are the bad ones. Now what does that say to you now?

NY: It could be the ultimate worldwide co-production.

PV: I think the financing should come from Saudi Arabia! I doubt if it will come from the United States—at least not from the Catholic church.

NY: If you get the controversy, then you get the protests, then you get the box office.

PV: Like with *Basic Instinct*.

NY: You're receiving the Lifetime Achievement award here, and they're showing some of your films, including *Starship Troopers*. It's amazing to see how that movie is being received now, compared with some of the reviews it got when it first came out.

PV: Yes! After being accused of being Fascist, or Nazi I would say, a correction has taken place I think, to a certain degree. And fortunately so, because it was very disappointing when the film came out that I was attacked. Less in England, I must say, but in Europe very much so, and also in the United States based on an article in the *Washington Post*, where in an editorial the film was discussed as being done by a Nazi.

NY: And now?

PV: People have understood that it was about American politics.

NY: This reevaluation has even extended to *Showgirls*: Jacques Rivette picked it when asked to choose the most underrated recent movie. Did you take that as a great compliment?

PV: Absolutely. I read that! One of the few good reactions I ever got about *Showgirls*.

NY: Do you watch Rivette's movies?
PV: Of course! He's the best!

NY: Did you expect such a compliment?
PV: No! I'd given up hope! I should write it on the ceiling like the guy in *Hollow Man*.

NY: Do such reevaluations make you feel good, or are you sad that it takes a while?
PV: Sad only from a commercial point of view. It doesn't help, that *Starship Troopers* article in the *Washington Post* was basically used by all the European newspapers, even before they could see the movie. It was put on the front pages, so when I came to Holland and to Europe to promote the movie, the decision was already made, to a large degree. European newspapers followed the American newspapers' spin—all American papers, including the *New York Times*, are heavily "spun."

NY: Even now, though, some people still describe *Starship Troopers* as a silly bit of science fiction about giant bugs?
PV: That's true—there has always been a pleasure of mine to work in the B-genre and elevate that, or use that as a vehicle for other thoughts. It's like the paintings of Karel Appel, our Dutch guy, who was copying all these children's paintings. That was a heavy influence—or you could even look at Dada. It's a normal thing in art, to use the "mediocre" and the "banal" to make a statement. That kind of sophistication in art is rare in filmmaking.

If you look at painting or even in music—especially at the beginning of the 20th century. Even the titles of some of these pieces: "Musique en forme de poire" by Satie. Using the banal—something that is everyday, which is used in a different way. This is normal in a lot of the arts, only in filmmaking it isn't, because of the high entertainment value, where everything has to be immediately understood. It's rare, and if you use that, this method of hyperbole and irony and alienation, it's very difficult for the audiences and even for the film critics to see through that. Often they are not even basically educated in the other arts, so they can only look at movies in the same way they've been looking at movies for the last fifty years or so.

NY: Do you still have faith in cinema?
PV: Sure, yeah. But I have to continuously run old movies to keep my faith. When I feel very depressed I look at *Ivan the Terrible* or *The Rules of the Game* or *Metropolis* or even *Blade Runner*, say, or *The Terminator* or something like that, or every Hitchcock movie—or maybe fifty percent of them. I *need* them—sometimes I come home completely depressed and I have to put them on. It's so difficult in

an industry where the parameters have become so much those of pure entertainment, to still keep your belief that cinema is an art.

It doesn't have to be "art" art all the time, but there is a possibility to express yourself beyond just basically entertaining and that might be values that you want to touch upon. It's very depressing I often feel, when you go through days and weeks, when everything in the conversation about your new movies has to do with the fact that the story should be changed because it's too "edgy." We have to change that because "people won't like that. That's not what the audience wants—the audience really wants *this*." That kind of statement all the time.

It's highly depressing and I need classics to convince myself that I started my career for a reason. Often I think, "Why do I do this? Why am I exactly now where I am? How come I got to this point where I start to disbelieve my own work?" Or where I start to disbelieve that I can do movies that still have a meaning to myself, as well as having a commercial meaning to others.

NY: Are there any other movies being made *now* that you would watch?
PV: I just saw a movie which I really liked, a Mexican movie—*Y Tu Mama Tambien!* Another movie I very much liked was *Sexy Beast*—which is English, so now I've mentioned a Mexican one and an English one. I thought that was an extremely interesting movie, it took me by surprise—I was like, "Wow!" Of course, these movies are made. But are they made often in the United States? No, rarely.

NY: Any American movies recently that have been interesting in that way?
PV: Not in that way, no. There's enough American movies that I respect for different reasons, but it's rarely the case that I see something that I didn't expect. Even the best American movies, or the most successful ones—whatever you want to call them—are not very surprising to me. It's more like "OK, that's very well made, but." *The Terminator* surprised me, for example—I was taken aback by that. It was like, "Wow—that's somebody who really thought about something!" And really did it, with cheap means, relatively, and made something very original. If anything influenced me when I came to the United States, it was that movie, because *RoboCop* is not derived from *Terminator*, but I studied it very very well before I embarked on *RoboCop*, because *RoboCop* was of course still very outside my Dutch genre. I didn't know much about that kind of filmmaking.

NY: It was a script that you received?
PV: Yes, I changed it just a little bit and shot it. But it was something that I had no expertise in and not much knowledge about. So I think *The Terminator* was a very good education for me—from a philosophical point of view it's an interesting, audacious statement. Yes, it's science fiction, but not completely. Of course,

Jim [Cameron] has done a lot of work that is highly innovative—*Terminator 2*, it's a little bit the same story as the first one, so story-wise it isn't so innovative, but from a digital point of view what he did there was all applied to a much greater degree in *Starship Troopers*. He again built on all that stuff with *Titanic*—he's one of the directors who I find very interesting in a technological way.

NY: With *Starship Troopers* and *RoboCop*, you're dealing in media satire. Now we're perhaps seeing the satire become reality, post September 11. Do you watch CNN and think, "I made that fifteen years ago?"

PV: Other people say that. It's more *Starship Troopers* than *RoboCop*. With *RoboCop* the ironies are about urban situations, *Starship Troopers* is more to do with foreign politics. It's about propaganda, and the function of propaganda versus reality, and how it spins reality, and et cetera. *RoboCop* is mostly about the idiocy of American television. These kind of people that flip-flop between extreme sadness, and fun, and a commercial. I always thought that *RoboCop* was my reaction to being thrown into American society, and looking around with wide eyes, thinking, "This is completely crazy." That's all in *RoboCop*. A lot of what we could call the "sociology" was already in the script—this was something that the American writers have brought in. *Starship Troopers* was more me reflecting on American politics—to a certain degree, domestic American politics. There's a lot of parallels with what happened after September 11, of course—not just in the obvious way of shooting rockets in tunnels at the Taliban, or the "arachnids" in the movie—but also in the function of propaganda and spinning. In some ways it's a pleasure that it all became true, but on the other hand there's not much pleasure that it came true.

NY: You're now living in America at the time of Bush. Do you see any grounds for optimism?
PV: No.

NY: Do you see in the future that America will be a place where you will be able to live?
PV: I think it's much more difficult to live in the United States for me, than it was a couple of years ago. With all the craziness of the Clinton administration I could easily identify with Mr. Clinton. Even with Lewinsky—that could be me. I could do that kind of stuff. I'm what you might call "weak" or "interested" or "curious" or "a lover of the female"—however you want to express it. I identify with that completely.

NY: Do you feel a real difference in the atmosphere after Clinton, under Bush?
PV: Yes, yeah, sure, because it's much more gung ho and it's much more dangerous.

NY: Do you think you could make a movie about this change of atmosphere, in America?
PV: Well, if I didn't already do that with *Starship Troopers*, then basically I don't think so. Not at the moment—it would be impossible to get it off the ground. The American studios are already asked by the government to be as patriotic as possible, and to participate in this "fight against terrorism." It would be very difficult to make a critical movie. If I would do it, it *would* be extremely critical of that.

NY: But *you* could do it, by making a movie that seemed patriotic but in fact is a critique.
PV: If I found something, I would try to do that. But during the period I was making *Starship Troopers* there were six different regimes at Sony, and the film always "switched through," so by the time people started to realize what the movie was about it was too late! Then the new people came in, and they would only stay for three or four months, one after the other: Mike Medavoy was there, then Mark Platt, then Mark Canton, then Bob Cooper, then Jon Calley. So there were five regimes, during one movie.

NY: The rumor was that Calley was such a fan he wanted to do a sequel, even though the box office wasn't so great for the movie. Is that true?
PV: I strongly doubt that. But at least he supported it. He's always been a little bit of an outsider, in a way that he has done quote-unquote "dangerous projects," also when he was with other studios. He was a good friend of Kubrick, of course. He is one of the few people in the industry who are more willing to take risks or do something a little outrageous. Unfortunately Sony has not been doing so well, and this has forced the whole regime into making movies that are not representative of the ideas that Jon Calley, or Amy Pascal, really have in their minds, and would have liked to do. They have been frustrated, because the movies that were, in the beginning, when they started in that direction, those movies didn't work.

NY: Now they're doing *Stuart Little 2*, and *Spider-Man*.
PV: *Spider-Man* could be interesting—Raimi is an interesting director, so that could be something. I think it's difficult with the American politics of this moment. Though not only this moment—my problems with American politics are to some degree colored by the present Afghanistan situation. But my anger and my resistance to American politicians have much more to do with their support of Israel than anything else. That's where I really feel that American politics are inconsistent and, basically, not honest. The pumping of enormous quantities of money, and technology, and military, into Israel every year—this has created a fascist state. Unfortunately—in my opinion, I think Israel has become a fascist state.

NY: Have you considered examining these subjects in a non-fiction movie? Could you make a documentary that would bring these arguments forward?

PV: I think other people might be better at that, because that's also a profession that you have to learn. It's not something that just "falls out of your hands" like that. I made documentaries when I started my career, about the Dutch marine corps, and another one about the Dutch national-socialist Mussert, but since then I've been doing features. If you want to go back to documentaries it's a completely different technique, and others are much better at that than I. On the other hand, I'm really *struggling* with my position in the United States—of course, I'm as guilty as everybody else, by participating and paying my tax there. I'm as much to blame, perhaps, by staying there, instead of raising my voice or whatever.

A lot of the history of the Palestinian-Israeli conflict is on the table, of course, though it's not discussed in the mainstream. The American vision of the history of this conflict seems to start with the last suicide bomber. It's rare that any American newspapers described what happened after Oslo—how the settlements were basically crisscrossing through Palestinian territory, and making life and autonomy completely impossible. That's what happened—if you see where these settlements are, you'll see that the whole West Bank is crisscrossed with all kinds of enclaves which makes all the Palestines almost separate ghettos. And this is not even on the table! Even now, when Powell is there, it's not on the table—it starts with the last suicide, or it starts a little earlier. But it never starts where it should start—it's like history doesn't exist.

Paul Verhoeven

Bruce LaBruce / 2003

From *Index Magazine*, November 2003. Reprinted by permission of the author and courtesy of *Index Magazine*.

Paul Verhoeven started out directing movies for the Dutch navy. He's obsessed with greed and corruption. After getting a Ph.D. in mathematics, he made Arnold Schwarzenegger an icon. (Verhoeven spoke to fellow director Bruce LaBruce from his office in Hollywood.)

BRUCE LABRUCE: Your film career began in Holland, a country people generally associate with tolerant attitudes about sex. But you couldn't get funding for your work there after you made *Spetters* in 1980.
PAUL VERHOEVEN: Yes. All Dutch movies were fifty to sixty percent subsidized by the government. I was denied government funding because my movies were considered to be decadent, perverted, and antigovernment. That's when I had to leave. The problem was the leftists—they are so fucking dogmatic. At that time in Holland, they were often more fascistic than the right.

BLB: *Spetters*, of course, is about three amateur dirt-bike racers who try to emulate their pro motorcycle hero, played by Rutger Hauer. In the DVD commentary you confess to participating off-camera in the scene in which the dirt-bikers pull out their dicks to see whose is the longest.
PV: Oh, yeah. And my director of photography, Jost Vacano, was also part of the contest. In fact, he won. *Spetters* prompted the formation of a Dutch group called NASA, or the National Anti-Spetters Association, which targeted my work.

BLB: You've talked about having a nervous breakdown early in your career that made you question your identity as a filmmaker.
PV: Well, my sanity too. When I was twenty-six or twenty-seven, I almost went

mad. It was as if my subconscious had broken through. Nietzsche had the same experience and he just didn't recover.

BLB: What was it like?
PV: I had continuous dreams in which I was in a pit filled with water. The walls were at the point of breaking and there were all sorts of things behind them. I think I kept my sanity because of my wife.

BLB: Because of your art, as well?
PV: After that experience in my twenties, I forced myself to resist the irrational, and rely on reality as much as possible. My Dutch work was often based on true stories. The American films I made later are mostly fantasies, but I never completely lost the tendency to look at the dark side of reality.

BLB: After the *Spetters* witch-hunt in Holland, how did you like working in Hollywood?
PV: For a long time I just worked with small studios, so I was protected from the real Hollywood. For *Flesh+Blood* and *RoboCop*, I worked with Orion, which has since gone bankrupt and disappeared. Then I segued over to Carolco.

BLB: Which is gone now, too, right?
PV: Yes, but I did *Total Recall*, *Basic Instinct*, and *Showgirls* with Carolco. After that, I worked with a really big studio, Sony/Columbia. With *Starship Troopers*, the studio regime was changing every four or five months so nobody cared what we were doing. We just moved through the maze of the corporate net. But with *Hollow Man* there was no escape anymore—it was a corporate movie.

BLB: Didn't you have problems with the way that *Starship Troopers* was marketed?
PV: The studio promoted it like an edgier *Star Wars*. And it's clearly a different type of movie. It's got more depth.

BLB: Definitely. It's about a fascistic, hyper-militarized society whose enemy is a race of giant insects from another galaxy. The insects are viewed as a worthless life form that must be exterminated. It's more like a Leni Riefenstahl movie than *Star Wars*.
PV: Yes, there are a lot of quotes from Leni Riefenstahl in the film, but she actually believed in the propaganda and I don't. I felt that the soldier characters were all idiots. They were willing to die for their country because of the propaganda they had been fed.

BLB: As for the idea of utopia, would your ideal be some form of socialism? You smash the state apparatus in *Total Recall* . . .
PV: Well of course I'm a socialist, no doubt about that. I come from a socialist country. A few days ago I heard someone complaining about Western Europe, and the maximum insult he could come up with was "Those countries are socialist!" He was talking about France and Germany and I laughed because it's so stupid to think that. Socialism is probably the best possible compromise between capitalism and communism.

BLB: Watching your movies always turns me into a total film geek. There's something extremely cohesive and obsessive about your themes and narratives—you're like an auteurist's wet dream.
PV: That's the nicest description I've ever heard.

BLB: I also have to tell you, video store clerks are your biggest fans. The audio commentaries on your DVDs have a cult following of their own.
PV: *(Laughs)* Yeah, I've noticed that. I spend a lot of time on them. People who listen to these commentaries are often interested in making films themselves. I want to let them know that the things they struggle with are quite normal, and that they can learn from my mistakes.

BLB: I loved when you said that a director should humiliate himself in front of the cast and crew because it relaxes everyone. When I was younger, I directed some art/porno films in which I also performed sexually in front of the camera. One of my rules was never to make anyone do anything on film that I wouldn't do myself.
PV: With sex scenes, I feel that the actors have to be fully prepared—no surprises. They have to know exactly what the director has in mind. No one should be sitting on a set naked and suddenly hear from the director that he is supposed to do something he didn't know about.

BLB: With the famous scene in your sex thriller *Basic Instinct*, in which Sharon Stone uncrosses and crosses her legs, there have been rumors that she wasn't really aware of the camera angle.
PV: I've been trying to set the record straight about that for years! *(Laughs)* At different times, Sharon has said a lot of contradictory things, but my recollection of the scene has always been very consistent. The shot had been thoroughly discussed with her, of course. I was there with perhaps four people, including a boom man and Jost, the DP. She had told me that she wanted to work with a very small crew.

BLB: That's standard for a scene of this nature, I would think.

PV: Yes. So we shot it at around seven p.m. And she saw all the angles, because we taped it. Since Jost and I are both Dutch, she was in the presence of two liberal people who would not be shocked by a shot like that. At the time, she had no problem with it.

BLB: People have debated the scene endlessly—one side says it's exploitative, while the other calls it the ultimate moment of pussy power. Essentially it made Stone a superstar.

PV: During the filming, the atmosphere was very relaxed. When Sharon saw it in a theater for the first time, it was completely different. She brought in about twenty people—all kinds of managers, agents, and friends. I think they were afraid that the explicit shot would cancel out the strength of her star-making performance. So Sharon came up to me and said she wanted it out.

BLB: She had a history of doing nudity in her early films, didn't she?

PV: I think she had done nudity before. She later said she was going to sue me, but of course she never did because she knew that she had agreed to it. In all honesty, she initially loved the idea because of how it symbolized female dominance.

BLB: Have you ever considered making a porno movie?

PV: Not really. Ultimately, porn movies are unwatchable. They're so boring. No story line, bad acting and basically no pleasure. I have the rights to a book that could easily be treated in a provocative way, which is Bukowski's *Women*. It's not fully fleshed, but there's enough narrative to make it interesting. The episodes are not pornography but the tone is so explicit that it could be considered pornography anyhow. I always wanted to do it and just two weeks ago I started to talk about it again with actors and friends. I'll study your work, perhaps it will give me some inspiration.

BLB: I love all the sexual sight gags in your movies. There's a scene in your second feature film, *Turkish Delight*, in which Rutger Hauer and Monique van de Ven are having sex in a car. Just before he comes, he accidentally turns the windshield wipers on with his foot and the cleaning fluid spurts out. It's as if the car is having a sympathetic orgasm.

PV: Right. I'm not so sure how subtle that is.

BLB: It's just a perfect moment. Or that scene in *The Fourth Man* in which Jeroen Krabbé uses his hands to flatten Renée Soutendijk's breasts so she looks like a boy. It works so well in the context of the movie which is about a writer, played

by Krabbé, who begins an affair with Soutendijk's character, a mysterious female hairdresser, but ends up more interested in her sexy young boyfriend.
PV: That's all based on personal experience.

BLB: Throughout your oeuvre, the theme of homosexuality is extremely strong. Some people think you're a rabid homophobe. I'm curious what draws you, as a heterosexual, to this subject.
PV: I strongly believe that everybody is born with the possibility to go either way. I remember when I was thirteen or so, there was a water-polo player who had the most beautiful body I had ever seen. It was like a Greek statue of Hermes—I couldn't keep my eyes off that man. You could call that Platonic homosexual love. I think the possibility was there for me, as it is for everybody, but circumstances made me move to the other side. I'm not homophobic. Just look at my movies, like *Flesh+Blood*. The only people in that film who sincerely care about themselves or each other are homosexual. Everyone else is driven only by opportunism or by money.

BLB: In *Spetters* you explained homophobia so clearly. The character that beats up homosexuals is repressing his own homosexuality.
PV: *Spetters* was based on a series of articles published in Holland about the violent behavior of homosexual gangs in Rotterdam.

BLB: Even in your early Dutch films, there seems to be a certain Hollywood influence. For example, your film language seems very influenced by Hitchcock.
PV: Perhaps all of my movies are unconsciously influenced by Hitchcock because I studied him so thoroughly in my twenties. I probably watched *Vertigo*, *North by Northwest*, and *Rear Window* fifteen or twenty times each.

BLB: *Basic Instinct* clearly references *Vertigo*.
PV: I saw *Basic Instinct* as a Hitchcock film for the nineties. I'm sure that if Hitchcock had been alive, he would have immediately bought that script and made the movie.

BLB: What about *Total Recall*?
PV: I would compare it to *North by Northwest*. There's a lot of moving around, there's a dangerous woman who might be a prostitute. Arnold Schwarzenegger is on an adventure that's not his own, and he's mistaken for the wrong guy. At the end of *Total Recall*, when Ronny Cox and Arnold are standing opposite each other in the alien oxygen provider, they kind of rotate around each other. That's identical to the scene in *North by Northwest* where Cary Grant enters James Mason's

villa. Mason and Grant rotate around this imaginary axis—the figures are always circling left or right.

BLB: So Hitchcock is a stylistic reference.
PV: Not exactly. I used that technique because it's a really good tool for creating a sense of unease. The scene in *Total Recall* when Dr. Edgemar tells Arnold that he's still living in a dream is another Hitchcock reference. First the camera is at eye level, and then, when the doctor makes this statement that's so difficult to swallow, the camera descends. Hitchcock used sudden low camera angles in several movies to emphasize a moment of alienation or weirdness.

BLB: One of your writers called your movies fascism for liberals. That's an interesting oxymoron.
PV: Yes, it is. In his novel *Starship Troopers*, Robert Heinlein envisioned a kind of military fascist utopia. Although we liked a lot of things in the book, I needed to present the extremity to which that kind of utopia would lead. It's not very far away from the Bush government, in fact.

BLB: Why does your irony elude people so easily? In *RoboCop* and *Starship Troopers*, where the irony seems so obvious, some people miss it.
PV: Irony is a lost art. Sarcasm is known in America, but American audiences are not very well versed in irony. I've used it all my life.

BLB: You use irony as a critical tool. Both *RoboCop* and *Starship Troopers* are very critical of American culture. *RoboCop* is all about corporate malfeasance and the privatization and militarization of the police force. These themes are even more relevant today than they were when you made the film.
PV: *RoboCop* was an ironic treatment of Texas's ultraconservative justice system, in which it can seem like criminals get condemned in a minute and are executed just a couple of hours later.

BLB: One thing I love about *RoboCop* is that it's not anti-technology. The *Terminator* and *Matrix* series are somewhat paranoid about technology, portraying it as a menacing, horrible thing that oppresses everybody. But *RoboCop* is about people coping with technology and incorporating it into their lives.
PV: There has been a tendency in liberal existentialist thinking, coming from Heidegger, to say that technology is basically bad. I disagree. I think science is the only religion you can really trust. Technology that comes from science should not be vilified. We can certainly question the ways in which technology is misused or overused, but technology is not the problem. It's the people who use the technology.

BLB: It's how it's wielded.
PV: Clearly. Our life spans are now considerably longer than they were in medieval times. The earth is a wonderful place, and if technology can help you to enjoy it longer and disappear into the darkness later, so much the better. Of course, I come from a science background. I have a Ph.D. in Mathematics.

BLB: But there is a kind of mystical transcendentalism in your movies that would seem to refute strict rationalism. I love the way mysterious, unexplainable things insert themselves into your films, like in *Spetters*, when a halo appeared above the boy in the wheelchair in a Christian revival hall. That was a nice way of debunking the rational.
PV: That halo was created by sheer coincidence. It was a gift of god. There was a little break in the camera lens, and at a certain angle it created that effect. The question of the existence of the divine and looking for the divine will always be part of my thinking. On the other hand, *Showgirls* is an exercise in looking into the pit. For me, the kingdom of the devil is described there.

BLB: *Showgirls* is a vision of hell. You've been threatening to make a movie about Christ the man. Mel Gibson is also doing his Christ movie . . .
PV: Yeah, but it's probably going to be a very Catholic, verbatim interpretation of the gospels. My Jesus story would deconstruct the gospels and the church's lies, examining exactly what happened.

BLB: So it would be more scientific . . .
PV: It would be very political. The context was the Roman occupation of Israel. Jesus was condemned by the Romans, not by the Jews. The title on the cross says "the king of the Jews." It was a political charge—that Jesus pretended to the crown of Israel. He was crucified as a guerrilla. It was not so different from Che Guevara.

BLB: I also think you should make the Harvey Milk story.
PV: Should I? I never thought about it. Ed Neumeier and I are working on a contemporary piece about the LAPD. It's a real-life version of *RoboCop*.

BLB: Is it about police corruption?
PV: Everybody's corrupt in the movie—the council people, all the politicians. There are some good people, but a lot more bad people.

BLB: Is that what you're working on right now?
PV: No. I'm currently working on a movie for New Line called *Solace*. I don't want

to say too much because it's not clear yet whether or not they're going forward with it.

BLB: Can you just tell me the theme in a few broad strokes?
PV: It has to do with clairvoyance and serial killings. It's a good combination of dark and light.

Paul Verhoeven: Back in Black

Alex Simon / 2007

From TheHollywoodInterview.com. Reprinted by permission of the author.

Paul Verhoeven has returned home to Holland for his latest film, which ranks among the best of his career. A sort of companion piece to his 1977 masterpiece *Soldier of Orange*, which told the true story of a Dutch aristocrat who is forced to come of age during WWII, *Black Book* tells the harrowing story of a young Jewish woman (Carice van Houten, who deserves to become an international star) who finds herself thrown by circumstance into the resistance against the Nazis, where she is asked to pose as a sexy cabaret singer in order to get close to Holland's head of the SS (*The Lives of Others*' Sebastian Koch, also excellent). *Black Book* is one of the most harrowing WWII stories every filmed, and deserves to be recognized in Oscar's Best Foreign Film category at next year's awards. Paul Verhoeven sat down with us recently to discuss his latest addition to the cinematic canon.

ALEX SIMON: *Black Book* returns you to your roots, both as a Dutchman and as a filmmaker. It's an amazing companion piece to *Soldier of Orange*, and it also reinforces the fact that all of your films, going back to *Turkish Delight*, deal in some way with fascism, whether it's fascist politics, or fascist relationships. When we first met, ten years ago, you said something I'll never forget: "When I close my eyes, I see buildings on fire, and dead bodies."
PAUL VERHOEVEN: That's correct. I was a small boy during the war, but the mind takes these images like a sponge at that age, and the images were so extreme: bombs exploding, buildings collapsing, the whole sky turning red because the city was on fire . . . I felt these things coming back to me when I stood on the roof of the Bellagio Hotel watching the riots (in 1992). I felt these things coming back when there were those big fires in Malibu, and I was driving to my house in the evening, and driving into this horizon of reds. There is something childlike, something almost exciting for me, seeing those images at first, although I know as an adult

to correct my thoughts, because people are dying and burning. But in a primitive way, these images are always there.

AS: Obviously the fascism you experienced as a little kid is something you're still trying to process.
PV: Yes, process and understand it. By now, there are six hundred to seven hundred books I have collected and read on WWII. This goes for me and my old friend, the screenwriter Gerard Soeteman, as a child you don't understand. If you grew up in an occupied country, in a violent atmosphere, war was more natural than peace.

AS: That was certainly the case for the character of Rachel, your protagonist in *Black Book*.
PV: One of the elements that was extremely important to me in this film, was this feeling that when liberation day comes, everybody would be happy, but the protagonist would be in more danger than ever. That feeling was propelling me to make this movie for many years now, and I don't know where it comes from. It might be something very personal, but I always thought it would be so compelling to see all these happy, dancing people, and in the middle of it all would be these two people who were in more danger than ever before.

AS: One of the compelling things about the film is how it's all about gray areas, whereas *Soldier of Orange* was much more about black and white.
PV: Right, there were good guys and bad guys. Here, we're more morally ambiguous. There was an enormous amount of latent anti-Semitism in Dutch society then, some that was even ingrained into the Dutch language, expressions that used the word "Jewish" in a denigrating sense. This was true through the fifties and sixties, until people were finally confronted with the realities of the Holocaust, and slowly this disappeared. There was even a notorious incident with the Dutch Prime Minister around that time where he used one of these anti-Semitic expressions, and he was nearly forced to resign.

AS: It's interesting that it took twenty years after the war for this to happen.
PV: Well, it really took that long for people to realize what had happened in the Holocaust in the first place. We didn't realize it very well in Holland at all, especially during the war. Did we know that the Jews were being sent to Poland? Yes, because we saw it. But people were so occupied with surviving themselves, particularly during the last years of the war, they didn't think about things like Jewish people who were being put on trains to Poland. It didn't occur to them that it was something other than labor camps.

AS: But one thing that this film illustrates graphically, as do most of your films, is that fascism can only exist through the complicity of the masses. *Soldier of Orange* even opens with a college fraternity hazing.

PV: Yeah, that was the idea. It was supposed to look like Auschwitz, with the shaved heads and closed-in spaces. You weren't supposed to know what it was at first, then it turns out to be a fraternity ritual. I was in that fraternity at University of Leiden, and I always felt when that hazing would go on "this is fucking fascism that's happening here."

So once I got through the hazing, I really wanted nothing to do with the fraternity. And it still goes on. Look at Abu Ghraib, and what happened there. So yes, there is something evil in our nature that seems to goad us on to abuse people that we seemingly have power over.

AS: It was great to see you go home, so to speak, with this film, reuniting with your former screenwriting partner, and several actors who were in your Dutch productions. How did you and Gerard, over twenty years, come up with this story?

PV: The scene at the end of the movie, in the prison, I discovered that when, in 1966, I was doing research for a documentary about the Nazi leader of Holland, who was executed by the Dutch in '46. So that scene had been in my mind for forty years: what happened in Dutch prisons after the war, what they did with the Nazi collaborators. It really shocked me the way the Dutch behaved when I did that research. Then, at the time we did research for *Soldier of Orange*, we came across a lot of great material about the end of the war that we couldn't use in the film, such as the story of the little black book, which really existed, as did many of the characters in the film. So it was created step-by-step over the years, with long intervals of time where we'd leave it alone, and then come back to it. The final structure we came up with in 2002–3, by making the protagonist a woman, which was a dilemma we'd had for a long time: whether to make the character a man or a woman. The character of the Jewish girl was always there, but once we made her the protagonist, everything fell into place.

AS: You've been a big studio moviemaker for the past twenty years here. What was it like to go home and make a comparatively small picture?

PV: It's much less of a sensation than you would expect. The Dutch and German crews were excellent. There have been lots of movies made in both countries in the past fifteen years because of the tax incentives, so the crews were much better than when I made films in the sixties and seventies. There was a lot of freedom, more freedom than you would get in any of the studios here, because nobody was dictating what I could or couldn't do. The only negative side of working in Europe is the enormous difficulties in getting the money together for an independent movie of this size. The budget was $21 million. This is really a European, as opposed to a strictly Dutch, film because the financing came from four different countries: Holland, England, Germany, and Belgium.

AS: Not only that, but a lot of the moral ambiguity, sexuality and violence in the film would have been watered down, had it been an American studio picture.

PV: Yes, absolutely, not to mention the fact that it would have cost $70–$80 million, as opposed to twenty-one. And it wouldn't have been the same film without those elements you mention. One thing we wanted to do with this film was to show that sometimes the people we think of as "good guys" can be really evil, and that the "bad guys" can have a heart. There's an old joke in Holland: "Everyone (during WWII) was part of the resistance." Well, if that had been true, would the Nazis have been able to overthrow the country? Not as easily, certainly. There were good and bad on both sides, and we need to recognize that.

AS: The other thing I love about the film is that it combines your two schools of filmmaking: it has the European elements we just discussed, but also the narrative drive that's characteristic of American pictures.

PV: Yeah, I think I learned that in the United States, and brought it back to Europe. I asked Gerard, whose sensibilities are more European, and therefore the narratives might be a bit less compelling, I asked him if he would write this movie with that kind of narrative drive. I think the combination of the two is interesting and compelling to the audience, as well.

AS: Do you tend to give lots of direction to your actors, or do you prefer to cast well and stay out of the way?

PV: It depends upon the actor. Sharon Stone, for example, I would give lots of direction and I would be continuously busy with her. With Carice, I found the less I did, the better it got. If I gave her too many instructions, it would limit her too much, whereas if I just let her go, she was limitless. She was like Meryl Streep that way. So I got whatever I wanted from her, but ultimately I had to tell her to not listen to me, and just to do what she felt, which was always the perfect solution.

AS: I always felt that *Starship Troopers* was your unheralded masterpiece: no one on this side of the pond understood that it was a satire.

PV: Not only that, but there are several different layers to it. The one that we added to (Robert) Heinlein's novel, which was a satire on American society, was also a real stab at fascism. I think it was too unusual a film, and not what people expected. Perhaps we should have pointed out that these elements existed before we screened it. In many countries, including the US, the film was accused of being fascist or neo-Nazi. It addressed what I felt were the possibilities of American fascism, but it was anything but pro-fascist.

AS: And of course, if you look at what's going on now, it was prescient.
PV: Yes, we didn't realize that at the time, but we could see the beginnings of it even in the late nineties. I mean, these last five years didn't come out of nowhere. It was ways of thinking that had been rampant in the eighties, even before Clinton. The whole neo-conservative philosophy has a long history in this country. I was aware of that, and certainly (screenwriter) Ed Neumeier was too. We went that way to counter Heinlein's narrative a bit, which was very militaristic, and perhaps a bit fascistic, as well. So the ironies were invented to counter the original narrative in some way. We borrowed a lot of imagery from Nazi propaganda, like Leni Riefenstahl's films, and the designs of the uniforms, so perhaps that's where the accusations of Nazism came from. What I like about the film, is that we did it in a playful way: I don't think we were grabbing the audience by the throat, trying to choke them with our viewpoints.

AS: Now that you've "gone back home again," do you want to continue to work on both sides of the pond?
PV: Sure, oh yeah. I can see that you can make European movies, which I used to be not so sure about, but the nightmare of the financing for this one would probably dictate that I would need to see more solid ground from the beginning. But yes, you can make interesting movies there, and in the United States, I'd prefer to go a bit more into realism, instead of doing so many science fiction and fantasy types of films. I'd love to do a film like *The Departed*, for example. I've never done that in the United States, really. *Showgirls*, perhaps was realistic that way ... (*Both laugh.*) Okay, okay, so I mean that in a somewhat amusing way, but *Showgirls* was based on a lot of research!

AS: Maybe we should end this conversation with your desire to do a film like *The Departed*.
PV: Good idea! (*Laughs*)

Devil's Advocate

James Hughes / 2007

From *Stop Smiling*, November 2007. Reprinted with permission from Stop Smiling Media.

A decade ago, the Dutch-born provocateur Paul Verhoeven had scraped the furthest reaches of his tumultuous tenure in Hollywood. After a series of science fiction mindbenders and erotic thrillers—*RoboCop* (1987), *Total Recall* (1990), *Basic Instinct* (1992) and *Showgirls* (1995)—had made him one of the most profitable directors of the nineties, Verhoeven unleashed *Starship Troopers* (1997), an allegory on fascism set against a backdrop of intergalactic warfare (with perfectly chiseled humans battling a race of alien insects that substitute for Brownshirts—or perhaps it's the other way around). The film is a hybrid of essential Verhoevian landmarks: a critique of jingoism and brutality—as a boy raised in occupied Holland in the early forties, he witnessed the repercussions of both firsthand—and an indulgence in special effects, disfigurement, transformation and, to coin Verhoeven's own phrase, "fantasy vengeance." The result of this cocktail is a catalog of American films that are crowd-pleasing, multiplex manifestations of the comic-book pulp of the twentieth century and the apocalyptic, medieval landscapes of fellow Dutchman Hieronymus Bosch.

Yet running throughout each film is a singular intelligence that subverts the trappings of genre escapism. The *New York Times*, while acknowledging his work can make "virtue of vulgarity," also celebrated his films as "well-oiled contraptions, taut and propulsive as vintage Hitchcock." What other action director who would helm a film about insect invasions can also boast a double major in mathematics and physics, and inclusion as a Fellow in the Jesus Seminar, a group of theologians and scholars who meet biannually to explore the authenticity of Christ? The influence of such an eclectic background is apparent in his work, often obscured by buckets of blood and toxic waste. Verhoeven, for example, described his first Hollywood feature, *RoboCop*, as a "search for lost paradise."

At the twilight of the nineties, Verhoeven—a man defined by his boundless energy—was beginning to show signs of fatigue. With *Hollow Man* (2000), a modern take on the oft-told invisible man parable, Verhoeven was confronted with a story that lacked his usual arsenal of stimulants. Struggling for a focal point, he seized on Plato's hypothesis that "if a man were invisible and could do anything, then he would act like an evil god." Despite a fondness for the film's technical achievements, Verhoeven still harbors regrets. "I felt I had made a movie that was not personal anymore and didn't have very much to do with me," Verhoeven said during our interview this summer. "I'd become, basically, a puppet of the studio, which I never wanted to do with my life. I wanted to make movies because there was something personal to me. To a large degree, I felt that a lot of these movies, like *RoboCop* and *Starship Troopers*, were personal enough for me to have pleasure. But after *Hollow Man*, I felt I should take a break from that style of American filmmaking."

After the release of *Hollow Man*, Verhoeven pulled a disappearing act of his own, returning to Holland to contemplate his own interpretation of an "evil god." The result, after a six-year absence, was an all-European production, *Black Book*, which may be the most personal work in his four decades of filmmaking. Based on a story he uncovered in the eighties along with screenwriter Gerard Soeteman, *Black Book* raises serious questions about the Dutch Resistance and their actions after triumphing over the Nazis who stormed their homeland. Along with providing a vehicle to connect with his art-house roots, Verhoeven viewed *Black Book* as an opportunity to counterbalance the more "heroic" portrayal of the Resistance in his 1977 film *Soldier of Orange*, which was an international hit and remains one of the cornerstones of Dutch filmmaking. Verhoeven's other Dutch works include *Turkish Delight* (1973), *The Fourth Man* (1983) and his most controversial film— even surpassing the picket-lines that *Basic Instinct* provoked—*Spetters* (1980), a study of teenagers struggling for redemption after a steady diet of street-crime and deep-fried dog food.

Ready to seize the momentum and critical acclaim that *Black Book* afforded him, Verhoeven went into production on *Azazel*, a thriller set in Russia. While in pre-production, the film's star, Milla Jovovich, announced she was pregnant and the project was put on hold. Never one to remain idle, Verhoeven plunged back into a book he's been writing for years about the life of Jesus Christ, tentatively titled "Jesus of Nazareth." (The book, he claims, is seventy-five percent completed, and is to be a stepping-stone for a larger project: a film about Jesus.) The break also provided him a window of time to open up to *Stop Smiling* from his Los Angeles office about life back among the visible.

JAMES HUGHES: You've said in the past that the most accurate portrayal of Jesus Christ on film is Pasolini's *The Gospel According to St. Matthew*.
PAUL VERHOEVEN: Not accurate, of course—accurate to the gospels. I thought Pasolini did an interesting job spinning the Gospel of St. Matthew into a Marxist

direction. He presented the story of Christ in a Marxist idiom. At the same time, he was not really deviating from the narrative or the text of the Gospel of St. Matthew. He was not looking at Jesus in any historical way. He was just following the Gospel, which is Christian spin, and he changed the reality to the reality of the times to promote the myth of Jesus.

JH: The structure of Pasolini's film is systematic. It has the feel of a procedural, where you're seeing a character's progression, step by step. Would you take a similar approach if you were to make a film about Jesus' life?

PV: I would not follow any of the gospels, because they are all, basically, untrue. They were all written by people who wanted to promote Christianity, so they're all propaganda material. In some way, you have to go back and find out what's behind these gospels: What was the reality of Jesus' life? That's what I'm going to do. I'm not going to follow any of these gospels, unless I feel there are elements of the gospels that look to me—and, let's say, to scholars nowadays—authentic. Whatever you want to call it—authentic sayings, actions or deeds of Jesus. So I would keep that. All the things I consider to be secondary, redactions or mythology: I would like to skip that. It's a completely different approach than Pasolini's film, or Mel Gibson's movie, for that matter.

JH: Are you the only filmmaker or artist who's a member of the Jesus Seminar?

PV: Oh yes. It's basically theologians who come from a church background, even John Dominic Crossan, for example, who is one of the famous members of the Seminar. He is an ex-priest, so he certainly comes from a Christian background. He is still a Christian—most of the members of the Seminar are Christians anyhow, though there are some from Jewish backgrounds, who of course are not Christians. I'm not a Christian either.

JH: Being that you're the lone filmmaker within that group, perhaps this question is appropriate: What is the reaction within the Seminar to the idea of Jesus becoming a kind of pop-culture icon through products like *The Da Vinci Code*?

PV: That is seen at the Seminar as very comedic. (*Laughs*) I don't think a serious scholar would look to *The Da Vinci Code* for any information or any interpretation that has anything to do with reality. Of course no one in the Seminar would comment on that. *The Passion of the Christ*, however, they did. Several scholars commented on that film, but not *The Da Vinci Code*. That was nonsense from the beginning.

JH: When Pasolini was casting his lead to play Christ in *The Gospel According to St. Matthew*, he considered offering the role to Jack Kerouac or Allen Ginsberg,

because he wanted to convey to young people that Jesus was a charismatic, revolutionary figure. If you were to get your film about Jesus made, what approach would you take?
PV: I would go for the best actor. It's already difficult enough, you know? It's a difficult and demanding part. An actor would need a lot of insight and talent to do that. I would not go for a non-actor. I would try to find an actor of thirty or thirty-five that could act in the most magnificent way. Pasolini ended up casting a student of theology for the main part, which worked very well. I admired Pasolini's approach. He made an interesting movie, which had nothing to do, in my opinion, with the historical reality of what happened. Personally, I would be more interested in making a movie that represents what I think was the historical reality, not one that follows the gospels, which are already contaminated by Christian spin.

JH: While making *The Battle of Algiers*, Gillo Pontecorvo held up production for weeks, searching the casbahs for a lead actor who had the right face.
PV: Yes. You're talking about a situation that was pretty close by. For the authenticity of that situation, he could basically grab someone, because he still had a link to that time because of photographs. He knew how the people really looked. There are several books, of course, written about the battles in Algeria. He wanted to stay close to reality and was looking for lookalikes or [someone] coming close. In the time of Jesus, we have no materials, no image of Jesus. There are few images, even of Joan of Arc—most of them were painted long after she died. We don't even know how she looked, let alone Jesus, John the Baptist or any other disciples. It's all fantasy.

In the last movie I did, *Black Book*, seventy or eighty percent was based on real events and things that happened during World War II in Holland. I went for good actors instead of thinking I needed to be close to the reality of the time. For some of the people [I portrayed], I had photographs, but I stepped over that. Everyone has their own approach. Pontecorvo was trying to be as pseudo-documentary as he could. *The Battle of Algiers* is one of the most interesting movies ever made—there's no doubt about that. Pontecorvo was fully right to do it that way. Every artist is different. There are many different ways, of course, of portraying elements that have historical backgrounds. Look at *Ivan the Terrible*. To a certain degree Eisenstein used a little bit about reality, but even when he was constructing the story, he omitted a lot of historical elements. He didn't like them. He constructed his own film that was meaningful to him. You could put many questions toward the historical value of that movie, but there are no questions about the artistic value of the movie. Nor is there any question of the artistic value of *Lawrence of Arabia*, where Robert Bolt changed a lot of elements: overlaid things, took things out, accentuated things. Bolt's script of *Lawrence of Arabia* was not complete reality—a lot of things have been adapted for dramatic or visual reasons. That's the right the artist has—to make his own interpretation of history without being a slave to it.

JH: After *Showgirls*, you said you were in "Hollywood jail." With *Black Book*, however, you received many positive responses from the press. But some critics, like Anthony Lane in The *New Yorker*, questioned precisely what you're saying now: The Resistance fighters were too elegantly dressed or had too much meat on their bones.

PV: They're wrong. The man who wrote that was wrong. He basically did not go through the elaborate process of documentation that I went through. The people in the Resistance basically had better food to eat than anyone else, because they were continuously hitting German trucks and getting food. That's nonsense. Of course there were people starving in The Hague, the city where I lived, and they were slim by the end of the war, but they didn't look like someone at Auschwitz. That is highly exaggerated. I think the writer was thinking of all the dead bodies you see at Auschwitz. The writer's view of people at that time is based on a lack of knowledge, really. (*Laughs*) People think they know something about the Second World War, but they know the clichés. I was living at that time—I know how people looked at that time. I have photographs of my parents in 1944 and 1945. They didn't look like skeletons—it's nonsense. People take things much too literally.

I think that writer is at fault. But many people are—they pretend, for example, that there were no bicycles at the time. Of course there were bicycles at that time. Once in a while the Nazis would close the quarter, and whoever had a bicycle, the bicycle would be taken and given to the German soldiers so they could move around, because there was no gasoline anymore. But they didn't do that every day. They did it every two or three months. Through the Resistance and all the channels of gossip, you knew in advance if this would happen, so a lot of people were hiding their bicycles. In fact, my parents had bicycles. I love the cliché that the Germans took the Dutch bikes. It's always a joke in Holland: If you see a German person on a bike, you say, "Oh, that's my bike. You've had it for fifty years."

JH: What is the reaction to America in Holland at the moment?
PV: Bad.

JH: Is there any turn in opinion now that several elected Republican officials have been voted out, or members of the Bush administration have been removed or resigned in disgrace?
PV: Certainly a lot of people are happy that the American people and the American media, who have been continuously following the president for five years, are

coming to their senses and starting to realize what happened. I think people in Europe who have been opposing the war—not so much the Dutch government, unfortunately, which I would say has been backing Bush and Blair—feel vindicated, of course, that the American people have begun to see the manipulation, lies and cheating that took place. In *Starship Troopers*, there was propaganda, propaganda, propaganda until you believe it's true. That's what happens. Many European people were skeptical from the beginning. There are still another six hundred or so days to go, and you don't know if the American government is going to launch further madness in Iran or anywhere else. Hopefully they would have a hard time pushing the House and Senate to follow them. I think it's a good thing that many of these neocon people, including Mr. Wolfowitz, are slowly moving to the side. The neoconservative thinking, if you read it and see what the themes are—that the United States should be the only power in the world and nobody should ever be able to come close to the military of the United States and the US can take everything they consider in their interests—it makes neoconservative thinking nearly identical to neofascist thinking.

JH: And it's made torture acceptable in the United States.
PV: Which is extremely medieval.

JH: In *Spetters* and *Turkish Delight*, there's a similarity between the aggressiveness of youth behavior and the droogs in Stanley Kubrick's *A Clockwork Orange*. How did you react to Kubrick's film when it was released?
PV: I thought the first part of the movie was excellent, and the second part I didn't buy. I don't think looking at shots of Nazi Germany and Hitler, basically, was convincing [enough] that it would cure this boy. I didn't believe that for a second. I don't think that's how you convince people of evil, or where evil is leading to. It's true in reality that evil led to the ultimate evil, which was the Nazi regime and the killing of about 50 million people in Europe. But I don't think in the movie he expressed that in a dramatic way. I think he expressed it by the visuals of the thirties. But that's really a very intellectual thought—it's not an emotional thing. Shots of parades are not, to me, evil. The evil is not the parades; it's what the soldiers did after the parades.

JH: When you were filming *RoboCop*, you searched high and low for the city that best fit your vision. I'm curious what you feel is the greatest skyline in America?
PV: At the time, I thought it would be Houston or Dallas. We shot *RoboCop* in Dallas, as you know. The end of the movie, at the steel factory, was in Pittsburgh. I would have loved to combine the skyline of Houston with the skyline of Dallas, but that was too expensive, so I had to shoot it in Dallas. Houston has a lot of

very modern architecture based on the enormous amount of money from the oil industry there. I also looked at Chicago, which has many modern buildings. I would not know at this moment what city has the most, let's say, impressive architecture. Normally I look at these things when I make a movie. So when I made a science fiction movie, like *Total Recall*, I was also looking again at Houston and Dallas, but there was a money problem, so I shot the movie in Mexico City. There were no skyscrapers or glass and steel in Mexico City, I found another style there called New Brutalism, which is all concrete. There were several buildings that had that. We shot a lot at the military academy. Then I tried to adapt the style as much to that concrete New Brutalism as possible in my sets. Location scouting is always a compromise between what would be the best artistically and what is logistically possible.

RoboCop was supposed to be Detroit, but the city didn't look good in any way. Detroit would in no way give us the impression of a futuristic city, so we went to Chicago, Dallas and Houston. The choice of Dallas was mostly for economic reasons. Chicago is a very interesting city—there are a lot of possibilities both ways. It has a lot of New York things, and a great railway system and a certain darkness like New York, and there's the beauty of the water around it. If you were to give me a city that is modern and a bit gritty and is beautiful, then I think Chicago would probably be the best choice. But I have never been able to shoot there. If you were to do a detective story and you didn't want to go for the obvious, which would be New York, then you should always go to Chicago, in my opinion.

Jesus of Nazareth

Rüdiger Sturm / 2009

Phone interview. Reprinted by permission of the author.

The seventy year old director is known for sparking controversy with cult classics like *Basic Instinct* or *Starship Troopers*, but none of this is as controversial as his efforts as a historian: For more than twenty years he has been exploring the historical roots of the Gospels, as the only non-theologian member of the scholarly circle, the "Jesus Seminar." His findings, published as *Jesus of Nazareth* are already in its seventh printing in his native Holland and have now been translated into German. Further international editions—also in English speaking countries—are bound to follow in the next few years.

RÜDIGER STURM: Why are you so interested in Jesus instead of, let's say, Buddha?

PAUL VERHOEVEN: Probably because my parents were Protestant and I was educated in Western Europe: Jesus was closer than Buddha. I started reading the Gospels instead of the teachings of Buddha. We in the West have been surrounded by Christianity for most of our lives. Society does that to you. It is arbitrary. Islam or Buddhism are as important as Christianity. But I have been intrigued by the life of Jesus, which is for me more dramatic than Buddha: the crucifixion seems more interesting to me than growing old.

RS: How did it come about that you wrote a book about Jesus?
PV: It started out as research for a movie about Jesus. I wanted to know what Jesus had really said and done—what can be considered historical reality in the Gospels. That's why I joined the Jesus Seminar in California in 1986—it's a group of (mostly American) theologians who study the historical Jesus. However, after doing research for fifteen years I felt that what I had discovered could be better formulated in a book than in a movie. In a book you can give arguments for your views, you can mention counter-arguments, you can make it clear that some

thesis is just a possibility or a probability, you can write "I think" or "I believe," you can use the word 'perhaps'. In a movie there is no "perhaps." A screenwriter has to make a choice between different (historical) possibilities, and a scene can only be shot one way. There is only one reality in a movie. You are not able to give arguments. You can't say: I based it on this, I have read that, these are the arguments of different theologians, this is what I think—it's not possible in a movie. You have to make a choice, whatever other possibilities might be available. Was Mary raped? Was Joseph the natural father of Jesus, or did Mary have an extramarital relationship? This is all possible. In a movie, however, there is only one possibility.

Around 2000 I started to feel that it was more interesting to present arguments than to use only the *result* of these arguments. That's why I wrote the book and did not make the movie. I hope that the book can convince the reader of my vision of Jesus more than a movie—with its overbearing impact—would do. What I have written about Jesus should not be read as a fantasy, even when I speculate—it is a possible reality.

RS: But couldn't you do the movie now? Or would it be more conceivable to make a documentary?

PV: My co-writer Rob van Scheers and I are working on a documentary. But that wouldn't be more than a visual aid to the book. I would talk about "my" Jesus while visiting the different locations in Israel/Palestine where he dwelled. If I were to make a film I would be forced to use dramaturgical tools to keep the audience—who will be sitting in the dark for two hours—interested. One must assume that the movie would—necessarily so—be a distortion of historical reality, as much as David Lean's film *Lawrence of Arabia* is. But I do not think that this movie will be made soon—this should reassure many good Christians. After working on the book for so many years I am pretty exhausted. It was quite an effort and I am happy with the results. At the moment I don't feel compelled to go to a studio and ask for money to make a Jesus movie. The next step in my life will hopefully fulfill an old dream; to make a movie about a woman in Munich in 1923. The year of hyperinflation (and a nice metaphor for our economy in 2009) and the beginning of Nazism—Hitler's Putsch. The working title is *A Most Improper Woman*. It suits me well.

RS: The press coverage of your book has focused mainly on your argument that Mary was raped by a Roman soldier, and that Jesus was his son . . .

PV: You know how the press works. They simply go for the most obvious—but certainly not the most original—thought in the book. Jane Schaberg already pointed out almost twenty years ago that there could have been a rape, which was a big scandal in the US at the time. In my book it's only a possibility, albeit a plausible one.

RS: Why aren't you interested in studying the mythology of Jesus, like the virgin birth or the resurrection?
PV: My book is not about what people *made* out of Jesus, it is about what he *did* and what he *said*. Thousands of books have been written about the mythological aspects of the story, and I have no interest in that matter. I am only interested in Jesus himself, as a human being. I tried to visualize him, get close to him—as close as you can possibly get to someone who has been dead for two thousand years. That was my objective; that is what I studied for twenty years: the book provides an overview of what I discovered. To a large degree it also deals with the political implications of his acts and words.

Jesus was crucified for *political* reasons, as an enemy of the Roman Empire. He was accused of pretending to be a "king of the Jews." According to all four of the gospels, that is the accusation that was written on the *titulus*, the piece of wood that was nailed on the cross above Jesus' head.

Many people, many theologians, even the gospel authors have tried to downplay this accusation. They say that the Romans were misguided; that they *thought* that Jesus tried to become "king of the Jews" but that in reality Jesus was talking about a *spiritual* kingdom, not "of this Earth." Whereas I state in my book that the kingdom (of God) that Jesus was always talking about, was in fact a *real* kingdom on Earth: the kingdom of Israel. Jesus' claim that God would put him in charge of this kingdom meant insurrection against the Roman Empire, which would immediately be punished by crucifixion. From the Roman point of view Jesus was crucified for good reasons. In their eyes he was guilty of *perduellio*: being a public enemy.

RS: The Gospel of Mark is the most original, as you also state in your book. But why in other instances do you base your argumentation on John—regarding, for example the number of Jesus' visits to Jerusalem?
PV: Most theologians think that John offers a lot of theological discourse that has nothing to do with the historical reality of Jesus, but I point out in my book that some fragments of the gospel stand out like a foreign body. They come out of nowhere and are not connected to the rest of the text. One example is the *fight* that Jesus had with John the Baptist (3:26), which stands in total contrast to all of the positive things that the gospels report about the relationship between these two men. A second example can be found in John's description of the famous

"multiplication of the loaves"—suddenly the people try to grab Jesus to "make him king by force" (6:15). These events are clearly disconnected from John's theological discourse and I therefore believe them to be historical.

The other gospel writers either did not know these facts or did not like them. They did not want to show that Jesus and John the Baptist had a falling out, neither did they want to portray Jesus as a revolutionary—which the kingship implies. It wouldn't be helpful in the Roman Empire to worship a man as God, who was then crucified as an insurrectionist.

RS: Certain of your convictions place you in the minority within the Jesus Seminar. Why is that?

PV: From the beginning the Jesus Seminar had the idea that Jesus was not expecting the Kingdom of God, he was more like a Jewish cynic in the vein of Diogenes. In the twenty-first century it is clearly a difficult thing to grasp that Jesus was expecting the Kingdom of God, that he even thought it was already partially present—in the form of his exorcisms—but ultimately realized that it wasn't going to come anyway. That's not very constructive for a modern Christian audience.

I am convinced that Jesus really saw his exorcisms as *proof* that the Kingdom of God had arrived. You can see that as the naive attitude of Jesus, and it was in fact a big mistake—the Kingdom of God did *not* arrive, as we well know, and Jesus ended up hanging on a cross.

But we should accept Jesus' naiveté. Fashioning him as a Jewish cynic as the Seminar did makes Jesus more modern than he really was. For me it is not about finding the best theology for the twenty-first century, but trying to see Jesus in all his naiveté, in all his wrong interpretations of reality.

What is most important to me—and perhaps this is not emphasized enough in the book—is the following: although Jesus interpreted the exorcisms wrongly, although his strong conviction that the Kingdom of God came to nothing, he nevertheless—simultaneously—created these wonderful and powerful parables in which he showed us *glimpses* of that Kingdom. Thereby he introduced a completely new ethic that involves a concept of human behavior that is even now—in anno 2009—hard to accept, let alone to follow. Instead of focusing on the cliché "love your enemy"—which is nearly impossible—we should look at the *behavior* of the Samaritan or the father of the Prodigal Son. It is exactly this behavior that can provide an ethical guide.

In short: Jesus made big mistakes but at the same time he created something that is absolutely marvelous.

RS: So one might say that your initial fascination has developed into a deep appreciation for Jesus?

PV: Yes. Pretty late in my research I started to study the parables and what Jesus said within the sphere of ethics and I realized how innovative and important that was. For me it explains why this man has continued to inspire us and why he is still so important to us today. Unfortunately the church, very early on, in the first four hundred years after Jesus' death did not focus on Jesus' ethics at all, but chose instead to elevate him to the status of God. So now we can worship Jesus (which is easy) instead of applying Jesus' ethics (which is difficult).

For me Jesus is like Mozart. He is the Mozart of ethics.

RS: Can you elaborate on that a little more?

PV: Take, for example, the parable of the Samaritan. A Jewish man is attacked by robbers who take all his money, even his clothes, beat him up and leave him naked and half dead on the road. Then a Jerusalem priest passes by. He sees the wounded man, but walks a big curve around him and continues on his way. The same reaction comes from a Levite [a lower priest] who passes by: he doesn't have any interest in the naked, severely wounded man either.

Then a Samaritan passes by. Understand that the Samaritans were *enemies* of the Jews. Nowadays you would think of Palestinians or even Hamas or more specifically, Barghouti. (For the priest and the Levite: think State Secretary Liebermann or Prime Minister Netanyahu.) The Samaritan sees the wounded man and walks immediately towards him. He revives him with wine, takes care of his wounds and places him on his mule—the Samaritan himself will walk. He brings the victim to an inn and pays for his stay there. He says to the innkeeper, "I am going away now, but I will be back in a couple of days. If there are additional costs I will pay that too." The Samaritan/Palestinian shows great compassion for the Jew, he crosses the boundaries of animosity and hate.

Similar ethics are visible in the parable of the Prodigal Son. The son wants to go abroad, start a new life there. He asks his father for his part of the heritage. The father complies and lets the son go to a foreign country. There the son squanders his money on prostitutes and becomes completely destitute when a famine breaks out. He decides to go back to his father and ask him for forgiveness.

But when the father sees his son return he does not reproach him for anything. On the contrary, he runs towards his son and embraces him. He gives him his own costly robe, puts the family ring on his hand, and slaughters the fattest calf so they can have a great party. This is again a transgression of the conventional boundaries of mistake/reproach and instead a showing of compassion, forgiveness, and love.

The father and the Samaritan both stand for Jesus' new ethics: whoever the victim is, whatever his background, his belief, his social or cultural position, if he needs help they will give that to him. This is an ethical ideal that has yet to be accomplished in our Western civilization.

RS: Have you promoted these ideals in your movies?

PV: Perhaps, I hope so. I can give you an example from *Soldier of Orange* that points in that direction: Eric, the main character of the movie played by Rutger Hauer, becomes a resistance fighter during the German occupation of Holland in World War II. However, a student friend of his, Alex—who has German parents—joins the German army. Halfway through the movie these two people meet again by coincidence: in The Hague Eric walks into a parade of soldiers who are on their way to Germany to fight against the Russians on the Eastern front. It turns out that Alex is one of these soldiers.

Eric recognizes his friend and yells out his name. Alex (who is marching) turns around. And then they wave at each other. Although they are at the opposite sides of the political spectrum, they reach across it. Their friendship is stronger than their political differences. That wouldn't be so far away from what Jesus was preaching.

RS: Do you see an irony in the fact that the prevailing notion of Christianity was implemented by your namesake?

PV: People have advised me to call my book the Gospel of Paul. But I am not a big fan of Paul's thinking, especially because I feel that Paul did not know enough about Jesus and did not even care.

Paul started preaching after he had apparently "seen" Jesus in a vision on his way to Damascus. That is already weird because Paul had never met Jesus, so how did he recognize him? Immediately after that vision he went off on his own and started to preach about Jesus. But he didn't know anything more about Jesus than what he could have heard from the Christians whom he had earlier persecuted. Only three years later did he go to Jerusalem and met Peter, James (the brother of Jesus) and one or two disciples. They probably gave him some *real* information about the historical Jesus.

What Paul did with that information was a distortion of Jesus' life and teaching. Paul put all of that emphasis on the cross, on Jesus' suffering, which he then transformed into evidence of God's will because Jesus, now seen as the *Son* of God, had to die for our sins. With this theological concept he tossed the historical Jesus overboard along with his ethical teaching. This, in my opinion was a disastrous development for Christianity. Although I have to admit that Paul did a pretty convincing job fabricating this distortion.

RS: Are you tempted at all to teach and preach your historical version of Jesus?

PV: In a church in Holland I had an interesting, warm, positive discussion with the liberal Dutch-protestant community that had invited me. I might have sounded preachy by talking too enthusiastically about Jesus' ethics but I would not call that real preaching, which is generally connected to being a Christian and "believing" in Jesus.

RS: If you had to choose between making a movie and going on a speaking tour about the real Jesus, which would you decide?
PV: I prefer to stay away from such plans. I have done enough "Jesus" work in the last couple of years. Even while I was filming *Black Book* I was working on the Jesus book. I want to abandon Jesus for a year and then see how I feel about a movie about him. It's possible that publishing this book will change my life and that I decide to stop being a film director and become a preacher of the secular Jesus. That's a possibility. At the moment I still see myself as a film director. But who knows? Life might bring me to places other than I foresaw.

RS: Did you know Ancient Greek before you began your research?
PV: I had five years of Greek and six years of Latin at my "classical" high school. I studied each language for five to seven hours a week. I could read Plato and Homer at that time. Reading the gospels in Greek is a lot easier than reading Plato—the language is simpler.

RS: Did you also do archival work?
PV: I tried to visit theology archives to study the original codices. But to get access to these, say to the archives of the Vatican, would be very difficult. I assume you have to be an extremely respected scholar to get in there. I did not try. It really isn't necessary: all the codices have been published in one way or another. I have for example in my library the published *Codex Bezae Calabriensis*, a very special codex that often seems to have more original texts than famous codices like *Vaticanus* or *Sinaiticus*.

Everything is available now. Even the Gospels of Judas and Thomas, which caused such a stir when they were discovered are all published now. By the way: the importance of these two texts has been enormously exaggerated by the media. They contain very little information about the historical Jesus.

RS: Apparently your house was swamped with books about Jesus while you were writing the book. Is your furniture still covered with your reading material?
PV: I cleaned it all up. I have about a thousand books, most of them bought through the Internet from antiquarian bookshops. I have moved all of these books to the second floor of my house, out of sight, against one long wall. So now my wife can move around again. (*Laughs*)

RS: How much did you travel for research? Did you go to Israel?

PV: Yes, I went to Israel a couple of times. But nearly all historical sites from Jesus' time are gone. For me it was important to feel the atmosphere, though. I also realized how small the famous Lake of Galilee is, how narrow the streets of Jerusalem are, how close the walls of the city are to the Mount of Olives. I saw the cave where Jesus was probably hiding when he was arrested. I went into the Church of the Holy Sepulchre where they show you the (presumed) grave of Jesus. These visits gave me some sense of reality.

RS: Did you feel anything particular in the chamber where Jesus was supposedly buried?

PV: It was a small room with a niche in the side of the rocks where someone can lie down. It was pretty dark.

RS: But did you sense anything beyond that, perhaps a certain energy?

PV: No, and if so it would just be a projection. There is little evidence to show that this was really Jesus' grave—the Crusaders simply decided that it was. Jesus might never have had a grave—normally the Romans would toss the bodies of crucified people into a pit and throw some earth over them. Then the dogs—always present at execution sites—would come and eat the bodies.

I had a much stronger, emotional reaction when I went to see the rock graves along the Nile back when I was scouting locations for a movie that was never made. These rock graves are much smaller than the enormous burial chambers of the Pharaohs in the Valley of the Kings. They are the same size as the alleged grave of Jesus in the Sepulchre Church. On the walls of these very narrow, small rock graves along the Nile were a lot of murals. The deceased—the Pharaoh's secretary for example—had ordered that all of his belongings, including his wife, cat and geese should be painted on the wall of the burial chamber. Four thousand years ago the Egyptians believed that everything painted on these walls would "travel" with the deceased to the other world (the afterlife), where they would again be at his disposal. For me that Egyptian dedication to their belongings was very moving, even tragic—I'm assuming their beliefs turned out to be wrong.

The most frightening experience I had in the Jesus cave was when I noticed a Greek orthodox monk standing in a corner and dressed all in black so you didn't notice him when you entered. I suppose the monk stands there to make sure that people don't chop off a piece of rock. At first I didn't see him, then suddenly I realized that I was not alone. That was a frightening discovery that really made an impression.

RS: Have you ever been spooked by Christian imagery or had visions when you were working so intensively on this subject?

PV: I have seen visions in the night many times. I wake up and see monsters, aliens or scary people bending over me and I scream. Fortunately they disappear after one or two seconds. Jesus, however, has never visited me. That would be really scary. It might mean that all of my thinking has been wrong, that I made a big mistake in believing that I could shut Christianity out of my life. There is always the frightening possibility that all thinking is hubris, a fata morgana posing as reality. But at the moment I think that what I wrote in my book is true.

RS: Can you envision making a movie which is a little more ambivalent—that doesn't show for example what happened to Jesus' body or what happened to Mary?

PV: Sure I can. In fact, I think that the last shot of the movie should be Jesus breathing his last breath. He dies, and cut to the end of the movie. Nothing about what happened to his body, which is anyhow sheer speculation. Neither would I start the movie during the revolt in Sepphoris, and certainly not with the rape of Mary, which is speculation as well.

I would probably start with John the Baptist. Jesus comes to him to be baptized and seeks repentance for his sins—as it is written in my favorite gospel (of Mark). And I would certainly make it clear that a *fight* occurred between John and Jesus. I would explain that the meeting of the five thousand at the Lake Genezareth, the so-called "multiplication of the loaves," was a *reaction* to the execution of John the Baptist by the ruler of Galilee (Herod Antipas). This execution made people very angry and inspired them to take up arms against the ruling class, Antipas and the Romans. They tried to make Jesus the miracle worker their leader; they wanted to make him into the "king of Israel." This was basically an insurrection. But Jesus fled, away from the territory of Antipas.

Later I would show Jesus entering Jerusalem. He is not expecting his death at all—he is convinced that the Kingdom of God will unfold in that city. By now he has changed—he expects to become a placeholder for God in that city, he even promises his twelve disciples that they "will sit on twelve thrones and judge the tribes of Israel." But the Kingdom of God does *not* unfold. Nothing happens in Jerusalem. Instead the Sanhedrin, the Jewish council, goes after Jesus wanting to arrest him. Jesus has to flee the city. The Sanhedrin pronounces his death sentence *in absentia*.

Jesus is a fugitive now. Six months later he organizes a meeting of militants in a safe house outside Jerusalem. One of the participants works secretly for the Romans and betrays the entire group. Jesus and the other militants are arrested and crucified the next morning. These are the story elements that I would use for a movie, that would give me a compelling narrative with solid drama.

But there is a big problem. How do you integrate Jesus' ethics into your narrative? These ethics are represented in his parables, but how do you visualize the parables? I have yet to solve that problem in my head. Without the parables it becomes an action story about a man who is being chased by the authorities for attempting to achieve his utopia, the Kingdom of God, which ultimately turns out to be fiction, but they kill him anyhow. True, that sounds like an (perhaps even interesting) action movie, which would be a terrible mistake. Because, without the ethics, the audience would ask, "Why is this man, Jesus, of any importance?"

RS: Do you mind the reaction of the public that says, "What does the director of *Basic Instinct* and *Starship Troopers* have to do with the historical Jesus?" Or do you accept that people might not take you seriously at first?
PV: There is not much that can be done about that. In Holland it turned out okay. Of course I got extra publicity because of my movies, even though the publicity was not always positive. But mostly they took the book seriously, and it is already in its seventh printing.

RS: Do you find something fascinating in the ritualistic, mythological-mystical elements of Christianity?
PV: I don't care about those. I was not raised a Christian, so I didn't have to make an effort to get rid of my Christianity. If you are raised a Christian it is not so easy for your brain to get rid of the Christian programming of the first ten years of your life. Often residuals are left behind. For better or worse, I was not pre-programmed, so my brain works in a secular way. I look at Jesus' story in a pragmatic and secular way. That's something that might be interesting about the book—very few nonbelievers have bothered to study Jesus—this I have noticed during all twenty years of my American film career.

RS: Can you envision yourself joining any religion?
PV: No. My religion is science.

RS: Do you believe in salvation?
PV: My brain can't believe that, even though my heart tries to seduce me. Intellectually I have a hard time. The only salvation that might ultimately happen is for us to evolve into beings that are more benevolent, more generous, less antagonistic than who we are now. I think that science will play a big part in that evolution. So if salvation comes, it will come through science.

RS: Has Christianity contributed anything to human progress?
PV: Honestly, it has contributed very little. Christianity has obscured science, has killed people left and right, has organized the most horrible crusades, has brought us the Inquisition and an infallible Pope. Christian theological thinking has been more harmful than benevolent. If people would have taken Jesus' words more seriously, things would have turned out better.

RS: So—briefly—what is the basic message of Jesus that is most prevalent today?
PV: I would say: take your enemy seriously. Try to figure out what the enemy wants. Are his goals understandable? Would you perhaps do the same if you were in his position? Are they really enemies? Are they really terrorists? Or are they fighting for a worthy goal?

Step over the axis of evil. Barack Obama said during his trip to Turkey, "Peace begins [. . . .] by learning to stand in someone else's shoes in order to see through their eyes." So when he says, "I want to talk to Iran"—that is the message of Jesus.

49 Minutes with Paul Verhoeven

Mark Jacobson / 2010

From *New York* Magazine, April 9, 2010. Reprinted by permission of the publisher.

In *Basic Instinct*, director Paul Verhoeven filmed probably the most famous crotch shot in the history of cinema. Nonetheless, Verhoeven dismisses the most sacred of all sex dreams: the penetration of Mary by the Holy Spirit, which resulted in the miracle of the virgin birth. In his new book, *Jesus of Nazareth*, a scholarly treatise on the historical Christ, Verhoeven, maker of such fantasy movies as *RoboCop*, *Starship Troopers*, *Showgirls*, and *The Fourth Man* (which includes a Jesus-on-the-Cross fellatio dream sequence), cuts the Prince of Peace and the more than a billion people who believe the accounts of his time on Earth very little slack, using close readings of the Gospels to fairly convincingly cast doubt upon such marvels as walking on water, the "multiplication of the loaves," and the Resurrection.

"Jesus was a human being, bound by history and the natural world; an extraordinary man, to be sure, but still a man," says the now-seventy-one-year-old Verhoeven as he sits in the coffee shop of a midtown hotel, his lank silver-gold hair swinging about as he staccato-fires his argument. "Jesus may have had an immense sense of importance or destiny, but he never claimed to be the Son of God." Verhoeven's here to plug his book at the Hudson Union Society. Then why care about Jesus if he's not the Son of God? Verhoeven says, "Because of his ethics. His thought. It isn't because of the healings, because now humans possess the healing technology to do one hundred times, one thousand times what Jesus did. What we are left with is what he said, the parables, the moral thinking, because when you begin to study Jesus' life, as the miracles fall away as physical impossibilities, you learn that the quotes, the speeches, and the reasoning behind them, for the most part, are genuine."

As to how he came to write such a book (the notes, bibliography, and various indexes take up eighty-seven of the 288 pages), Verhoeven, who grew up in The Hague during the Nazi occupation, smiles slyly and says, "You mean when I'm supposed to be spending all my time making another version of *Total Recall*? There are other things to think about, you know." The fact that he had a degree in both math and physics didn't prevent him from becoming the best known of all Dutch filmmakers, so the fact that he spent months shooting Elizabeth Berkley thrusting her crotch didn't keep him from also being the first nontheologian Fellow in the prestigious "Jesus Seminar," a group of scholars dedicated to sorting out likely fact from the obfuscations and flat-out fibbing that appear in the Gospels of Mark, Matthew, Luke, John, and Gnostic Thomas.

For Verhoeven, Jesus is as much a political figure as a spiritual one. "The Romans saw him as an insurrectionist, what today is often called a terrorist. It is very likely there were 'wanted' posters of him on the gates of Jerusalem. He was dangerous because he was proclaiming the Kingdom of Heaven, but this wasn't the Kingdom of Heaven as we think of it now, some spectral thing in the future, up in the sky. For Jesus, the Kingdom of Heaven was a very tangible thing. Something that was already present on Earth, in the same way that Che Guevara proclaimed Marxism as the advent of world change. If you were totalitarian rulers, running an occupation like the Romans, this was troubling talk, and that was why Jesus was killed." As far as Verhoeven is concerned, Jesus is a similar figure to Joan of Arc, a spiritually oriented political being who just might have been a "borderline" psychopath.

In the end, however, Verhoeven is a moviemaker, and he readily admits that his Jesus book, for all the footnotes and often speculative arguments about which Gospel rings truer than the others (in the opinion of the Jesus Seminar, the Gospel According to John is considered to be the least reliable), is essentially "a treatment for a film I have been thinking of making for the past thirty years." This is problematic, however, "because to make a film you must have action. In America I am known as the director of *RoboCop* and *Starship Troopers*; these are what are usually referred to as action films. Yet here I am trying to make a historical film in which some of the best-known action scenes will not be portrayed because they didn't happen. That gives me a lot of talking. I don't know if I can make a film with people standing there talking for five minutes at a time. Who wants to watch that? This is a dilemma."

Verhoeven sighs. One day, he hopes, he will figure out how to make his Jesus film, if for no other reason than to answer the picture of Jesus presented in Mel Gibson's *The Passion of the Christ*. "If that's God," Verhoeven says, "then we are really fucked."

According to Verhoeven: *Vertigo*

Rob van Scheers / 2011

From *Volgens Verhoeven*, De Bezige Bij, 2012. Reprinted by permission of Rob van Scheers, cultural reporter and film critic. Translated from the Dutch by Julia van den Hout.

Vertigo is a fim that engages the viewer in an expert game of chess, at first glance an occult tale that in the end reveals itself to be a classic murder mystery in disguise. I'll summarize the plot briefly: Gavin Elster (Tom Helmore) wants to murder his wife and devises a plan so that it looks like suicide. The story is fairly traditional, but *Vertigo* owes its reputation, of course, to all of the wonderful details that are built around it.

My childhood friend Andrew van Nouhuys, who later became a painter, discovered the movie for the both of us. He took me to the theater to see it and I was immediately blown away. Before the era of the VHS, if you wanted to study a movie you simply had to return to the theater again and again. I think I went to see the film about twenty times and now, everything I know about film, I learned from *Vertigo*.

Such as:
—How long you can maintain a single take.
—How to achieve continuity.
—How to trick the audience into suspending their disbelief.
—The important role of music, as exemplified by the magnificent, uncanny score by Bernard Herrmann.
—But above all: It is not the dialogue but rather the imagery that needs to tell the story in a film.

When it comes to visual storytelling, Alfred Hitchcock is clearly the master. Compared to the visual sequences in *Vertigo*, the dialogue carries minimal weight. Those images are burned in my brain and it is from them that I draw all of my inspiration. And while over the years I've developed a preference for the more upbeat *North by Northwest*, I'll always cherish *Vertigo*.

It's no secret that *Basic Instinct* is my homage to *Vertigo*. I like to imagine that if Hitchcock were a young man today, he would have liked to direct a sexually explicit movie like *Basic Instinct*. I mean, in the Hollywood of his time there was still the Hays Code, the form of self-censorship the film industry imposed on itself from 1930 to 1968. Just as Billy Wilder had to do with *Double Indemnity*, Hitchcock had to camouflage everything with language, always making sure to avoid trouble with the Hays Office.

Meanwhile, it was known that Hitchcock loved all kinds of beautiful, sexy women. You can read about it in the memoir of one of his screenwriters, David Freeman: *The Last Days of Alfred Hitchcock*.

For his last and never completed project in 1980, *The Short Night*, Hitchcock even proposed an elaborate masturbation scene between two adulterous lovers while the woman's husband approaches them in a motorboat. Sadly, this spy thriller was never completed.

In *Vertigo*, everything lies in the power of suggestion. James Stewart—as John "Scottie" Ferguson, former inspector for the San Francisco police department—develops an obsessive love for platinum blonde Madeleine (Kim Novak), the woman he is hired to follow by her husband Gavin Elster (Tom Helmore). Elster claims his wife is exhibiting signs of suicidal tendencies, and Ferguson reluctantly accepts the job at the behest of his old college friend.

Scottie's shadowing leads us into occult territory, where Madeleine appears to be possessed by the ghost of her great-grandmother Carlotta Valdes, who we find out committed suicide in the 19th century. Madeleine visits her grave, gazes at her portrait in the museum, and buys the same flowers that Carlotta holds in her hand in the painting. It comes as no surprise when Madeleine attempts suicide soon after; abruptly jumping into the water at the foot of the Golden Gate Bridge. Scottie dives in quickly after her and saves her just in time. He takes her home and the sparks begin to fly between Kim Novak and James Stewart.

Typically Hitchcockian, this romance greatly complicates everything else in the film. The mutual love between Scottie and Madeleine doesn't fit into Gavin Elster's evil scheme—that Ferguson likes her, alright, that is still acceptable, but that she loves him back . . . she won't go blabbing, will she? Elster's precise intention is to make Ferguson aware of Madeleine's second suicide attempt, this time a jump from the church tower. It is again staged; this time so that he can throw the body of the real Mrs. Elster across the balustrade while Kim Novak stays hidden up in the tower.

Gavin Elster was cunning, and didn't hire Ferguson simply for his skills as a private detective. As old college friends, Elster was aware of Ferguson's vertigo and accompanying dizziness, so the tall church tower of the San Juan Bautista Mission in California was the perfect location for the deadly switch. Indeed: when Madeleine unexpectedly (but precisely according to Elster's plan) runs up the stairs of the church tower, Ferguson follows her. He feels overwhelmed by his acrophobia, his vertigo. He cannot possibly go any further and he starts to sweat. He hears a scream and suddenly he sees a blonde wearing the same outfit as Kim Novak go hurtling down past the window. Ferguson of course thinks it was Madeleine, and is so deeply in shock that he is unable to see through the deception. And neither does the judge, who takes Ferguson's word for it as an ex-policeman.

Scottie is tormented by guilt. He blames himself for Madeleine's suicide and winds up in a psychiatric institution. With help from his ex-fiancée Midge Wood (Barbara Bel Geddes) he is released, but begins to see Madeleine everywhere. Each time proves to be a false alarm, until he meets a woman who will later introduce herself to him as Judy Barton.

Judy reminds him of Madeleine, which is odd since she is a brunette who looks nothing like the blonde Madeleine who was always dressed in fashionable suits and pearls. My mother would have called Judy a "trashy" girl, with her heavy make-up and ample cleavage—all necessary for the story, of course. As a working class girl in need of money, Judy was easily roped in by Gavin Elster. I must say that up until this point the movie is very inventively put together.

The key to *Vertigo* is in the metamorphosis of blonde Madeleine into the brunette Judy. And that transformation is very convincing, all thanks to Edith Head, the costume designer and Hitchcock's frequent collaborator. Throughout her career she won eight Academy Awards and earned thirty-five nominations. She worked on great films like *Sunset Boulevard* and *Roman Holiday*, and Kim Novak's transformation in *Vertigo* could not have been any more effective. When you see Judy for the first time, you hardly realize that she was once Madeleine.

You think: Madeleine is dead and Ferguson, delirious, must be pursuing the wrong woman. He sees Judy walking down the street, follows her, goes into her hotel, knocks on her door, and then talks his way inside. She lets him in but keeps him at arm's length, accuses him of stalking her, but—as we soon discover—she knows full well who he is: the man she unintentionally fell in love with during the murder plot. That's why she agrees to go out with him, and what follows is a fantastic shot: a satisfied James Stewart steps through the doorway as Judy sits in the foreground. In silhouette, we see her from behind before she turns to the camera. We instinctively understand the spotlight on Judy—it alerts us to the fact that something remarkable has happened to her—but what, exactly? It is a mystery due in part to Hitchcock's direction, but above all to the merit of Edith Head.

Pure suspense, but with forty minutes left until the end of the movie, all of the sudden Hitchcock curiously gives the whole plot away. Unlike the source novel by

Boileau-Narcejac, *D'entre les Morts*, where the big reveal doesn't happen until the very end, Hitchcock uses a flashback to show the audience what really happened in the church tower. Madeleine did ascend the stairs, but Gavin Elster was waiting for her there and threw his wife's body over the edge. The viewer now knows more than the protagonist of the film. Apparently Hitchcock thought that was the right time to let the audience know that Madeleine and Judy are the same woman. That it would somehow make the rest of the film more exciting.

Now when we watch Ferguson's slow and obsessive transformation of Judy, we know that she has already played the role of "Madeleine" before. Ferguson has her style her hair in the same way, and wear the same grey suits. Every detail has to be perfect, and this is all revealed to us in rather drawn-out scenes.

Some reviews of the film associated Ferguson's obsession with necrophilia but I have my doubts about that. Those long sequences primarily suggest that Judy's transformation must have held a very personal significance for Hitchcock, because they go on for much longer than you'd like to watch. Apparently he wanted to incorporate this theme into the film so badly that he was willing to sacrifice the buildup of tension and suspense. On the other hand, if we weren't already aware of Judy's true identity, the entire dressing-up would feel more like a psychological interlude. Hitchcock was trying to avoid that; it would only delay the thrill. But the caveat of Hitchcock's solution lies in the reduction of suspense into frustration—as a viewer you keep thinking, "Ferguson, you still haven't figured it out? They're one and the same!" And: "How much longer can Judy keep this secret?"

Eventually, Judy gives herself away with the amulet, the same one that Madeleine used to wear. The jewel was part of Judy's payment for her role in the murder plot. The first time I saw *Vertigo*, in 1958, I was able to go along with all of it. But rewatching the movie fifty years later, I'm thinking: sorry, but this is *too* obvious. All of a sudden, the suspension of disbelief doesn't hold up anymore. That's also one of the reasons why these days I prefer *North by Northwest*.

Finally, Ferguson realizes who Judy really is, and we think: jeez, it's about time! Outraged, he drags her back up to the church tower. He questions her aggressively, and startled, she falls: this time she really does fall to her death. I used to think this doubling was beautiful, so tremendously literary! It makes *Vertigo* not only a thriller, but also a tragedy—a tragedy about the loss of a woman, after which the main character reunites with her, only to lose her again in the end. It's more of a double tragedy, actually.

Now, those last forty minutes are hardly the best of the film. Emphatically straining toward that literary device, the final section of the film undermines much of what came before. That's not to say that those first ninety minutes aren't extraordinarily fascinating and, above all, strikingly visual. And again, Hitchcock's flirtation with an occult, gothic sensibility was quite ahead of his time. His followers include Roman Polanski's *Rosemary's Baby* (1968), based on the book by Ira Levin, and Stanley Kubrick's *The Shining* (1980), based on the novel by Stephen King. With the number of recent film adaptations of Stephen King novels alone, the examples are endless.

The silent hero of *Vertigo* is Hitchcock's trusted cinematographer Robert Burks, whose shot compositions are filled with atmospheric detail. When Madeleine and Ferguson go to Pebble Beach, Scottie worries that she'll try to attempt suicide again. The two converse in front of the camera with the turbulent ocean crashing behind them, evoking a sense of uncertainty and impending doom. I eagerly recreated that image in *Basic Instinct*, when Michael Douglas visits Sharon in her villa, situated on a cliff. He comes to question her, they go onto the terrace and in the background you see that same menacing Pacific.

You have to be careful with those references, of course. The Golden Gate Bridge plays a very important role in *Vertigo*, so I felt it better to leave it out of the frame, instead showing the bridge next to it. I must admit that *Vertigo* is so imprinted in my subconscious that I've made many unintentional references to the film. Luis Buñuel calls this "hidden continuity": to unconsciously steal, in utter sincerity. Something makes an impression on you, only to come back out again suddenly, though you might not remember where the idea originated. The subconscious works like a junk shop containing all sorts of information. It's like one of the fleamarkets that line the streets of Holland on Koninginnedag (Queen's Day).

I'll give you another example: James Stewart is shadowing Kim Novak in *Vertigo*. At some point, he watches her from outside as she closes the blinds of her hotel room, at a location that would have had significance for Madeleine's great grandmother Carlotta Valdes. There is a small church in the background, and as it turns out, I filmed that same church in *Basic Instinct* when Michael Douglas goes after Sharon Stone . . . though I didn't realize that until after the fact.

In that scene, as research for her book, Sharon goes to visit Hazel Dobkins (Dorothy Malone), a murderess who killed her husband and kids for unknown reasons. I simply told my location scouts: I want a church in this shot, right over there. It seemed to me like a good contrast: Christian symbolism and a ruthless murderess. In retrospect, clearly what I meant was: I want a church in the background, just like in *Vertigo*. Hidden continuity.

Minus those last forty minutes, *Vertigo* has continuously provided me with an endless source of inspiration. Even in my first movie, *Eén Hagedis Teveel* (*One Lizard Too Many*), I included a kind of transformation à la *Vertigo*. And *Basic Instinct* in essence is no different; *Vertigo* is my alpha and omega.

My Filmviews Interviews . . . Paul Verhoeven

Nostra / 2013

From myfilmviews.com, February 8, 2013. Reprinted by permission of the author. Translated from the Dutch by Nostra.

Tricked is the new movie by Paul Verhoeven, which has been made through crowd-sourcing. Everyone had the chance to participate in the project by writing part of the script, composing music or simply by voting. The movie was made in eight episodes. My Filmviews talked with Paul Verhoeven about making the film, the challenges he faced and his thoughts on the remakes of his most well known movies.

NOSTRA: How was your experience making this crowd-sourced movie, *Tricked*?
PAUL VERHOEVEN: It's a very intensive and long way to create a story. It is cheaper to start with a real story/script instead of doing it this way. It costs a lot of time, you really need the time you have between episodes to look at the scripts. When doing that you need to be honest to your audience—the users—by using what they suggest as much as possible, but you also have to be keen to change what isn't right or doesn't work structurally. You ask yourself: "Are we going to have a problem with this?" or "If we are going to do it this way is it going to be an endless road that we won't be able to finish in eight episodes?" It's hard to take control without getting the feeling that you change it too much to reflect your own vision. Working with user generated content is something that works up to a certain extent—but not how we thought. We thought we would receive a couple of scripts that would really stand out and that we could use as a starting point. We thought we would—together with Robert (Alberdingk Thijm)—be able to turn those scripts into one script and that it would be something that could be done in half a day. That wasn't the case. It took us two weeks every time and we had to take the good parts from a lot of different scripts. For the second episode we used forty out of seven hundred scripts.

N: Was the script the biggest challenge?
PV: Yes, because shooting it was fantastic and I worked with a great crew. The atmosphere on the set was probably the best since *Floris* and *Turkish Delight*.

N: What was the reason for that?

PV: It was because everyone was so spontaneous and we didn't know where the story would go, it was all very adventurous. Everyone was willing to try, and over half of the people were young. There was no stress, we had great locations and it was fantastic. I should do it again, but with a "real" movie that has the same "lightness" as *Tricked*. You can't work that way when you are doing a thriller, that's too hard. It isn't possible to shoot a movie like *Basic Instinct* so loosely, where everything has got to go like clockwork.

N: How did you decide on the cast?

PV: We tested around a thousand amateur actors and actresses. But when I received the first five pages of the script—written by Kim (van Kooten), who is really able to write between the sentences where there is a lot of ambiguity in what the characters are saying and where it is more important what they *don't* say—I immediately thought: This is going to be difficult; only real actors are able to express that. Kim's script almost floats through the story and it is very difficult to realize that with amateurs.

N: Would you consider doing a project like this again in the future?

PV: I would do it, but then it would have to start with the idea of it becoming a full length movie. The question then would be how much more expensive it would be instead of developing the script yourself. You would have to be able to keep filming. We had to wait a lot. We could shoot for two or three days at a time, after which we would need to wait three to six weeks before we could continue and had to set up everything again. That's something you don't have when the script is ready before you start filming. Therefore, doing it again is really an economic question—can you afford it? Ziggo (a Dutch company) was able to make that investment, because PR played an important role. But you have to realize that for the money they invested, you would have been able to make a full length movie—if the script had been available at the start. During the project they tried to make it a ninety minute movie, but it was already too late. The story was already heading toward its ending and it wasn't possible to change it. By then a lot of the story was established, relationships were made clear, secrets were shared and at that moment you can't say "let's make up some scenes where the character heads to Germany where something else happens" and then return back here and finish the story.

Before this interview I asked readers of My Filmviews to send in questions for Paul Verhoeven. Below are the questions I was able to ask him.

N: Several remakes of your movies have been made or are being made, like *Total Recall* and *RoboCop* . . .
PV: *Starship Troopers* was recently bought.

N: Did you have any advising role in those movies?
PV: No, I wasn't asked for advice.

N: Would you be interested in working on a remake?
PV: I wouldn't do a movie over again. I probably would have done something like it, to give feedback, but I'm always interested in doing something new.

N: What did you think of the remake of *Total Recall*?
PV: It wasn't good. With *Total Recall* all of the lightness was taken out. It's all played straight and it only has chase scenes and shootouts. In that setting the story seems idiotic. If I look back at the way we did it, the character who is selling Schwarzenegger that dream is kind of a comedic car salesman. Because of that, you buy into this crazy story. If you take it all seriously from the outset you're approaching it in the wrong way. Philip K. Dick's stories have a lightfooted-ness about them, where he plays around with the elements, and that's the way that I filmed it. By leaving that out and making it very serious—which is something that could also happen to the new *RoboCop* movie—you really are left with a ridiculous story. If you film it while slightly making fun of yourself, with the right perspective while winking at the audience, you protect yourself against the danger of it becoming ridiculous.

N: How did you do that with *RoboCop*?
PV: We had to think for a long time about how we would introduce *RoboCop* in the movie. The idea eventually came from the maker of the suit, Rob Bottin. He suggested to not immediately show the whole suit, but just bits of it. When you watch the movie you see a flash of it on a TV, then a shot of it filmed through a matte piece of glass and the next moment you see RoboCop, but only very briefly. If you present all of it immediately, no matter how good that suit is, people will start to laugh. If you look at the first two *Star Wars* films you also see they have that lightness to them. That's why you believe everything, you believe in those aliens from other galaxies and it makes the "princess" something ordinary.

N: Are you a member of the Academy?
PV: Yes, I am a member of the Academy, of the Director's Guild and I vote.

N: Since you are, I thought it was interesting that you appeared at the Razzies. How do you look back on that?

PV: Well, that's different, it was kind of a joke. It really was a fantastic evening. I didn't know what those "Razzies" were, but René Mioch (a famous reviewer in the Netherlands and also the producer of *Tricked*) asked me to go. It turned out to be a lot of fun, although it initially started very unpleasantly because people were laughing so much when pieces of *Showgirls* were shown—to show how "bad" it was. When they realized the director was there and that he had to head to the stage six or seven times to receive an award for Worst Movie, Worst Directing, Worst Actress, etcetera, the mood changed. People started yelling "*Showgirls!*" and it really was a change of values. Going in I expected a slaughter, but it ended in a victory and I'm really happy that I attended.

The new movie by Paul Verhoeven, *Tricked*, will premiere in the Netherlands on March 28. The movie was created together with the public and that same public can influence its release by buying tickets at wewantcinema.com and decide in which cinemas it will be shown.

Verhoeven in Venice

Margaret Barton-Fumo / 2014

Printed by permission of the author.

When I first met Paul Verhoeven in 2014 at a cafe in Venice Beach, I intended to update this book with new content and catch up on his activities over the past seven years since the release of his last feature, *Black Book*. The general curiosity in the US continued to build as meager remakes of first *Total Recall* and then *RoboCop* petered out at the box office. Before traveling to Los Angeles I researched the basic details of the *Entertainment Experience* and was intrigued by the idea of Verhoeven judging a reality show in the vein of *American Idol*, except for aspiring filmmakers. I soon found out that the "reality" was quite different, wherein Verhoeven matter-of-factly shot down thousands of contestants who were attempting to compile a screenplay, one scene at a time. In this case, the *Entertainment Experiment* might have been a more fitting show title.

MARGARET BARTON-FUMO: Tell me about the *Entertainment Experience*, which led to the production of *Tricked*. We have similar reality-style shows in the US that aren't quite as democratic, in which an established artist or celebrity acts as a mentor for contestants in some sort of competition.
PAUL VERHOEVEN: Right. So we tried. They're exporting the show now to China. They have a very famous director attached to it (John Woo), but I think he's just supervising. I was actually doing it. I jumped into it and basically erased everything, because that's what had to be done.

MBF: Is it true that you had to rewrite the crowd-sourced script?
PV: I wouldn't say that I rewrote it but I rearranged everything with a television writer (Kim van Kooten) who wrote the first five minutes of the film. The rest was written by the crowd in five minute segments. It was extremely difficult to find a way through all of the scripts, starting off with seven hundred that slowly diminished as the project moved forward. There were only fifteen or twenty scripts

that I was able to bring to the halfway point, when there were probably about two hundred people who were still writing out of the original seven hundred. I told them then that we had to structure towards an ending and acknowledge when certain threads could not go on.

I thought that I would be able to use at least one or two scripts for each segment as they were, or perhaps combine two or three together for a five minute episode but even that turned out to be absolutely impossible. We had to bend, change, restructure and invent whatever it took to keep it going, otherwise the story would completely deteriorate and characters would change into gangsters, or the mafia, or the Russians, the Romanians, aliens, or whatever, while the original story was really about six people.

MBF: Did that surprise you?
PV: Yeah. The scriptwriter and I were constantly trying to protect the continuity of the original script. We had to protect the style, protect the fact that it was an interior piece about six people and their plotting—not exterior events like the mafia blowing up the house, to give an example. I would say that there was a lot of intervention on our part and that our input was perhaps more creative than was acknowledged in the media.

MBF: At less than an hour in length, the completed film is rather short.
PV: No, not really because it was meant to be a short film. It was supposed to be twenty-five minutes but it turned out to be fifty-two. The whole seminar that my scriptwriter and I gave about how they should write and direct the story didn't help much either—there were one or two people who would sometimes come up with some good stuff but ultimately we made a mistake in allowing the crowd to be too large. Maybe if we could have drawn more applicants from film schools and perhaps academies or theater schools we would have had a group who knew more about structure and character.

MBF: Were most of the participants young people?
PV: People of all ages participated—including forty, fifty, sixty year olds. A few young people submitted work but I think there might have been a deliberate sabotage on the part of film schools to convince their students to *not* participate. I can't prove it, but I felt like that was the case.

MBF: And yet *Tricked* turned into a good film.
PV: Yes, I like *Tricked* very much and in retrospect I think we did a good job. My DP's basically developed this new style, using two digital cameras and two boom

microphones at all times. With their help I started to realize what I could do with two cameras, and not in the normal way—for action scenes, for example—but by using two cameras that work with each other in a dialectic way. Instead of using one camera here and then taking another shot there, there were two cameras; each doing its own thing. It felt like a very different kind of style; very loose, always handheld with the camera carried on the shoulder. These were big cameras (Alexas), so there were no smooth Steadicam shots. I'm trying to adapt that style even further for the film that I'm preparing now.

MBF: I have to say that I thought of *Turkish Delight* when I watched the pivotal bloody-tampon-in-the-toilet scene in *Tricked*. It's similar to the scene in the earlier film where Olga looks in the toilet and thinks she has cancer, but Eric tells her it's just because they ate beets for dinner—that's not the kind of thing you'd ever see in an American film.

PV: Yeah! It's a very warm movie of course, in a harsh romantic style. Rutger Hauer's character is very lovely, although he's mean, too. I like it very much, it's a nice story. We shot that film handheld with a noisy little Arriflex, so the whole film was dubbed. Like all of Fellini's films, the actors came back during post production and recorded their dialogue, so we were able to use this small camera and do all kinds of different things with it.

This new electronic Arriflex that I mentioned earlier is very handy. It has two steel bars to hold onto that form three points, allowing the cameraman to do all kinds of movement. The Steadicam is similar; it's closer to the body and very difficult to handle, but with the Alexa you can do the movement with your arms because of its very complex system. It's a new approach to filmmaking that offers a lot of possibilities.

MBF: Did your experience with *Tricked* inspire you to keep up the momentum and continue to direct on your own?

PV: Sure. And it inspired me to write again with my friend Gerard Soeteman, who wrote all of my good movies. We're using *Tricked* as a template for a big television series. It will have a different story but we're going to tell it in that same style, with that same lightness. It isn't heavy, it's got what you see in those old comedies of Ingmar Bergman—Have you seen *Smiles of a Summer Night*? When we started out on *Tricked* I told the writers that I was looking for a style that was in between *Smiles of a Summer Night* and Jean Renoir's *The Rules of the Game* in modern language, of course, and with different camera styles. I'm a big fan of Ingmar Bergman, even though I use a different style. It's easy for me to watch and re-watch his movies; it's like listening to my favorite music. Of course I can't do it every day, but every year I can admire certain Bergman movies without getting bored. I've referenced one or two of his books before, and I've quoted him in newspaper articles that I've written about filmmaking.

MBF: Now that the medium is quickly gaining prestige, would you consider directing a film for television?
PV: Yes, and in fact there's often more interesting content on television than in film. I feel like film has lost its grip and created a lot of gaps where television has jumped in. And I think that when it comes to plot and characterization, television is more interesting.

There's a couple of television projects that I have been asked to consider, but the one that I'm working on with Gerard will at least be written, you know? All of the others are just pitches. I pitched a story in Paris about the Crusades, and a story about 1940's spy stuff to a television writer in England, and then there's a project about the French Revolution that was originally set up with Michael Hirst, who does the *Vikings* now and *The Borgias*. It's centered on a specific woman of that time whom we all know very well; her name is Madame Tussaud. So there are three television projects. Will they go forward? I don't know. I don't have much influence there, whereas with the Dutch stuff I have the power to get things done.

MBF: It sounds as if you're constantly working on one project or another.
PV: Sure. Which I hate, in fact. My whole life I've gone from project to project to project and now, having seen how easily the studios tend to kill projects off, I know that if you concentrate on one project it can be very difficult because you might work for it then wait for a year and it's lost.

MBF: Do you have any plans to direct another feature?
PV: I'm working on a French film based on a novel by Philippe Djian, a novel called *Oh . . .* , but the film will be called *Elle*. In fact, I leave tomorrow to go to Holland and then to Paris to do the casting. The main character is already cast, and she will be played by Isabelle Huppert. It's a new chapter in life, since it's been some time since I directed a feature. It's difficult here (in Los Angeles) to do what I want to do because I'm not forty-five anymore, you know? I want to work on other types of projects that are not available here—only rarely, or once in a while. So I've been thinking about making European movies lately, more so than American ones.

MBF: Have you noticed the slew of new biblical epics lately (Ridley Scott's *Exodus*, Darren Aronofsky's *Noah . . .*)?
PV: Yeah. They're all nonsense. They all follow the same mythological nonsense and it's all Christian-oriented. None have any interest at all in the political

situation of that time; it's as if Jesus lived outside of politics or something which in my opinion is completely impossible. As you can see in Israel right now, you'll never be able to *not* be political there—not now and not then.

MBF: Hollywood studios have always relied heavily on bigger, flashier films in times of financial desperation.
PV: Bigger films, and Christian. They realize now that there are still a lot of Christians in this country. I think it's eighty percent of Americans who believe they are going to heaven, so . . . they're all in for a big surprise. To follow these Old or New Testament stories as they are written is a disservice to civilization.

MBF: It's also intellectually lazy.
PV: Yeah, lazy or money-hungry. The basic thought is that it worked for two thousand years so let's grab a piece of that. I mean there isn't anyone interested in looking at the Bible from a critical point of view and that's so boring. There are elements of truth that the filmmakers could build up but they're not even looking in that direction. They make films out of stories like the Ten Commandments, and now they're looking to remake *Ben Hur*. . . .

MBF: It's Cecil B. DeMille all over again, but on the cheap.
PV: Yeah. Or digital.

MBF: Are there any contemporary filmmakers that impress you?
PV: Haneke.

MBF: Is that why you approached Isabelle Huppert to star in *Elle*?
PV: I think Isabelle Huppert approached the producers so no, I did not approach her. I've seen four or five of Michael Haneke's movies and I liked them all because they are interesting, and shot with a lot of long takes.

MBF: *White Ribbon* in particular is visually stunning.
PV: Yes it is. There were some long shots that kept going for a minute or longer as you watch the characters changing positions—I really liked that. I also liked *Amour* very much. It's shot in the same very simple style. I wrote an article about the film with my friend for the newspaper and just for fun I counted the number of cuts Haneke made in the first half hour and it was twelve or something, perhaps fifteen or twenty at most. Then I looked at twenty minutes of *Tricked* and there were something like two hundred cuts! (*Laughs*) It's so interesting to see the difference in style.

MBF: How do you maintain such a consistent style and image without acting like a tyrant on set? You've been known to tell your actors exactly how you want them to act, sometimes performing a pantomime for them . . .

PV: Well, sometimes. There are some actors you shouldn't do that with because they get very pissed off! It's best to keep your mouth shut with really good actors or actresses because they always know better. Improvisation and change is important. If the actors are not good than you have to be more adamant in your direction, but if they're really good you had better let them go, basically. Then you allow them to take over because they feel it so much from the inside that they're superior to me in their possession of the character. That was the case with *Black Book*, where I was working with really good actors, like Carice van Houten. I would ask her to act in a certain way and she would do it but it wouldn't be any good. She always followed my direction but after four or five misfires I finally said to her: go ahead and do what you want!

MBF: And yet Carice shares some traits with other of your leading actresses—she could have been in *Showgirls*, for example.

PV: Oh yeah, right. She's very good, probably the most talented actress that I've worked with, who's now spending her time acting on *Game of Thrones*. She plays a sorcerer or something.

MBF: Have you given up on your longstanding plans to make a film about Jesus?

PV: No, not really. I tried to meet with producers here but it fell apart about five months ago, because the writer we attracted was very interested but was not able to work on it. Another writer is interested now, Nicholas Kazan—he's the son of Elia Kazan and a very experienced writer—he's interested in writing it but he's still busy with other projects. No, I've not given up, it's more like I've postponed it. It's not easy to do and of course it's an extremely provocative subject because it's such a different story from what people expect.

The book I wrote on Jesus is largely about how he was seen by the Romans as a political terrorist, and perhaps for good reason. He was certainly killed for being a political terrorist. Crucifixion was historically a punishment for murderers but he was obviously killed for political reasons, for insurrection against the Roman empire. The Romans clearly saw him as an insurrectionist.

MBF: Are you interested in writing another book, perhaps on another topic?

PV: Yeah, there's another book that I started thirty years ago about John Leiden who lived in Holland and Germany in the sixteenth century, at the beginning of the Anabaptist movement. He was an innkeeper or something similar to that who went just over the border of Holland to the city of Münster and he started a big insurrection there based on the idea that Jesus would return to earth and Münster would be the new Jerusalem. Jesus did not come, of course, and ultimately John Leiden was tortured and killed. It's just a great story, very well known.

I read about John Leiden for the first time about thirty years ago in a book called *The Pursuit of the Millennium* by an English historian named Norman Cohn. I wrote a script about it and I always thought I should try to publish it, but I never did. I thought it would be a fantastic topic for a movie but very expensive, because the whole German army shows up and surrounds the city like the fall of Troy (*laughs*). If I write another book, it will be about that.

MBF: Do you intend to dramatize the story at all, or write it as a purely historical document?
PV: No, what I've written is historical. There's a very interesting eyewitness report from a citizen in (Münster) that was written in 1536 or 1537, immediately after the execution of these people. It's very informative and it reads more or less like a script, although I don't know if I'd ever be able to film that. I mean Jesus is cheap in comparison to the John Leiden story.

MBF: Have you continued to attend seminars at the Westar Institute since the end of the Jesus Seminar in 1998?
PV: I haven't gone much anymore over the last five or six years because they shifted away from Jesus and they went to Paul, then to the Acts of the Apostles, and then they started a seminar on early Christianity. The leader of the Jesus Seminar was Robert W. Funk, who died a couple of years ago and since his departure I think the seminars have become more and more spiritual. They're more interested in God and the seminars are becoming increasingly vague. When Funk was there the focus was, "What was the guy saying? What was he doing?" It was all very academic. There were no metaphorical interpretations—it was simply taking a line from the Bible and deciding whether Jesus said it or not. And I liked that; it was so precise. I've wanted to make a movie about Jesus since I was living in Holland, so I found it to be a wonderful education. It's been a bit difficult for me to appreciate the seminar since it's become spiritualized.

Shooting *Elle*

Margaret Barton-Fumo / 2015

Printed by permission of the author.

MARGARET BARTON-FUMO: When we last spoke about a year ago you told me how you experimented with the Alexa camera and new filmmaking techniques on *Tricked*, and that you intended to use those techniques again on *Elle*. How did the shoot go?

PAUL VERHOEVEN: The shoot went well and I shot it exactly as I did with *Tricked*. These days the amount of time a director is given to make a move has diminished by forty to fifty percent. Working with two cameras solves part of that problem while giving you the opportunity to do things that you wouldn't do before.

I received a lot of support from my producer Saïd Ben Saïd, who knew that I was trying to do something different and appreciated that. Even the cameraman, Stéphane Fontaine, had not worked in that style at all before. In fact he told me that it was really unusual in France to use two cameras simultaneously but we did it anyway and I am very happy with the results. Filming with the two cameras next to each other as close as possible gives you the same access point—that way you can do a long shot and a medium shot at the same time and you can cut anywhere because the shots are basically the same, just recorded in two different ways. It's really an old trick that was used already in *Gone with the Wind* and I do it all the time now. I started using this technique on *Tricked*, and hopefully I perfected it on *Elle*, where you have a long shot, medium shot, then a long shot and so on, in and out so that you don't notice it. The point is that it should be flawless but if you look precisely, you will see it. The shoot was about fifty days long and half of that time was spent on location in the house of Isabelle Huppert's character, Michèle. The rest was shot in Paris.

MBF: Was this a small scale production?
PV: Well, it wasn't that small of a scale. Although it certainly wasn't a special effects movie, either. I would call it a normal film with a lot of interiors. There

aren't any big action scenes but rather big scenes with actors sitting around a table. It's not all that simple . . . I am editing it now in Amsterdam with my editor from *Tricked* and *Black Book*, Job ter Burg. We shot it in France, as you know, with French actors and a completely French crew.

MBF: Did you have to brush up on the language before going into production?
PV: Well, when I was younger I spent a year in France. I had forgotten what I learned there but it wasn't completely gone, you know? So I took a course at a language institute here in Holland to establish a certain kind of routine. When I was young, my French was much better than my English but now I think they're about the same (*Laughs*). It's always a bit difficult to direct in another language, of course, but ultimately I think it worked out very well.

MBF: Are you planning to premiere *Elle* at any festivals this year?
PV: Well, the sound mix will be done in October in Paris, so the movie will be finished sometime in November. But I don't think that Saïd wants to show the movie until next year. I'm sure that he'll try to get it into some festival.

MBF: There's Cannes in the spring . . .
PV: Yeah sure, it could be Cannes. That's possible—if it's selected! I leave that completely to Saïd, who is a very capable producer and also very interested in what the director is doing. He makes a lot of critical remarks and in general makes very good points. I was impressed by him, he's really a special man.

MBF: There's a general excitement in the air; a rumor that Verhoeven has made another erotic thriller.
PV: Those people who think that this is an erotic film will be disillusioned. They are in for a strange confrontation with a movie that is . . . not ordinary. I don't think the story is erotic; it's about rape. An erotic thriller would be a bit weird, right? I mean, it might be erotic for the person doing it, but I don't think that rape in general is something you would call erotic.

MBF: The source novel, *Oh* . . . by Philippe Djian has yet to be translated into English, but the plot description alone is very provocative. I got the impression that the novel is written in a way in which information is initially withheld, then doled out selectively in the form of a mystery.
PV: It is partially written as a thriller, because the rapist wears a mask and the main character doesn't learn his identity until later on in the story. Djian gives you the information piece by piece and for a long time you don't even know exactly what happened so yeah, it is written like a thriller in a certain sense. But on the

other hand, it is also a story that has a lot to do with the main character's social connections. She is caught in a web that includes her father, her mother, her son, her daughter-in-law, her lover, her ex-husband, etc. These relationships are all rotating around her, most of which have nothing to do with the rape and nothing to do with the thriller genre.

MBF: You've filmed several rape scenes over the course of your career and quite a few of them were controversial, raising troubling questions of the characters' consent. The scene with Michael Douglas and Jeanne Trippelhorn in *Basic Instinct*, for example, or the scene with Rutger Hauer and Jennifer Jason Leigh in *Flesh+Blood*. . . .

PV: Well, in *Flesh+Blood* the consent is clearly fake: Jennifer Jason Leigh's character pretends to enjoy it so that Rutger Hauer's character will protect her from being gang raped afterwards. By pretending to enjoy it she took initiative and commited what I consider an act of survival. But it wasn't something that she actually enjoyed—not in any way.

MBF: Did you choreograph the rape scene in *Elle*?
PV: It had to be choreographed because it was so violent. You really have to figure out beforehand what can be done by the actors and what has to be done by stunt performers. You cannot have the actor—or the actress, in this case—thrown to the ground. She might break something! Then you won't be able to finish the movie.

MBF: Did you storyboard the film?
PV: Yes, I storyboarded this one myself. I showed the storyboards to the assistant director and to the DP, so they had a complete idea of what I was doing with these scenes from the first shot to the last. Every morning I would give them my drawings, so that basically every scene in the film was choreographed.

MBF: Did you collaborate well with the actors? Were you particular in your direction of the lead actors, or did you allow them room to improvise?
PV: No, I would never be so demanding with Isabelle Huppert—she knows what to do! She's one of the most brilliant actors I've ever met in my life. She's so extremely special and is able to avoid any cliché in any situation, always finding a different way of doing things. She comes up with all kinds of extra details that you wouldn't even dream of, that I would never come up with on my own. She's not only a great actress but she is also especially imaginative and creative in her approach to the character. I didn't have to tell her anything about Michèle because it was clear from the first shot that she knew exactly what her character would do

and how she would behave in whatever circumstance. She is extremely audacious and she really had no problem with anything that was in the script, so I have an enormous respect for her.

MBF: Reading through all of these interviews with you dating back to 1968, you've always claimed to incorporate what you call realism into your films.
PV: Sure, because in order to feel comfortable I want to give my films a certain amount of realism, or a sense of reality—within the framework of science fiction or action or whatever—but I still believe in researching for details, finding out what's more or less possible in the story and how things would go if the film were to go in a certain direction. I've said this before but it really comes from my Dutch background that includes the realist school of painting in Holland. If you compare the Dutch painters of the seventeenth century with the Italians or even the English, you can see that the Dutch had a better sense of representing reality than other Europeans. I think that if you come from a country where you are aware of that and you can feel that difference—I think that's something that I took with me to the United States. I certainly utilized it in *Elle*, which I shot in a completely realistic way—you don't even get the feeling that the film is lit. Of course I used lamps here and there but you can see that the cinematographer used as much natural light, or suggested natural light as possible throughout the shoot. The dark in the film is really *dark*.

MBF: You've always blended this type of realism with stylization, though, especially when it comes to the camerawork in your films.
PV: Well, everything is blocked of course. It's too distracting to move the camera all of the time while the characters are talking to each other, isn't it? When we shot *Elle*, both cameras were handheld throughout. The camera would be on the DP's shoulder so that it could be a free instrument, never on a dolly, or set on a pole, or whatever. It was basically just in the hands of the operator, never completely steady, which creates a sense of observation. If you're holding the camera on your shoulder and you're breathing or whatever there's always a slight movement of the camera that gives you a feeling of uncertitude—perhaps a bit voyeuristic—which I also did in *Tricked*. That film was also shot without dollies or poles or anything like that, all handheld.

Elle is more of what you might call a "European" movie because it's not completly plot-driven like say, *Basic Instinct*, where you're always trying to figure out the identity of the killer. Was it Sharon Stone, or perhaps Jeanne Tripplehorn?—Everything in the whole film is dedicated to that mystery. In *Basic Instinct* you don't meet any of the characters' families. You have no idea, for example, about George Dzundza's character—Is he married? Does he have any children? There's really none of that and as such *Basic Instinct* is more in the tradition of Raymond Chandler or Dashiell Hammett mysteries, where you never learn about the social environment of any of the characters because that's not really the point; it's about the detective solving the case. In *Elle*, Isabelle's character wants to find out who did this to her but that's only part of the story. The other part has to do with her place in the middle of this social network—what is she doing there, and how do all of these people around her relate to each other?

MBF: I expect the dialogue must be very important in this film.
PV: Much more important than in *Basic Instinct*. And certainly more than in any of the science fiction movies that I've made (*chuckles*), where the dialogue is mostly, "Let's go!" and the like, always very rudimentary.

MBF: You first left Europe to work on larger projects in the United States. The creative limitations here proved to be too strict, and now you're back in Europe . . .
PV: I don't think that a movie like *Elle* would ever be proposed in the US! They stay far away from such projects there. As I get older I've grown more interested in doing things that are beyond the norm. I've already made too many science fiction films, action-oriented movies or whatever in the United States and I think that to a certain degree this return to Europe has to do with being able to make the kind of movies that I want to make. I'm looking for things that I haven't done before, which is certainly the case with *Elle*.

Additional Resources

Books

Bouineau, Jean-Marc. *Le Petit Livre de Paul Verhoeven*. SpartOrange, 1994.
Bouineau, Jean-Marc. *Beyond Flesh and Blood*. Le Cinephage, 2001.
Bouzereau, Laurent. *The Cutting Room Floor*. Citadel, 1994.
Hickenlooper, George. *Reel Conversations: Candid Interviews with Film's Foremost Directors and Critics*. Citadel, 1991.
Keesey, Douglas, and Paul Duncan, editors. *Paul Verhoeven*. Taschen, 2005.
Sammon, Paul M. *The Making of Starship Troopers*. Boulevard Books, 1997.
Van Scheers, Rob. *Paul Verhoeven*. Trans. Aletta Stevens. Faber and Faber, 1997.
Verhoeven, Paul. *Showgirls: Portrait of a Film*. Newmarket, 1995.
Verhoeven, Paul, and Rob Van Scheers. *Jesus of Nazareth*. Trans. Seven Stories Press, 2010.

Additional Interviews

Bardin, Brantley: "How to Shoot a Sex Scene." *Premiere*, July, 2003.
Blokland, Robbert: "A Long Talk with Paul Verhoeven." www.AintItCool.com, April, 2002.
Carlsson, Mikael: "Starship Composer [Basil Poledouris Interview]." *Music From the Movies*, Summer 1997.
Crookes, David: "*SciFiNow* Talks to . . . Paul Verhoeven." *SciFiNow*, (Issue 4) 2007.
Florence, Bill: "Pumping Irony: *Total Recall*." *Cinefantastique*, May, 1990.
Frank, Alan: "Going Dutch." *Film Review*, February, 1988.
Holben, Jay: "Invisible Force." *American Cinematographer*, August, 2000.
Jeffries, Stuart: "Of course there are nude scenes . . . I'm Dutch!" *The Guardian*, January 11, 2007.
Kiang, Jessica: "Rome Interview: Paul Verhoeven on *Tricked* and What's Next Including *Rogue*, *Hidden Force*, and *Jesus of Nazareth*." *The Playlist*, blogs.indiewire.com/theplaylist, November 26, 2012.
Koehler, Robert: "Vulgar Moralism: Paul Verhoeven's *Black Book*." *Cinema Scope*, Spring, 2007.
Koppl, Rudy: "Paul Verhoeven." *Film Music*, February, 1999.
Lim, Dennis: "Triumph of the Ill." *Village Voice*, August 22, 2000.
McBride, Joseph: "Big Bugs! Big Bucks!" *The Director's Chair Interviews*, www.mrshowbiz.go.com, 1997.

Mendik, Xavier: "The (Un)Hollow Man: Paul Verhoeven Discusses the Politics of Pulp." www.kamera.co.uk, 2002.

Porton, Richard: "Undercover Showgirl." *Film Journal International*, March, 2007.

Puig, Claudia: "Paul Verhoeven Regroups." *USA Today*, November 7, 1997.

Reid, Craig D.: "*Hollow Man*: Paul Verhoeven, Parts I & II." www.cinescape.com, August, 2000.

Roddick, Nick: "Verholloven Man." www.urbancinefile.com.au, September, 2000.

Ryan, Mike: "Paul Verhoeven, *Tricked* Director, on the *RoboCop* and *Total Recall* Remakes." The Huffington Post, www.huffingtonpost.com, April 23, 2013.

Simon, Alex: "Paul Verhoeven Goes Buggy with *Starship Troopers*." *The Hollywood Interview*, www.thehollywoodinterview.blogspot.com, October, 1997.

Sloane, Judy: "Meet the Hollow Man." *Starburst*, October, 2000.

Smith, Adam: "*Empire* One on One." *Empire*, November, 2000.

Smith, Damon: "Back to Basics: Talking to Paul Verhoeven." *Bright Lights Film Journal*, www.brightlightsfilm.com, August 1, 2007.

Tobias, Scott: "Paul Verhoeven: The Interview." *Onion A.V. Club*, www.avclub.com, April 3, 2007.

Von Busack, Richard: "Sweet Jesus! Director Paul Verhoeven Discusses the Importance of Christ's Life on Film." *Sonoma County Independent*, February 26-March 4, 1998.

Williams, Linda Ruth: "No Sex Please We're American." *Sight and Sound*, January, 2004.

Wilmington, Michael: "On Dangerous Ground." *Film Comment*, July/August, 1990.

Index

actors, direction of, 17, 51, 83, 94, 110, 164, 200, 204–5; Arnold Schwarzenegger, 55–56; Rutger Hauer, xiii–xiv, 30–31, 61–62; Sharon Stone, 82, 98, 111–12, 115, 164
Alberdingk Thijm, Robert, xxii, xxvii, 191
All About Eve (Mankiewicz), 93, 137
Antonioni, Michelangelo, xi, 10
art, Dutch, 41, 57, 89, 148, 205
arthouse cinema, and commercial cinema, xi, xii, xv, 10, 27, 44, 50, 51, 94–95, 120, 135, 149, 205–6

Ben Saïd, Saïd, 202
Bergman, Ingmar, xi, 24, 197, 198
Berkley, Elizabeth, xiv, xvi, xvii, xviii, 104–8, 109–12, 114–16, 117–19, 136, 185
Blokker, Jan, xiv–xv, 19
Bottin, Rob, 45, 193

Calley, John, 151
Carolco Pictures, 55, 82, 95, 112, 154
censorship, xiv–xv, 33, 45, 53, 69, 72, 85–90, 95–96, 112. *See also* MPAA
Christ, Jesus, 16, 18, 19–20, 76–79, 159; crucifixion, 20, 45, 58, 77, 175, 200; in film, 167–69, 198–99; *Jesus of Nazareth* (book), xx, xxvi, xxvii, 167, 173–83, 184–85, 200; seminar, ix, xx, xxv, 76–77, 166, 168, 173, 176, 185, 201

Christ the Man. *See* Verhoeven, Paul: Unrealized Works
cinematography, xii, xvii, xxii, 16–17, 41–42, 50, 51, 83, 93–94, 103, 142, 158, 159, 190, 196–97, 205; Alexa camera, 197, 202; Jan de Bont, 30; Jost Vacano, 48, 51; Steadicam, 48, 94, 197
commercial cinema, and arthouse cinema, xi, xiv, 10, 11, 14, 27, 44, 50, 73–74, 89, 135

Da Vinci Code, The (Howard), 168
de Bont, Jan, xxiv, 30, 31, 41
DeVito, Danny, 76
Djian, Philippe, *Oh . . .*, xxii–xxiii, xxvii, 198, 203

editing, 16, 17, 80, 83, 241
Eisenstein, Sergei, xi, 24, 59, 80–81, 94, 169
El Cid (Mann), 38
Entertainment Experience, The. *See* Verhoeven, Paul: Works: *Tricked*
Eszterhas, Joe: *Showgirls*, xvii, xxvi, 64, 91–93, 106, 110, 112, 113, 118, 136; *Basic Instinct*, 82–83, 86

Fellini, Federico, xi, 24, 93, 95, 197
female characters, 26, 200; in *Basic Instinct*, 83–84, 139; in *Flesh+Blood*,

209

31–32, 33, 38, 76; in *Showgirls*, 93, 97, 99–100, 105, 117–18
Ferry, Bryan, 22, 24
film industry, Dutch, x, xi, xii–xv, 11, 14, 35, 60, 62, 63, 66–67, 68–69, 89, 153, 163–64

Ghost (Zucker), 73–74
Goldman, Gary, 55
Gospel According to St. Matthew, The (Pasolini), xxi, 167–68, 168–69

Haneke, Michael, xi, 199
Hauer, Rutger, xiii, xiv, xxiv, xxv, 23, 24, 25, 26, 30–31, 37, 44, 61, 67, 153, 156, 178, 197, 204
Heinlein, Robert, xviii, xix, 121, 122, 124–25, 127, 158, 164, 165
Houwer, Rob, xxv, 5–7, 11, 14, 60, 66
Hitchcock, Alfred, xx, 45, 75, 83, 101, 138–39, 148, 157–58, 166; *North by Northwest*, 24, 94, 157–58; *Vertigo*, xxii, 24, 81, 157, 186–90
Hitler, Adolf, 3, 12–13, 72, 144, 146, 171, 174
Hitchhiker, The, "The Last Scene," xxv, 47
homosexual and/or bisexual characters, 18–19, 22, 23, 26, 62, 84, 85–86, 157
horror cinema, xix, 17–18, 58, 123
Huppert, Isabelle, xxii, xxiii, xxvii, 198, 199, 202, 204

John of Leiden, 13–14, 31, 34, 37, 200–201

Krabbé, Jeroen, 16, 19, 156

Landis, John, 76
Last Temptation of Christ (Scorsese), xxi, 26, 77

Lean, David, 24, 44, 174
Leigh, Jennifer Jason, xxiii, 30, 38, 204
lighting, xii, 87, 103, 129, 188, 205
"lightness" (in tone), 29, 31, 75, 113, 160, 192, 193, 197
Lucas, George, xii

MPAA, xv–xvi, 33, 45, 53, 72, 86–90, 95, 112, 139
MacLachlan, Kyle, xvii, xviii, 113–14
Medavoy, Mike, xii, xiii, 151
Metropolis (Lang), xiv, 46, 148
Mol, Albert, 6, 8, 12
Morrissey, Paul, 137–38

National Anti-Spetters Action Committee (NASA). *See* Verhoeven, Paul: Works: *Spetters*
Nayman, Adam, *It Doesn't Suck: Showgirls*, xvi
Neumeier, Ed, xviii, xxvi, 46, 48, 121, 159, 165

O'Bannon, Dan, 55, 68

Passion of the Christ, The (Gibson), 159, 168, 185
Peckinpah, Sam, 36
Portrait of Anton Adriaan Mussert. *See* Verhoeven, Paul: Works
Prince, 108

rape, xi, xxii, 31–32, 37, 41, 87–88, 99–100, 135, 203–4
realism, x, 27, 39–40, 57, 70, 77, 82, 86, 96, 120, 135, 137, 154, 165, 205
remakes, 193, 195, 199
Reve, Gerard, 16, 18–19, 62
Riefenstahl, Leni, 133, 154, 165
Rules of the Game, The (Renoir), 148, 197

Schwarzenegger, Arnold, xiv, 55–56, 64, 68, 74, 79, 99, 144, 146, 153, 157, 158
science, xx, 33–34, 38–39, 91, 96–97, 158–59
screenwriting. *See* Soeteman, Gerard
sex scenes, x, xii, xvii, 9, 18, 27, 57, 81, 82, 86, 87–88, 90, 96, 98, 138–39
Shue, Elizabeth, 141, 142–43
Shusett, Ron, 55, 68
Soeteman, Gerard, xii, xxvi, 6, 7, 14, 18, 20, 22, 24, 29, 35, 66, 70, 162, 163, 164, 167, 197, 198
Soutendijk, Renée, 16, 17, 18, 25, 27, 32, 83–84, 156
special effects, 70, 124, 128–29, 141
Spielberg, Steven, xii, xiv, xxv, 44, 66, 76
Stone, Sharon, xiv, xvi, xviii, 81, 82, 84, 87, 88, 98, 111–12, 114, 115, 117, 118, 139, 155, 156, 164, 190, 205
storyboarding, xvii, xviii, 51–52, 102–3, 204
Streisand, Barbra, xii

television
  American, xv, xxv, 21, 73, 133, 198; in *RoboCop*, 52, 150
  Dutch, x, 9, 18, 24, 35, 59, 120; *Entertainment Experience*, xxii, xxvii, 195, 197; *Floris*, xiii, xxiv, 5, 30, 47; VPRO/TROS Networks, x, 3, 4, 7, 11–12
Terminator, The (Cameron), 149–50
Tippett, Phil, xviii, xx, 51, 52, 121, 122, 123, 135, 142
Touch of Evil (Welles), 93
Tours, Martine. *See* Verhoeven, Martine
Truffaut, Francois, 95

Vacano, Jost, 48, 51, 94, 153
van de Ven, Monique, 25, 156

van Houten, Carice, 161, 164, 200
van Kooten, Kim, xxii, xxvii, 192, 195
van Scheers, Rob, xii, xxi–xxii, xxiii, xxvi, 144, 174, 186–90
Verhoeven, Martine, xxiv, 48, 80, 140, 154
Verhoeven, Paul: career in the Netherlands, ix, xxiv–xxv, 62, 67–68, 69–70, 71, 100; Christian faith, xx, xxi, xxiv, 13, 20, 24, 26, 58, 182; education, ix, xvii, xxiv, 44, 47, 50, 58–59, 60, 94, 99, 120, 163, 179; European identity, ix, 24, 44, 57, 71, 82, 94–95, 101, 150, 152; influences, xi, 24, 45, 93–94, 148–49, 157–58, 197–98; mental breakdown, xx, xxiv, 24, 153–54

Unrealized Works
Azazel, 145, 146, 167
Batavia's Graveyard, 145–46
Bimbos (projected sequel to *Showgirls*), 110, 119, 136
Christ the Man (Jesus film), xx–xxi, xxvi, 76, 77–79, 134–35, 159, 168, 174, 179, 181–82, 185, 200
Crusade, 64, 79, 144, 146–47
Gangreen, 34
Harry's Tale, 25
Mistress of the Seas, 64
Most Improper Woman, A, 174
Official Assassins, 144, 145
Solace, 159–60
untitled John of Leiden book, 200–201
untitled Marquis de Sade project, 64
untitled television projects, 198
untitled Victoria Woodhull project, 144, 145

Works
Basic Instinct, xv, xxvi, 75, 83–84, 98, 205–6; directing Sharon Stone in,

111–12; influence of *Vertigo* on, 81, 157, 187, 190; leg-crossing scene in, 82, 155–56; and the MPAA, 86–89, 95, 112; working with Joe Eszterhas on, 82, 91

Black Book, xxi, xxvi, 161–64, 167, 169, 170, 200

Business Is Business, xxiv–xxv, 5–8

Elle, xxii–xxiii, xxvii, 198, 199, 202–6

Flesh+Blood, xxv, 25, 27–28, 29–34, 35–42, 61, 67–68, 157, 204

Floris, xiii, xxiv, 30–31, 35, 37, 47, 59, 120, 191

Fourth Man, The, xii, xxiv, xxv, 16–20, 27, 44, 57–58, 62, 83–84, 102, 156–57

Hollow Man, xix–xx, xxvi, 131, 140, 141–43, 166–67

Katie Tippel, xii, xxv, 12, 31, 67–68, 70, 100

Portrait of Anton Adriaan Mussert, x, xxiv, 3–4, 7, 12–13, 152

RoboCop, xiv, xxv, xxvi, 43, 44–46, 47–54, 62, 70–72, 80, 87, 149, 150, 158, 171–72, 193

Showgirls, xvi–xviii, xxvi, xxvii, 91–103, 104–19, 136, 159, 165; and camp, 137; at the Razzies, xvi, 136, 194; response to, 135, 147

Soldier of Orange, xi–xii, 11–12, 13, 20, 30, 59–61, 66, 68, 94, 122, 132–33, 162, 163, 178

Spetters, xi, 18, 22–27, 29, 32–33, 67, 92, 100, 135, 153, 159; homosexuality in, 23, 26, 85–86, 157; negative response to (NASA), xi, xxv, 27, 62, 137

Starship Troopers, xviii–xix, xxvi, 120–25, 126–29, 131–35, 147, 148, 150, 151, 154, 158, 164, 166, 193

Total Recall, xiv, xxv–xxvi, 68, 71, 72, 73, 81, 87, 157–58, 193; directing Arnold Schwarzenegger in, xiv, 55–56, 68; interpretation of, 74–75, 99, 139–40

Tricked, xxii, xxvii, 191–92, 195–97, 199

Turkish Delight, x–xi, xxv, xxvii, 6, 9–10, 12, 13, 15, 27, 57, 59, 138, 156, 197

violence, 40, 45, 53, 58, 64–65, 72, 85, 87–88, 90, 128, 134, 161–62

Warhol, Andy, 137
Weller, Peter, 43, 45
Westar Institute. *See* Christ, Jesus: seminar
Wolkers, Jan, x, 6, 9, 12, 15
World War II, ix, xxi, xxvi, 12, 20, 57–58, 60–61, 64, 121–22, 127, 161–63, 164, 170

www.ingramcontent.com/pod-product-compliance
Lightning Source LLC
Chambersburg PA
CBHW021836220426
43663CB00005B/275